Starting and Progressing in Powerlifting

A Comprehensive Guide to the World's Strongest Sport

By Gary F. Zeolla

ISBN: 978-0-578-02516-2

Table of Contents

Section Five:
Injuries and Back Pain ... 231

Section Six:
Nutrition and Supplements ... 251

Section Seven:
Personal Problems in Powerlifting ... 305

Section Eight:
Appendixes ... 337

Preface

This book is geared towards the beginner to intermediate powerlifter, along with the person just thinking about getting into the sport. This book will present sound training, competition, dietary, and supplements advice to aid the reader in starting and progressing in the sport of powerlifting. It will also help the reader to wade through the maze of federations, divisions, and supportive gear now found in powerlifting.

In addition, this book will detail some of the personal difficulties the writer has encountered in his many years of training and competition in the hopes that doing so will help the reader to avoid the same mistakes and problems. So this book is truly a compressive guide to powerlifting.

The author has a degree in Nutrition Science and was a state and national collegiate powerlifting champion and record holder back in 1979-82. Starting in 2003, he began to compete again and has continued to do so as of this writing. He is currently a top-ranked master powerlifter, holding 39 records set in four different powerlifting federations.

He is also the founder and director of Fitness for One and All, which is dedicated to helping people attain their heath, fitness, and performance goals, with an emphasis on powerlifting.

Disclaimers

The material presented in this book is intended for educational purposes only. The author, Gary F. Zeolla, is not offering medical or legal advice. Accuracy of information is attempted but not guaranteed. Before undertaking any training, dietary, or supplement program or participating in the sport of powerlifting, consult your doctor. Powerlifting can be a dangerous sport, so train and compete at your own risk.

It is also highly recommended that the personal services of a nutritionist, personal trainer, or other qualified health or fitness personal be attained when starting and following a dietary or exercise program. The author is in no way responsible or liable for any harm (physical, mental, emotional, or financial) that results from following any of the advice or information in this book.

All brand and company names are registered trademarks of the respective companies. The author is not employed by any powerlifting gear, weightlifting equipment, or supplement company and does not benefit in any way from the purchase of any particular product.

Recommendations for specific items are based on the author's research and personal experience. Mentioned products can be purchased from the companies listed in Appendix #1.

The author is, however, sponsored by APT Pro Lifting Gear. (www.prowriststraps.com ~ 888-236-1258). But he began to use and recommend APT products before being sponsored by them and would continue to do so even without their sponsorship. Pictures of APT gear are taken from APT's Web site.

The picture on the back cover is from NASA Northeastern States, June 7, 2008, at Washington High School in Washington, PA. It was taken by Eric Magnone, as are other pictures from that contest in this book.

Introduction

Like many, I began lifting weights as a teenager alone in my basement. But this meant I had no one to correct me on my form, as if I would have listened anyway. I also had no idea what a powerlifting contest was like, never having been to a one. And I had no idea what the rules were, never having read a powerlifting rulebook or a book like this one.

With that background, my first contest was a high school bench press meet in eleventh grade. I predictably did everything wrong.

The day before the contest, my gym class was using the school's weight room, so I worked up to a max single "to see what I could do." I then opened with just five pounds less than that weight at the contest.

For that first attempt, the two spotters handed off the weight, each holding the bar at the end. I wasn't ready when they let go, and the bar almost crashed onto my chest.

On my second attempt, I came up with the weight, but my feet were kicking in the air and the bar came up very uneven. The lift was turned down by all three judges.

On my third attempt, I wised up some and had one of the spotters handoff to me from behind. My form was also better for this final attempt. But at that point, I was too tired out and only got the bar halfway up. I thus bombed out of the contest.

It was very distressing at the time, but in retrospect it was probably the best thing that happened to me. After that disaster, I joined a gym. That gym furnished help and support from the other lifters and the owners in proper lifting techniques. I thus learned to use proper form and what the rules of performance were.

I then entered the same bench press meet my senior year. This time, I successfully completed all three attempts and won a 4th place trophy out of about 20 competitors. The organizer of the meet said that if they had a "most-improved lifter" trophy I would have won it as well. It should also be noted that I have never again bombed out of a contest, so I truly learned my lesson.

But hopefully, this book will prevent the reader from having to learn that lesson the hard way like I did. It will teach you the rules of a contest; instruct you on proper training and contest preparation techniques, and explain proper form on the powerlifts that is in accordance with the rules.

The World's Strongest Sport

The subtitle for this book claims powerlifting is "the world's strongest sport." Athletes in some other sports might dispute this claim, namely those competing in World's Strongest Man (WSM) contests and in Olympic weightlifting.

However, in powerlifting, the three powerlifts (the squat, the bench press, and the deadlift) are performed for one rep. The winner is determined by who lifts the most weight for that one rep for each of the three lifts. Ideally the lifter's last attempt will be a full maximum lift, meaning, the most weight he or she could have lifted on that day. Performing one maximal effort rep is a true test of pure strength, so the winner of a powerlifter contest is the lifter who is the strongest on that day.

But in WSM contests, the events never test the athlete's maximal effort strength. There is always an endurance aspect to the events. So, for instance, when a WSM contest has some kind of squat or deadlift event, the athletes usually lift a given weight for as many reps as possible. The winner is the one who does the greatest number of reps. When doing several reps on such lifts, muscular strength is definitely a factor, but so is muscular endurance. The winner is thus not necessarily who is the strongest, but who has the best combination of strength plus endurance.

Now at some powerlifting contest, there might be a separate "bench for reps" or even a "deadlift for reps" contest. But such events are not true powerlifting and will not be addressed in this book. Training for one rep max (1RM) strength is completely different than what the training would be for a "reps" contest. Similarly, training for powerlifting is different than training for a WSM contest. They are really two very different sports.

Meanwhile, in Olympic weightlifting, only one rep is performed in the two lifts, the snatch and the clean and jerk. However, both of those movements are highly skilled lifts and require a great degree of quickness. This is not to say the powerlifts do not require skill or quickness, but nowhere near to the degree that the Olympic lifts do. So the winner in an Olympic weightlifting contest is the lifter who has the best combination of strength plus skill plus quickness.

What this means is that of the three sports, powerlifting is the truest test of pure strength. Thus powerlifting is truly the world's strongest sport.

About the Author

I attended Penn State University from 1979-83, where I earned a degree in Nutrition Science. While a student, I was a member of the Penn State Barbell Club and competed in powerlifting contests. I was a two-time Pennsylvania Collegiate Powerlifting Champion, winning Best Lifter the second year. I won the National Collegiate Powerlifting Championships my sophomore year in the 114 pound weight class and was runner-up at Nationals my junior year at 123s. I broke every PA state collegiate record in both weight classes (except for the bench at 114s) and one national collegiate record (425 pound squat at 123s). I also had won a whole wall-full of trophies. The picture to the right is from Nationals Collegiates in 1981.

My best lifts when I competed in college were as follows (all weights here and throughout this book are in pounds):

114s:

Squat	352
Bench	205
Deadlift	410
Total	953

123s:

Squat	425
Bench	240
Deadlift	435
Total	1095

Unfortunately, heath problems prevented me from competing in State and National Collegiates my senior year in 1983. In fact, my last full powerlifting contest was in the summer of 1982. I competed in and won a couple of bench press contests in the summer of 1985. But then I didn't compete again until April 2003, when I was 43 years old, almost 21 years after my last full power meet.

When I started powerlifting again, the sport of powerlifting had greatly changed. Back in college, there was only one powerlifting federation (the United States Powerlifting Federation). With only one federation, there was only one set of rules, including allowing only one type of supportive gear. But now, there is a myriad of federations, each with slightly different rules, including different rules in regards to gear.

Including college, I have now competed in five different powerlifting federations, with plans to compete in at least one more. I have competed using single-ply gear, multi-ply gear, and unequipped, so I have personal experience with different federations and gear. However, all of this changing of federations and gear has caused me many problems. This will be detailed in this book.

My best lifts since 2003 are as follows:

114s; Multi-Ply Gear:
Squat	415
Bench	220
Deadlift	410
Total	1030

114s; Unequipped:
(Belt, wrist wraps, knee sleeves)
Squat	331
Bench	187
Deadlift	402
Total	920

123s; Unequipped:
(Belt, wrist wraps, knee wraps)
Squat	385
Bench	190
Deadlift	400
Total	975

I now hold 39 powerlifting records, set in four different powerlifting federations. For the years 2003 to 2007, I was the #1 or #2 ranked master (over 40 years old) lifter in the USA in the 114 pound weight class (*Powerlifting USA* magazine).

For 2007, I was the #9 ranked multi-ply lifter for all USA lifters 132s and under. In 2008, I was the #7 ranked raw/ unequipped lifter for all USA lifters 132s and under (PowerliftingWatch.com). Since I compete at 114s and am in my forties, these rankings have me competing against lifters up to two weight classes above me and against lifters sometimes half my age.

The picture to the right is the same picture as on the back cover, except not cropped. It is my opener at NASA Northeastern States, June 7, 2008, where I competed unequipped.

Back in college and in the years since I started powerlifting again, I have experimented with many different types of training methods, but I have finally found a system that works very well for me. This system will be detailed in this book.

With a degree in Nutrition Science, I have written books on nutrition (see Appendix #2). These can be pursued for a full discussion on this subject. But this book will summarize nutritional basics for powerlifting. I have also experimented much with supplements, so an overview of supplements will be presented.

I accomplished all of the preceding despite suffering from numerous health problems throughout my life. The worst of these have been:

Crippling low back pain
Near fatal bicycle accident
Various sleep disturbances
Fibromyalgia (chronic pain plus chronic fatigue)
Stiff Person Syndrome (a very rare auto-immune disorder)
Multiple Chemical Sensitivity (severe allergies)

I completely overcame the low back pain, as will be discussed in this book. I mostly recovered from the various injuries from the bicycle accident, except that my right shoulder is still weaker than the left, hindering my bench press.

The stiff person syndrome would often leave me completely paralyzed for hours to days at a time, but I am mostly over that problem now.

The various sleep disturbances include restless leg syndrome, neurological "tics" and others. One or more usually flare-up on any given night, so I have a difficult time getting a good night's sleep.

The fibromyalgia, especially the fatigue, and the multiple chemical sensitivity are serious problems that I deal with on a daily basis. I also have numerous less serious problems to deal with as well.

Together, these problems mean I am very limited in the amount of time and energy I have to spend in working out, so I have learned to be very efficient in my workouts. My health issues have also forced me to be very strict in my eating plan. I have also experimented much with different supplements, so I know what works and what does not work. My training, dietary, and supplement program enables me despite so many problems to be successful in powerlifting, so this program should be of great benefit to the reader.

I founded Fitness for One and All on July 12, 2003 (see Appendix #3). The Web site is dedicated to helping people attain their heath, fitness, and performance goals, with an emphasis on powerlifting.

Through my Web site, I have advised many people on various issues relating to health, nutrition, and fitness, along with many powerlifters looking for training advice. Those who have followed my recommendations report attaining very good results.

Also posted on the site are videos of various lifts done during my workouts. This book will provide an explanation and pictures of the proper performance of the powerlifts and of many different assistance exercises. But the videos will enable the reader to see the exercises being performed.

My experiences in powerlifting are wide and varied. These experiences enable me to present a unique perspective on the powerlifting scene. As such, this book should be of great aid to the reader in starting and progressing in the world's strongest sport.

Section One

The Sport of Powerlifting

Starting and Progressing in Powerlifting

Chapter One: Introduction to Powerlifting Competition

This first chapter of this book will provide an introduction to the sport of powerlifting and overview what a powerlifting contest is like.

The Three Powerlifts

Powerlifting is composed of three lifts: the squat, the bench press, and the deadlift. Anyone who has ever worked out at a gym has either done bench presses or at least seen someone do them. Benches are popular as you can handle greater weights in the bench press than any other upper body exercise. They are also a great exercise for chest, shoulder, and triceps development. The picture shows me benching at the IPA Iron House Classic, on Saturday April 16, 2005.

But the other two lifts are not quite as popular, but they should be! Squats are the best exercise there is for developing leg and hip strength while deadlifts utilize just about every muscle in the body, so they develop total body strength. In fact, the three powerlifts should be the core of any sound training program, and no other exercises will provide the strength and muscular gains that the three powerlifts produce.

The chapter "Proper Performance of the Powerlifts" explains details in that regard, so it will not be repeated here. But it will be said, if you are not incorporating these three lifts in your training program then you are not making the strength and muscular size gains that you could be. And of course, if you are thinking of competing in a powerlifting contest, you need to be performing the powerlifts in training.

Divisions, Weight and Age Classes

In powerlifting, there are separate divisions for male and female lifters. These divisions are then divided into weight classes. For men, at most contests, there are 12 weight classes. They are (in pounds):

15

114.5, 123.25, 132.25, 148.75, 165.25, 181.75, 198.25, 220.25, 242.5, 275.5, 308.75, and over 308.75. The odd numbers are due to the pounds being converted from kilograms. In fact, some contest will use kilos at weigh-ins while other will use pounds.

The 308.75 pound class might not be seen at all contests, while some will have 319.5 instead. For some contests, 114s has been dropped (much this writer's chagrin since this is my weight class).

For women, at most contests, there are also 97 and 105.75 pound classes, while the top class is 198.25, with heavyweights over that.

At all contests, there will be an "open" division that lifters of any age can enter. But at most contests there will also be age classes.

First, there will be teenage divisions. These are usually in two-year increments, starting at 12 or 14 years old, i.e., 12-13, 14-15, 16-17, 18-19. Some contests will allow kids under 12 to compete, though some-times under special rules. Some contests will also have a junior category for 20-23 year olds.

Then some contests will have a sub-masters division for 35-39 or maybe 33-39 year olds. Then masters divisions will start for those 40 and older, usually in five-year increments, i.e., 40-44, 45-49, 50-54, etc., but sometimes in ten-year increments, i.e., 40-49, 50-59, etc.

Usually, a lifter can enter just the appropriate age division or both the age and open divisions. But to enter two divisions usually requires a higher entry fee cost.

There is also usually a "Best Lifter" trophy. This is for the lifter from the entire contest who totals the most on a pound for pound basis. But this is usually not calculated by diving total weight lifted by body-weight. It is figured out using a formula, such as the Schwartz, Wilkes, or Glossbrenner formulas. These complicated charts are derived from looking at world records for the various weight classes.

Some contests will have separate Best Lifter awards for men and women, and some might even have separate Best Lifter awards for teenagers and for master lifters. But it depends on the number of lifters entered in the contest and in each category.

Some contests might also have separate divisions for collegiate lifters, police and firefighters, and a Special Olympics division.

It is by having so many different divisions and classes that power-lifting truly is a sport that anyone can compete in.

Weigh-ins and Contest Length

Before the start of a contest, there will be a weigh-in period. For some contests, this might occur as early as 24 hours before the start of the contest. In this case, for a contest on Saturday (which most are), weigh-ins might be as early as Friday morning. For other contests, weigh-ins might not begin until the evening before the contest. But for other contests, weigh-ins are only held the morning of the contest, usually starting about two hours before the contest and lasting until about half an hour before it starts.

Weighing in early is very helpful if you had weight to lose to make weight. This will give you more time to eat and re-hydrate before the contest starts. So personally, I only enter contests that have weigh-ins at least the evening before.

Powerlifting contests usually start Saturday morning, generally between 9:00 and 10:00 am. If there are a large number of entrants, there might be an afternoon session as well, starting after the morning session ends, or it might be a two-day event. Usually, lightweights and females compete first, then heavyweights. A very large contest (usually a national or world meet) can take several days.

Exactly how long a contest on a given day will last depends on the number of entrants and frankly, how well the contest is run. An average-sized contest would have about thirty lifters. If it is run well, it should take about six hours, so a contest starting at 9:00 am would not be over until about 3:00 pm. Calculating the winners and handing out the awards can take another hour or so.

What this means is, if you weigh-in the morning of the contest, you probably will have to arrive as early as 7:00 am, and you might not be out of there until 4:00 p.m.. So a powerlifting contest can make for a very long and grueling day. And this is for an average-sized, well-run contest. Larger contests and ones that are not that well-run can really drag on. The worst was a contest I entered in college. I had to be there at 8:00 a.m. for weigh-ins, and I wasn't out of there until after midnight! That is exceptional, but you have to be prepared for anything when you enter a contest.

Warm-ups and Flights

Even if you're not weighing in the morning of the contest, it is still best to arrive at the contest site at least an hour before the start time. This will give you time to change into your lifting clothes, familiarize yourself with the setting, and to warm-up. There is also usually a rules clinic held about half an hour to an hour before the start of the contest that all competitors are required to attend.

Most contests will have a warm-up room that is separate from the contest platform. But the quality of the equipment in the warm-up room can vary widely. Some will have two or three each of squat racks, benches, and deadlifts platforms, while others will only have one of each. And remember, you will not be the only one warming up. You will have to work in with the rest of the lifters. So again, you need to allot plenty of time. But timing your warm-ups can be difficult.

At a contest, each lifter gets three attempts for each of the three powerlifts. The lifts are contested in the order of squats, bench presses, deadlifts. There are also specialty contests where only just one lift, usually bench presses, or just two of the lifts, usually benches and deadlifts, are contested. Some contests will also have a separate bench for reps, deadlift for reps, or even a curl contest. But the descriptions that follow will be based on a full power meet where the three main powerlifts are being contested.

You want to be sure you are done with your warm-ups with plenty of time left to get to the contest area and be prepared for your first attempt. On the other hand, if you finish your warm-ups too early, you'll cool off before your first attempt. However, it is better to warm-up too early than too late.

To time you warm-ups, you need to find out when you will be lifting. For most contests, the lifters will be divided into "flights" of 10-15 lifters each. For a contest with 30 total lifters, there would probably be two flights of 15 lifters each.

The pattern is as follows: each lifter gets three attempts for each of the three lifts. All of the lifters in the first flight will perform their first attempts. The lifter opening with the lightest weight will go first. Then the lifter with the next heaviest attempt will go next, etc. In other words, the weight on the bar will always increase, never decrease. A list should be posted in the warm-up room with the order of lifters for the first round.

After all of the lifters in the first flight finish their first attempts, the weight will be decreased back to the lightest second attempt. All of lifters in the first flight will then perform their second attempts, again, in the order of lightest to heaviest attempts. But here is where you have to be careful. The order of lifters in the second round might not be the same as it was in the first round. So you have to be listening for the announcer to know when you are up.

Generally, it will be announced on a P.A. system who is "up." This is the lifter who should be ready to lift. It will also be announced who is "on deck" – the next lifter, and who is "in the hole" – the third in line. Once your name is called as being "up" and the bar is announced as being loaded, you have one minute to start your attempt. If you do not do so, your attempt can be disqualified. After your attempt, you then have one minute to give your next attempt to the scorekeeper.

At some contests, these limits are timed to the second, but at other contests, they don't really pay much attention to the time limits and may not even use a clock. So you have to see what it is like at the contest. But whatever the case, it is best to be prepared to start your attempt when you name is called and to give your next attempt to the scorekeeper as soon as possible.

After the second round for flight one, the same pattern will occur for the third round as everyone in flight one takes their third attempts. Then after flight one is finished, flight two will begin their attempts.

What this means is, if you are in the first flight, then you need to be ready to squat when the contest starts. However, if you are in the second flight, you will not need to start warming up until the first flight begins lifting. But this is where it can get difficult to time your warm-ups. You really have no way of knowing how long it will take for flight one to compete all three of its rounds. But you can generally figure on at least an hour for squats, and maybe a little less time for benches and deadlifts. The best you can do is keep an eye on what is happening on the platform and time your warm-ups accordingly.

When the second flight begins their squat attempts, it is time for the first flight to begin warming up for benches. But again, it can be difficult to time your attempts. Also be sure to check if there will be a break in the action between squats and benches. Sometimes, there will about a 15 minute break to give the judges and other meet personal a break. You need to figure this into when to start your warm-ups.

The same flight and rounds pattern will be used for benches as for squats. However, at some full power meets, lifters are allowed to compete in just one of the lifts, with separate awards for the single-lift lifters. This is usually just for benches, but sometimes there are some lifters performing just squats or just deadlifts.

You have to know about such lifters as they can foul up your warm-ups. Sometimes, for instance, there are enough bench-only lifters to constitute another flight. So there might be three rather than just two flights, with usually the bench-only flight going after the regular two flights. This can make for a very long break between benches and deadlifts. So you'll need to wait to start your warm-ups.

Then after benches, there again might be a break in the action for 15 minutes or so. Then the same pattern will be followed for deadlifts. If you're lifting in the second flight you need to be careful as deadlifts tend to move faster than squats and benches. This means you'll have less time to warm-up if you wait until the first flight begins lifting.

What it comes down to is you really need to keep abreast of what is happening and understand you are lifting under far different conditions than you are used to in training. It would be very helpful if you can have someone with you to keep an eye on how things are progressing on the contest platform as you're warming up.

Rules and Reasons for Disqualification

Around the contest platform will be three judges. One sits in front of the lifter and the other two on either side. The judges use a system of colored lights to indicate a lift is passed or failed. A "white light" indicates the lift is good, a red light that it is not. You need two white lights for the lift to be passed.

For contests competing in all three lifts, at the end of the contest, the lifter's best successful attempts for each of the three lifts are added up to give a "total." The lifter with the highest total wins. For single lifts contests, the lifter lifting the most weight wins.

What this means is, for a full power meet, you will have a total of nine attempts, three for each of the three lifts. A "perfect" day in powerlifting would be to go "nine for nine with 27 white lights." This means, the lifter successfully completed and got passed by all three judges all nine of his or her attempts. Going "nine for nine" is often abbreviated as 9/9.

If two attempts were missed, he or she would have gone "seven for nine" (7/9). Often, lifters will report how they did on a particular lift, so getting two out of three squats would be "two for three" (2/3).

The preceding points about not lifting under ideal conditions need to be remembered when picking your attempts for a contest. Also, you need to be aware of the rules for performing the powerlifts. Simply put, the manner in which people perform squats, bench presses, and deadlifts in most gyms would not pass under contest conditions. This is why those who have competed will just smirk when someone starts bragging about how much they lift in the gym. It's only what is done in a contest that matters.

On squats, the most important rule is "The lifter must bend the knees and lower the body until the top of the thigh at the hip, NOT the hip joint, is lower than the top of the kneecap"  (IPA Rulebook). Most people when they squat in the gym don't even come close to squatting down this far. The picture shows what this depth looks like.

Also on squats, in most contests, once you take the weight off of the racks and get set, you must wait for the head judge to signal

"Squat" before starting down. Then after you come back up, you have to wait for the head judge to signal "Rack" before racking the weight.

In regards to the squat racks themselves, there are two main types of racks that might be seen at a contest. The first are hydraulic racks. These operate similar to a car jack, but of course are much larger. They can be adjusted to accommodate the height of just about any lifter. But you need to check the racks before the contest starts to see how you will want them set for your attempts. Then this information needs to be given to the scorekeeper. The scorekeeper will then announce this setting when the weights for your attempts are announced.

Considerably different from hydraulic racks is a monolift, pictured to the right (from 2006 APF PA States).

A monolift is fully adjustable, so you still need to check your settings before the contest starts. But the big difference is that with a monolift you will not need to walk the weight out of the racks.

By this is meant, with hydraulic racks, as with squat racks and power racks at most gyms, after you lift the weight off of the racks, you need to take a step or two backward to get away from the racks so as not to hit the racks during the execution of the lift. This is called walking out the weight. Then after you're done with the lift, you need to walk the weight back in.

However, with a monolift, once you lift the weight off of the racks, a spotter will pull a lever that swings the racks out of your way, as seen on the left-hand side of the picture. This means, you can stay in the same place for the lift. Then after the lift, the head judge will call for the rack, and the spotter will pull the lever down, bringing the racks back in place for you to re-rack the weight. The monolift thus eliminates what was once an essential part of the lift, the walkout, and for that reason its use is controversial, and it is not found at all contests. But a monolift does lessen the chance of an accident occurring.

If a monolift is available, it would be prudent to take advantage of it. But be careful if you are not used to it, as it might throw you off balance. This potential problem will be address in Chapter Nine. But here, it is for this reason that at some contests you will still see lifters walking the weight out even with a monolift.

On benches, nothing can move except the arms. The butt cannot come off the bench, and the feet cannot come off of the ground. At some contests, the head also must stay on the bench. But most importantly, when you lower the weight to the chest, you must pause at the chest, holding the bar motionless, and wait for the head judge to signal "Press" to start pressing the weight back up. Once the arms are extended straight, you again have to wait for the "Rack" signal.

Note also that the bar must come up evenly, meaning both hands must come up together at about the same speed. You might get away with a slight uneven extension, but even then, both arms must lockout at the same time. If one lockouts first, you could be red-lighted.

At most contests, the "chest" is defined as finishing at the base of the sternum/ breastbone, so you cannot touch your body lower than that point. At some contests the bar is allowed to be lowered to the stomach, but it would be best to learn to bench with touching the chest.

But again, when people bench in the gym, they often do not even come close to following all of these steps. Butts coming off of the bench, feet kicking in the air, bouncing the bar off of the chest or not touching the chest, coming up and locking out unevenly, and racking the weight before the arms are straight are all commons sights in a gym, but all of these would get you disqualified in a contest.

As for deadlifts, there are three main issues to watch out for. The first is "hitching" which is supporting and bouncing the bar on the thighs at the end of the lift. Second, once you have lifted the weight, you have to wait for the head judge's "Down" command to lower the weight. Third, when you lower the weight you must do so in a controlled manner. Dropping the weight will result in disqualification.

But the biggest problem on deadlifts is fatigue. As indicated previously, most likely you will have arrived at the contest site in the early morning. But it will be the afternoon, possibly late in the afternoon or even the early evening before you are deadlifting. Or to look at it another way, there could easily be 5-10 hours from the time you first started warming up for squats to when you are pulling your last deadlift. Many a powerlifter, this writer included, has simply "run out of gas" by their final deadlift attempt. This is why, even though powerlifting is a strength sport, general conditioning is still very important.

One final point applies to all three lifts. Once you start lifting the bar up, it cannot drop back down again. It is allowed to stop and then start moving again, but it cannot drop down even slightly.

Having said all of this, going back to picking attempts, you need to be very conservative, especially on your openers (first attempts). You want to be sure you get at least one attempt completed and passed for each of the three lifts. Failing to do so will result in a "bomb out." This refers to missing all three of your attempts on a given lift. If this happens, you are out of the contest. And trust me, you will feel terrible.

Your opener should be a weight that you know you can get no matter what goes wrong. And on squats, it should be a weight you can sink so low there will be no doubt it will pass.

This is an important point as you never know what the judging will be like until the meet starts. At some contests, the judging might be much stricter than at others. What might be considered a good lift at one contest might not pass at another. But you need to be prepared to go very deep. After your first attempt, you should watch some of the other lifters, and if the judges are passing lifts that are not quite so low, then you can cut it a little higher on your next two attempts. Tips on picking your attempts will be given later in this book.

Picking a Contest

Before picking a contest to enter, you need to be aware of the mess that powerlifting is in today organizationally. This issue will be addressed in detail in Chapter Three. But here, it will just be said, there are over 20 different powerlifting federations, each with slightly different rules. This is why phrases like "at most contests" or "at some contests" are used in this chapter. Some federations, for instance, have a 24-hour weigh-in rule while others only allow weigh-ins the morning of the contest.

But as a new lifter, you do not need to get hung up on all of these differences and the politics behind them. When starting out, it would be best to just enter whatever federation is holding a contest near your home. There are two ways to go about finding a contest.

The first would be to check the list of "Coming Events" in *Powerlifting USA* magazine (see Appendix #1). The second is by checking the Web sites for the various federations. Most will have a "Schedule of Events" posted on their site. See Chapter Three for the URLs for these sites. Once you find a contest, it would be wise to read over the rulebook for that federation. Most federations have their rulebooks posted or available for download on their Web sites.

Whatever contest you decide to enter, you will need to send in the entry form for the contest beforehand. Entry forms are usually available for download off of the federation's Web site or can be ordered by contacting the meet director. Be sure to observe the entry deadline on the entry form and send it in before that date.

Supportive Gear

In checking out contests to enter, there is a difficult issue you will need to make a decision on. This would be whether to utilize various types of supportive gear. This subject will be address in detail in the next couple of chapters. Different powerlifting federations have different gear rules, so you need to check this out before a contest.

But suffice it to say here, you will need to abide by the rules of the federation that sanctions the contest you decide to enter. Find out what these are and purchase gear accordingly.

But I would suggest, if it is allowed, to wear a belt, wrist wraps, and knee sleeves or knee wraps. These will provide support for the given joints but are not very expensive. I would suggest holding off on other types of gear that is more costly. There is no sense in spending the money until you are sure you want to continue with powerlifting.

Atmosphere and Conclusion

At some contests, there will be heavy metal music blaring, lifters screaming to psyche themselves up, and others yelling, cheering them on. At other contests, there will be no music and little screaming and yelling. Personally, I prefer the loud and rowdy atmosphere.

But whatever the atmosphere, powerlifting contests can be exciting and challenging. At the very least, planning on entering a contest will give you an incentive to be consistent in your weightlifting workouts and to train with a higher degree of intensity.

There are many difficulties in competing, but these are far outweighed by the many joys and benefits. I hope this chapter will give the reader some idea of what a powerlifting contest is like so you will be prepared if you decide to compete. But even better would be to attend a contest as a spectator before competing yourself. That way, you will be able to see all of the preceding points in action and be even more prepared when it is your turn to get on the platform to compete in the world's strongest sport.

Chapter Two:
Gear Descriptions

This chapter will provide descriptions and pictures of the various types of gear that can be worn and used by powerlifters. Some of this gear is available from APT Pro Lifting Gear (www.prowriststraps.com ~ 888-236-1258). The rest of the gear to be discussed is available from a variety of powerlifting gear companies. A list of such companies can be found in Appendix #1.

Singlet and a T-shirt

At almost all contests, you will be required to wear a singlet. This is the same type of one-piece outfit a high school, college, or Olympic wrestler wears. Pictured is the singlet sold by APT. The only exception to this rule is at some contests teenagers are allowed to wear gym shorts and a T-shirt.

The purpose of requiring a singlet is two-fold. First, it looks nice for all lifters to be wearing the same type of outfit.

Second, and more importantly, it was mentioned in the previous chapter that on benches, your butt is not allowed to come off of the bench. If the lifter was wearing a loose fitting pair of gym shorts, then the judges could not tell if the butt is off of the bench due to the shorts hanging down. But a singlet fits snuggly on the body, so the judges can see if there is any "daylight" between the butt and the bench. Remember this in training and at a contest. You will not get away with even a slight elevation of the butt.

A singlet is rather inexpensive, costing about $35.

Most federations require a T-shirt to be worn under the singlet on squats and benches. This is for hygienic purposes, to keep sweat from getting onto the bar on squats and onto the bench on benches. But some federations do not require a T-shirts on deadlifts, since no part of the upper body ever touches the bar.

That is why I am not wearing a T-shirt in the picture of me deadlifting in the "About the Author" chapter. I didn't wear a shirt as it was very hot that day, so I was taking advantage of the rules to keep from getting overheated like I did at my previous contest on deadlifts.

But note that some federations are rather "picky" about the type of T-shirt that is worn. Some require that it has short sleeves, so a sleeveless T-shirt is not allowed. Also, some do not allow it to have a pocket on it. But some federations allow both. This is why it was said in the previous chapter that you should always read the rulebook before entering a contest. You don't want something stupid like a pocket on a T-shirt to cause you problems at the contest.

Along these lines, women are allowed to wear a bra underneath the T-shirt, but you need to be careful about what kind of bra you wear. The bra cannot "maintain its shape when placed upright upon a flat surface. It must not contain any wire or supportive device" (NASA Rulebook).

I mention this as I remember an incident back at Penn State. One of the Lady Lions in the Barbell Club who was (how should say this?) rather "developed" was not allowed to wear her underwire bra at National Collegiates. She had to borrow a bra from another woman who was not near as busty as she was. She said it was not very comfortable. Again, always read the rulebook before a contest.

Shoes

In the "About the Author" chapter, the first picture is of this writer squatting in college. It can be seen in that picture that I am wearing a pair of low-top sneakers (a.k.a. tennis shoes, or "tenners" here in the Pittsburgh, PA area). But that is not the best kind of footwear to wear on squats as they do not provide much support.

Later in college, I began to wear high-top work boots, and wearing boots of some sort for squats is very common. I remember back in college, one of the other lifters in the Barbell Club, an ex-marine, wore military boots. Such boots provide much better support for squatting, but they are rather heavy for walking out the weight.

Even better are today's specialty squat shoes. At some contests, such specialty shoes are required to be worn. They are usually high-top shoes, made of leather, with Velcro straps across the laces to provide even better support. The Velcro straps also enable the lifter to easily loosen the shoes between attempts or sets then be pulled very tight for the actual lifts. Most have some kind of small heal, usually ½" – 1". Such heals provide stability for the lift. I am wearing Crain Power Shoes in the picture on the preceding page (taken at 2006 APF PA States).

However, such shoes can be rather expensive, costing about $125, as of this writing. So if the contest allows, it would probably be best to wear some kind of high-top sneakers or boots for one's first contest or two. Once you are certain you plan on continuing with powerlifting, then it would be good to invest in a good pair of squat shoes.

For deadlifts, back in college, I wore wrestling shoes. The reasoning here is that wrestling shoes have very thin soles, so they do not add to the distance you have to pull the bar. Also, they do not have heals. Heals would cause you to lean forward, which is the exact opposite direction you are trying to pull the bar. Wrestling shoes are also high-tops, and thus provide ankle support.

I still had wrestling shoes from college when I started lifting again, so I initially wore them. But then later, when they wore out, I purchased a pair of Nike wrestling shoes. I can be seen wearing these Nike shoes in the deadlift picture in the "About the Author" chapter.

Most powerlifting gear companies sell "deadlift shoes" that they claim are not the same as wrestling shoes, but they sure look like they are to me. The price is about the same either way, but I preferred to buy the shoes locally rather than ordering them so I could try them on first. But either wrestling or specialty deadlift shoes would work.

Some federations allow gymnastic slippers to be worn. These are basically socks with thin soles. The idea is the same as with wrestling shoes, to keep the lifter as close to the floor as possible. But they provide little support, so I have never worn them. If you are using a close (conventional) stance on deadlifts, they might be okay, but I would not recommend them if you use a wide (sumo) stance. With that stance, you need the ankle support that high-top wrestling shoes provide.

For benches, sneakers work just fine. Just be sure they fit snuggly and do not slip on the floor. See the picture on the next page for the Nike "tenners" I wear for benches.

Powerlifting Belt

The most basic support gear is a powerlifting belt. Most people who lift weights are familiar with a standard weightlifting belt, seen in many gyms. Such a belt is four inches wide in the back, tapering to two inches in the front. It is one quarter of an inch thick and is generally brown or black and made of leather.

However, a powerlifting belt is different. It is four inches (10 cm) wide all the way around and is twice as thick, half an inch (13 mm). It is made of leather and is usually covered in felt and can be ordered in just about any color or color combination the lifter wants. The belt you see me wearing in most of the contest pictures in this book is a bright red Crain power belt. But pictured above is APT's "Woodland Camo" colored belt.

The purpose of the belt being 4" wide all the way around is to increase intra-abdominal pressure, thus more effectively supporting the torso. A belt adds little to how much a lifter can lift, but it does provide stability and support.

The standard belt and the one I have always worn has a single prong buckle. But double-prong buckles are also available, as seen in the picture. Also available are belts with a lever instead of a buckle.

Some specialty belts are also available. The first would be a bench belt. This belt has the same basic design, but is only 2" wide all the way around. The reason for the thinner belt is so that the belt does not get in the way of the lifter arching on the bench press. I am wearing such a belt in the picture (taken at NASA Northeastern States, June 7, 2008). My arch is not as pronounced as some, but for those who really arch, then such a belt is essential.

Also available is a specialty deadlift belt that is similar to a standard weighting belt, 4" wide in the back but tapering to 2" in the front, but still ½" thick. The thinner front is so the belt does not get in the way of getting down to the bar for the start of the deadlift.

A belt is not required, but all federations and divisions allow a belt to be worn, and it is wise to do so for the support and protection.

A belt will cost from $40 – 100, depending on the type and brand, more if you want your name embroidered on it, as some companies will do. But be careful as some federations do not allow you to have your name written on the outside of your belt, but some do. Most federations allow the name of your nation, state, club, or sponsor or the manufacturer's name on it, but nothing else. This restriction applies to not just the belt, but also to the t-shirt, singlet, and any other gear.

If you take care of it, a belt with last a lifetime, so it is a worthwhile investment. In fact, when I started powerlifting again, for my first contest in 21 years, I used the same belt I used in college. But by my next contest, I bought a new one, but only because I wanted a different color! In college, my belt and all of my gear were blue due to attending Penn State. But red is my favorite color, so I wanted to switch to red for my gear and got myself the bright red belt.

Wrist Wraps

Wrist wraps, as the name implies, wrap around wrist. They are usually held in place by Velcro. Most have a thumb loop to hold the wraps in place until you tighten them. But be careful as some federations do not allow the thumb loops to remain over the thumb during the execution of the lift. So after tightening them, get in the habit of pulling the thumb loop off of the thumb.

In most federations, wrist wraps are allowed to be up to 8 cm (3") wide and up to one meter long. But they are available in a variety of lengths, from 12" up to 36". I can be seen wearing APT 24" Black Mamba wrist wraps in the bench picture on the previous page, and pictured to the right is APT's Strangulater wrist wraps.

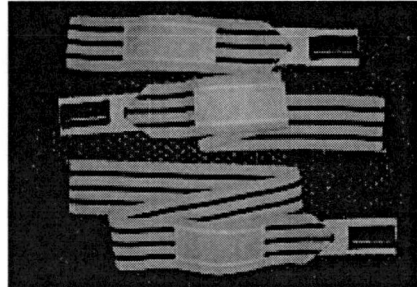

Wrist wraps obviously provide support to the wrists, but they do not add anything to how much a lifter can lift. Wrist wraps are most commonly worn on benches, but some lifters wear them on squats and even on deadlifts.

But for deadlifts, you need to be sure they do not get in the way of the pull. For that reason, in college I just wore the basic "Ace" type of wrist wraps that can be purchased at a pharmacy or sporting goods store. More recently, I wore APT's wrist bands, which slip over the wrist like sweat bands.

In most federations, you are allowed to wear wrist wraps or wrist bands or sweat bands, but you are not allowed to wear any kind of combination of wraps and bands. Wrist wraps cost from $15 – 40 a pair, depending on the quality, length, and brand.

Knee Sleeves

In college, for deadlifts, I generally wore the type of knee sleeves that can be purchased at a pharmacy or sporting goods store. These can be easily pulled up and down over the calves onto the knees. But more recently, I have worn APT's original knee sleeves for deadlifts. I can be seen wearing them in the picture of me deadlifting in the "About the Author" chapter. However, these are no longer available.

APT's now instead offers heavy knee sleeves that are about twice as thick as the pharmacy type knee sleeves or their original knee sleeves. I have found they provided plenty of support even for squats, but they add little to the performance of either squats or deadlifts.

APT also has available Convict knee sleeves (pictured to the left). These are thicker and longer than their heavy knee sleeves. They thus provide even more support, but they still add little to how much can be lifted. And they are more difficult to put on and take off.

For these reasons, I prefer the heavy knee sleeves. They are the type of knee support I would recommend for a lifter's first contest. They provide more than sufficient support to protect the knees but are inexpensive and very easy to use. They can be easily pulled up onto the knees for the lift then pulled down between lifts.

Considerably different and more expensive are Inzer's Knee Sleeves XT. They have three Velcro straps going across the front that can be tightened over the knee. This design enables them to evade the main limitation of knee sleeves.

Knee sleeves must be pulled up over the feet and calves, and that limits how tight of knee sleeves a lifter can get on. But the Velcro straps enable the knee sleeves to effectively fit very tight. With doing so, they can add significantly to one's squat. Never having used them, I cannot say how much, but it would probably approach that of knee wraps (to be discussed next).

The controversy over such knee sleeves will be discussed in Chapter Five. But here, it will be said that the above mentioned knee sleeves cost from $30 for a pair of the APT knee sleeves to $55 for a pair of the Inzer knee sleeves.

Knee Wraps

Knee wraps are somewhat similar to an "Ace" bandage, but they are much stronger and thicker. The allowed width is the same as for wrist wraps, 8 cm (3"). But they can be 2.0 meter, 2.5 meter or even 3.5 meters long. Different federations differ in their rules as to how long of a wrap is allowed. This will be addressed in the next chapter.

The knee is wrapped in a spiral or crisscross fashion. For the spiral fashion, you start a little above the knee, then wrap around the knee going downward, overlapping each wrap, then back up again. The end is then tucked underneath a previous wrap.

But I have always used a crisscross method. You wrap just once above the knee, leaving some of the end of the wrap sticking out. You then cross over the knee in a diagonal fashion, then make one wrap around just below the knee, then cross over the knee in the opposite fashion as the first cross, thus making an "X".

The crisscrossing is continued until you run out of wrap, leaving just enough to tie the wrap onto the first end that you left handing out.

But it should be noted that not all knee wraps will work for the crisscross method of wrapping. Most of today's wraps are too stiff to allow the crossing and tying of the wraps. The only wraps I've found that work are Crain Genesis Power Wraps, Titan THP wraps, and APT's Blue or Black Mamba knee wraps. Pictured is APT"s Blue Mamba knee wraps.

Whichever method is used, throughout the wrapping process, the leg should be kept straight and the wrap should be pulled out so that once wrapped, it fits very tight around the knee. In fact, you should not be able to bend you knee if it is wrapped properly. But once you put the weight on your back, the extra weight will "push" you down and then the wrap will help to "lift" you back up.

The original purpose of knee wraps was to help protect the lifter's knees from injury. But due to the "lifting up" effect, knee wraps can also add significantly to how much a lifter can squat.

When I powerlifted in college, all lifters used "Super Wraps." These were white wraps, 2.0 meters long and about twice as thick as an Ace bandage. They probably added about 10-15 pounds to one's squat. I can be seen wearing such wraps in the picture of me squatting in college in the introductory chapter "About the Author."

But today's wraps are much stronger and thicker and can easily add twice that amount or more to one's squat. Adding even more are 2.5 meter and 3.5 meter wraps. This again leads to much controversy that will be addressed in Chapter Five. But even greater controversy surrounds the rest of the gear to be discussed in this chapter.

The cost of knee wraps varies from $15 – 80 a pair, depending on the quality, length, and brand. Knee wraps tend to wear out rather quickly. Many lifters will purchase a new pair for every contest, and then afterwards use that pair for training until the next contest.

Squat and Deadlift Suits

A squat suit or deadlift suit looks like a singlet. But that is where the similarity ends. Squat and deadlift suits are made of much thicker and stronger material.

In my college lifting days, all lifters wore a "Super Suit." I can be seen wearing this suit in the picture to the right (taken October 1981 in the old "Rec Hall" at Penn State Main Campus for an article in *The Collegiate* school newspaper).

The original purpose of the suit was to provide protection for the hips and groin area. But a Super Suit also added to the squat about the same amount as the Super Wraps, about 10-15 pounds. So together, the gear added about 20-30 pounds to one's squat. But the suit did little to add to one's deadlift.

Looking at a properly fitting squat suit before you put it on it looks like it is a couple of sizes too small. But that is the idea.

Picture an attractive woman wearing a very tight pair of jeans (a pleasant thought I know). Now picture her trying to squat down. Most likely, she will have a difficult time doing so. But put a couple of hundred pounds on her back, and the weight will push her down. But then the tight jeans, if they don't rip, will help to push her back up.

It is the same idea with a squat suit. But with the suit extending up the torso and with straps going over the shoulders, the effect is much greater. And the material is such that it is not that likely to rip (although blowouts do happen and can be dangerous).

Now, back up and picture that attractive woman trying to get the too tight jeans on. She might need to lie on a bed and kick her feet in the air. But that is nothing compared to the difficulty of getting a squat suit on.

With today's suits, it can sometimes take a couple helpers and 10-20 minutes to get the suit on. In fact, it can be quite a workout in itself. But they add considerably more to one's squat than the old Super Suits. But how much depends on the type of suit and the lifter.

The old Super Suit was what would be called today a single-ply, polyester suit, and such suits are still available today. In fact, the first suit I got when I started powerlifting again was such a suit, a Crain Genesis Power Suit to be exact. It seemed to add about twice what my college suit did. But that suit was made of what would now be called old-style polyester. There is now available a newer "super-poly" that can add considerably more, and that is just for single-ply suits.

But also now available are double-ply polyester suits. My second suit was such a suit, the same brand as my first suit but in double-ply. I can be seen wearing this suit in the first picture in this chapter. That suit added probably about 50 pounds to my squat. But again, that was using the older style polyester. Crain and most every other gear manufacturer now uses the new "super-poly" that reportedly adds much more to one's squat.

But polyester is only one type of material that suits can be made of. Suits can also be made of denim or canvas. To the right is a picture of me wearing a Ginny's Powerwear canvas squat suit. I got out of this suit about what I did the double-ply poly suit, about 50 pounds. But some report getting much more.

In fact, some report getting as much 100-200 pounds or more put out of either the newer double-ply, super-poly suits or a canvas suit. But it should be stated, not all federations allow double-ply or canvas suits. Many only allow single-ply, poly suits. But still, even with that restriction, with today's super-poly material, 50-100 pounds is commonly reported. And it is because of such numbers that the use of squat suits has gotten very controversial.

However, I should mention that I never found even today's deadlift suits to add much of anything to my pull. But some report getting as much as 50 pounds out of a deadlift suit.

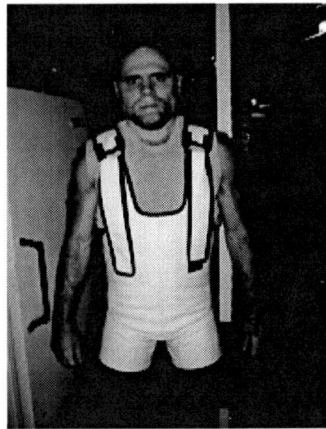

The price of a squat or deadlift suit can vary greatly, depending on the material, the number of plies, the quality, and the brand. A basic, single-ply poly suit can be found for as little as $50, while a top of the line, double-ply super-poly or canvas suit can cost up to $300.

Adding to this cost would be any alterations that might need to be made, and almost certainly that will be the case. It is unlikely that a suit will fit you just right "off of the rack" so to speak. Once you try it on, you will most likely need to send it back to the manufacturer to get it altered. And that will cost money for both the shipping and the alteration itself. You also must remember this when ordering a new suit. Allot plenty of time before your next contest.

You could just take the suit too a local seamstress or alter it yourself if you are so skilled, but doing so could void the warranty. Most new suits are guaranteed against blowouts for something like one year.

Briefs

Standard brief underwear or a jock strap is allowed to be worn under the suit or singlet. But some federations also allow supportive "briefs" to be worn.

As the name implies, these originally looked like "tighty whities" but were made of the same material as a basic squat suit, single-ply polyester supportive material. Those types of briefs added little to one's squats, but they are still available.

But the briefs evolved to look more like boxer briefs, having legs, and then to extend much further up the torso than briefs of any sort normally would. So now, your standard powerlifting briefs are basically a squat suit without straps.

Briefs are generally made of single-ply or double-ply poly. The first briefs I used were Titan "boxer briefs," which are single-ply poly. But later, I got a pair custom made by Ginny Phillips of Ginny's Powerwear, using her specialty "stretch denim." I can be seen swearing these in the picture.

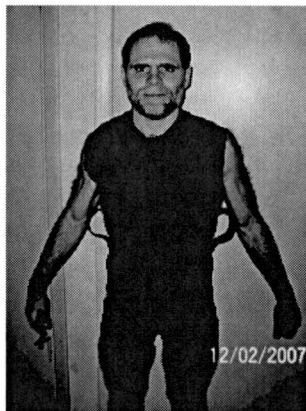
12/02/2007

Note that the loops on the side are not standard for briefs. I had Ginny add these special to give me something to grab onto when putting the briefs on. But such loops would not be legal in all federations that allow briefs.

34

Without the loops, briefs can be even more difficult to get on and off than a suit, since there are no straps to use as "handles" to pull on. But I should mentioned that it really is not wise to use the straps as handles as that can stretch them out, but most lifters do anyhow.

As for how much briefs add, that is hard for me to say. When I was experimenting with different briefs, I was also experimenting with different suits. But it didn't seem to me that they really added that much. Since I was already wearing a double-ply poly or canvas suit, I don't think having another layer or two of briefs make that much difference. But some lifters seem to think that briefs can add almost as much as a suit, on top of what the suit adds.

As for the cost, that can range from as little as $20 for the basic single-ply briefs without legs, to $150 for double-ply super-poly boxer-type briefs.

Summary of Squat Gear

Combining all of the gear mentioned so far can add considerably to how much a lifter can squat. Personally, I probably get close to 100 pounds out of 2.5 meter knee wraps, a double-ply poly or canvas suit, and briefs. But some lifters report getting much more than this, especially those in the heavier weight classes. Some heavier weight lifters report getting as much as 300 pounds out of their squat gear.

To put that in perspective, a lifter who can squat 600 pounds without gear could squat as much as 900 pounds with gear. That type of poundage would put someone into an altogether different level of performance, and that is why there is such controversy over gear. Again, this subject will be addressed in detail in Chapter Five.

But here, it will be said all of that gear can be quite expensive. That lifter getting 300 pounds out of his gear could easily have spent over $500 on all of that gear, and that is another reason for the controversy. Not every one can afford to spend that much on gear.

It should also be mentioned that putting on all of that gear and taking it off can also be very time consuming. This needs to be remembered when warming up for squats at a contest. You need to allot plenty of time for getting into your gear, along with the time it takes you to do your actual warm-ups sets.

For your actual contest attempts, you need to start getting ready before your name is called as being "up" to give yourself time to wrap your knees, tighten your wrist wraps, get your straps pulled up, and tighten your belt. Then as soon as you are done with your first attempt, you need to loosen all of that gear, roll up your knee wraps, and start getting ready for your next attempt.

All of this focusing on gear can make it difficult to focus on your actual attempts. It can also be very exhausting. And that again, is why some find the gear to be so disagreeable. I'll discuss my problems in this regard later in this book.

Bench Press Shirt

We now come to probably the most unique and controversial piece of powerlifting gear, the bench press shirt. Such shirts were just coming out when I stopped powerlifting back in college, so I never wore one back then. But I remember that my roommate got one. It looked rather stupid to me, and he said it didn't do much, so I just never bothered with it. But the idea behind it was that it would protect the shoulders.

When I started powerlifting again, I ordered a bench press shirt when I ordered my initial squat and deadlift suit. It was a Crain single-ply poly Power Shirt. That shirt was a basic bench press shirt, which looks like a short sleeve T-shirt. But that is where the similarity ends.

A bench shirt is made out of the same type of material as a squat suit and can be single-, double-, or even triple-ply. Along with polyester, they can also be made out of denim material.

Unlike a T-shirt which has the arms going out to the sides, the arms on a bench shirt angle more towards the front. If the shirt is fitting properly, which is to say, very tight, it should be difficult if not impossible to pull your arms back without any weight. But as with a squat suit, add some weight, and the weight helps to push the bar down to your chest, and then the shirt helps you to lift the bar back off of your chest.

These points can be seen in the pictures on this page. I am wearing a Crain Double Xtreme Power Shirt. In the first, you can see how my arms are pushed to the front by the shirt. In the second, I am pulling

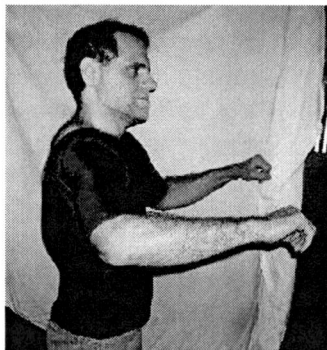

my arms as far back as I am able, but as you can see, that is not very far. And it should be noted, many lifters wear shirts that would not allow their arms to be pulled back even that far.

The first shirts were all closed back shirts, like a T-shirt. Getting such a shirt on and off can be very difficult and cannot be done by yourself. It takes one or two helpers to get the shirt on and off. It is also very uncomfortable to wear. The tightness in the chest can be almost unbearable, and I found it very difficult to breathe with it on. But such closed back shirts are the only type of shirts that are allowed in some federations.

Generally speaking, federations that only allow single-ply polyester shirts also only allow closed back shirts. But now at least, most manufacturers make shirts with stretchy material on the back. This makes it a little easier to get the shirt on and off, and makes wearing the shirt not quite so oppressive.

But along the way, some lifters figured out that a shirt with an open back was easier to get on and off, and it actually added more to the lift. It was also found that denim was an even more advantageous material. As a result, most federations that allow multi-ply poly shirts also allow open back shirts and shirts made of denim.

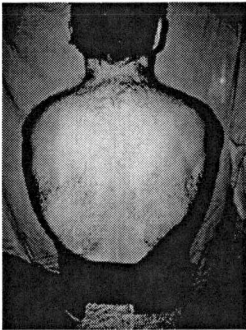

My Double Xtreme shirt was initially a closed back shirt, but after my first contest wearing it, I had it converted into an open back shirt. I can be seen wearing this shirt in the bench picture earlier in this chapter.

The picture to the left shows what is meant by open back. At the bottom, near the belt area, is 4" wide Velcro that helps to hold the shirt in place. Wearing a tight belt also helps in this regard. But it is worth noting how very little such a shirt resembles a T-shirt.

The open back shirt is relatively easy to get on and off. I can even do it myself. But it still feels very tight when wearing it, and is anything but comfortable. Wearing it for an extended period of time can be tiring due to the tightness. But then, the same can be said for a tight squat suit.

How much a bench shirt adds to one's bench press can vary greatly, depending on the type of shirt and on the lifter. It takes a lot of practice to get used to using a bench shirt, and getting a lot out of it is a skill that needs to be developed. One's training even needs to be adjusted to accommodate the shirt, as will be addressed later.

Personally, I never got that much out of a shirt. My first shirt probably only added about 10-15 pounds to my bench. The pictured shirt

shirt added about 30-40 pounds. But that is minuscule to what some report getting from their shirts.

Some lifters report getting as much as 100 – 200 pounds out of a single-ply shirt and as much as 300 pounds out of a multi-ply shirt. This means, the amount a bench shirt can add is about the same as all of the gear together on squats.

Add up what some lifters get out of their squat gear and bench shirt, along with a few pounds out of a deadlift suit, and such lifters are totaling up to 600 pounds more with gear than they would be able to do so without gear. And again, this is why gear is so controversial.

But I should say that these really high amounts are for heavy-weight and very experienced lifters. Again, I never got anything near this poundage. But then, I'm a lightweight. And how much gear adds is best figured out on a percentage basis. Gear can add from 20-40% to one's squat and bench press, depending on the number of plies, the material, and the skill of the lifter

As for the cost of a bench shirt, again, this varies widely. A basic, single-ply shirt can be found for as little as $40, while a top of the line, double or triple ply denim shirt can cost as much as $250.

But again, this is before alterations. Even more so than with a squat suit, plan on having to get your shirt altered at least once, maybe several times to get it to fit just right. That will add to the total expense. Add this amount to the cost of squat gear, a deadlift suit, and miscellaneous other gear, and the total cost can come to over a grand.

However, it must be emphasized that none of this gear is necessary to compete in powerlifting. The only specialized gear that is required is a singlet. Everything else is optional, so I do not want to scare off anyone from powerlifting by mentioning such expense.

But that is why it was recommended in the previous chapter that you lift with limited gear for at least a contest or two before investing in more expensive gear. And it is more than possible to continue to compete with little gear. In fact, some believe that doing so is more legitimate than lifting with gear, as will be discussed in Chapter Five.

Tips on getting gear on and off will be presented in Chapter 23.

Elbow Sleeves and Wrist Straps

It would be good to inject here a few comments on two kinds of gear that are *not* allowed in any federation.

The first would be elbow support of any sort. This rule has always seemed a little strange to me, even back in college. It just made no sense to me to allow heavy duty knee wraps but not to even allow drugstore-type elbow sleeves. Was the knee somehow a more important joint to protect than the elbow?

But whatever my thoughts, the rules back then and still today universally in powerlifting is that nothing whatsoever can be worn on the elbows during bench presses, not even elbow warmers. You can wear support on every other joint of the body, but not the elbows. So if you have elbow pain that prevents you from doing heavy bench presses without some support, you are out of luck.

To be clear, some federations do allow elbow warmers or even elbow sleeves to be worn during squats and deadlifts, although, why you would want to is beyond me. But no such gear can be worn on the elbows for benches.

The second type of gear that is not allowed in any federation is wrist straps. These are pictured to the right.

Wrist straps make it easier to hang onto the bar on pulling exercises. They are commonly used on deadlifts and upper back exercises, like rows, lat pulldowns, and pull-ups. However, if you have any aspirations to be a powerlifter, do not use them on such exercises.

If you have problems hanging onto your deadlifts, then you need to work on your forearm and gripping strength. Exercises for doing so will be discussed later in this book. But here, it will be said, just doing your deadlifts and upper back work without wrist straps will increase your gripping strength, so frankly, it is not wise to use them on such exercises even if you are not a powerlifter.

However, there are two exercises where wrist straps are needed, rack pulls and shrugs. These exercises will be discussed in Chapter 12.

Chalk and Baby Powder

Before closing this chapter, it would be good to mention a few additional items that will be of help to the powerlifter. The first is lifting chalk, which is the same as gymnastic chalk, which is magnesium carbonate. It is used on the hands of powerlifters, gymnasts, and other athletes to ensure a sound grip.

Chalk is especially important to use on the hands for deadlifts, but it can be helpful on squats and benches as well, along with other exercises done in the gym.

In addition, for squats and benches, it is a good idea to chalk your upper back. This will help keep the bar from slipping on squats and your upper back from slipping on the bench. The latter is especially important if you have a pronounced arch. In that case, it is also good to chalk you butt. Unfortunately, many commercial gyms do not allow chalk to be used anymore.

I will address such nonsense later in this book, but here I will say, if you are at all serious about powerlifting, then find a gym that will at least accommodate powerlifters to the degree of allowing chalk. To try to pull a heavy deadlift without it can lead to many missed pulls due to a loss of grip.

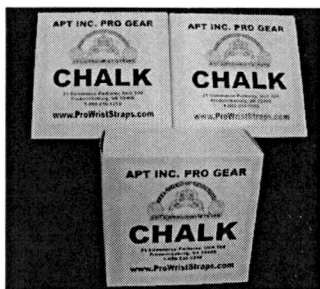

At most contests, chalk will be provided in some type of bin for all lifters to use. But I would strongly suggest you take your own, just in case the chalk runs out. That could be disastrous if it happened right before your final and heaviest deadlift.

Chalk is very inexpensive. A pound (8 – 2 ounce blocks) can be purchase for about $15 from APT or just about any other gear provider. Get yourself a pound of it. It will last a long time.

But be very careful when putting chalk on your hands for deadlifts that you do not get any on your thighs. That is last thing you would want as the chalk would make it much harder to drag the bar up your thighs at the end of the lift.

In fact, what you should put on your thighs for deadlifts is baby powder, which has the opposite effect of chalk. Baby powder will make it very easy to slide the bar up your thighs.

However, you must be very careful when using baby powder. You do not want to get any on your hands as that could cause you to lose your grip. Also be sure to not get any on the floor, as if you or someone else were to step on it, that could cause you to slip then or your feet to slip while on the platform. For these reasons, I can understand gyms not allowing lifters to use baby powder.

In any case, shake a very small amount of the baby powder in the middle of your thigh, then use the side of the bottle to spread it over your thighs. I would suggest keeping a hand towel in your gym bag to wipe your hands off after using the baby powder and to wipe up any that might spill on the floor.

I would also suggest not using baby powder in training, even if your gym allows it. That way, it will make the top part of the lift a little harder in training. Then come contest time with the baby powder, it will give you a little "edge" and the confidence that if you can get the bar above your knees, there is no way you'll miss it at your thighs. The bar will just seem to fly up from there.

But it should be noted that chalk and baby powder are the only substances that are allowed to be applied to the lifter's body during a contest. Oil, grease, or other lubricants are not allowed.

Gym Bags

It goes without saying that you will need something to carry all of the preceding gear in, and most lifters use a gym bag, or two, or three. I say this as if you are using all of the gear mentioned in this chapter, you will not be able to fit it into one bag, unless it is a very large bag, like a duffle bag.

When using full gear, I've found it best to take three gym bags to a contest—one for all of my squat gear, one for all of my bench and deadlift gear, and a third, smaller bag to keep my chalk and wraps in that I will be using for a given lift.

If you're lifting raw or unequipped, you will not have near as much gear to carry. But still, if you're using a different belt and shoes for each lift, then you will need a gym bag larger than the standard size seen at most gyms. I recently got the pictured APT "mid size" bag for this purpose, and it fit all of my gear for lifting unequipped just fine.

Food and Water Containers

You will also need a container to store food in for the contest. What to eat during a contest will be addressed in Chapter 21. But it will be said here, with the length of a contest, you need to plan on packing enough food to get you through the day. Of course, if you take anything that needs to stay cool, you will need a cooler with ice.

I would also strongly suggest taking a water jug with you. You do not want to depend on a water fountain or purchasing bottled water. Trust me, with the length of most contests, and especially if it is hot, you will end up drinking a lot of water.

In fact, for my last two contests, both in the summer heat, I went through a half gallon jug of water by the time benches were done. But fortunately, I had the foresight to take an extra gallon of water that I left in my car, so I went out to the parking lot to get it before deadlifts. Staying hydrated is vital as even a small amount of dehydration can adversely affect your performance.

Paperwork, Calculator, Cash

Before the contest, I strongly suggest you write down all of your planned attempts, along with all of the weights for your warm-up sets. But to do so, you need to find out beforehand if the contest will be in pounds or kilograms. Also be sure to ask about the warm-up room. Sometimes, the contest will be in kilos, but the weights in the warm-up room will be in pounds. But whatever the case, have it all written down and take that with you.

If the contest is in kilograms, then take a kilo conversion chart with you in case you need to change an attempt. Such a chart will probably be found on the Web site of the federation.

A calculator will also help with the conversions (1 kilogram = 2.2046 pounds). A calculator will also be helpful in figuring out subtotals and totals, which might be important if you're in a close contest. I know of one lifter who lost a contest because her coach didn't calculate correctly what she needed to pull for her last deadlift attempt. He ended up calling for five pounds less than she needed for the win.

Also be sure to check beforehand what the records are for your division in the federation sanctioning the contest and have those written down. If there is a chance you will be breaking a record, be sure to inform the scorekeeper so that proper documentation can be made.

You need to purchase a membership card for the federation hosting the contest. If you purchased it beforehand, be sure you take it with you. If not, be sure you have cash on hand to buy one at the contest. Also at some contests, companies will be selling gear and other products, so take some extra cash in case you see something you like.

And finally, if you are entering an age division, you might need to have on hand some proof of your age, like a driver's license or birth certificate, so be sure to take that as well.

"Just in Case"

Extra laces for your shoes in case one breaks, a watch to keep track of time during your warm-ups in case there is not a clock in the warm-up room, and even an extra pair of socks in case you manage to misplace them while changing gear between lifts (as I stupidly did once) are all things you might want to take "just in case."

You might also want to take some bandages in case you manage to cut yourself, or more likely, cause bleeding by hitting the bar against your shins on deadlifts (you are not allowed on the platform if you are bleeding, for obvious reasons). Personally, I often cause bleeding on deadlifts, so I usually put bandages on my shins in the appropriate spots beforehand to prevent bleeding.

You also should take along backup gear for every piece of gear you're planning on using. That way, if something goes wrong, like say a suit blowout, you will have something to fall back on. I usually take an extra gym bag with me with older gear that I leave in the car. I only had to resort to it once, when I had problems with a newer suit and briefs, so I had to go back to an older suit.

Like going on vacation, you need to think ahead about everything you will need and plan for anything that might go wrong and pack accordingly.

Chapter Three
Powerlifting Federations

It was mentioned earlier in this book that there are over 20 different powerlifting federations in the USA. This chapter will present an overview of 21 of these federations.

But first, it would be helpful to present some terminology to summarize the different levels of gear that are allowed in the federations.

Gear Terminology

The following terminology will be used in this chapter and consistently throughout this book. However, as will be noted, not all powerlifters and federations utilize such precision in terminology, and this adds to the confusion about gear in powerlifting.

But most generally, the term "raw" refers to lifting without supportive gear, while the term "equipped" refers to utilizing gear. But more specific terminology will be utilized in this chapter and book. Following is what each term refers to.

Completely raw = No supportive gear whatsoever.

Raw = Belt only, or a belt and wrist wraps.

Unequipped = Belt, wrist wraps, and knee support (knee sleeves or 2.0 meter knee wraps).

Equipped, Full Gear, or Assisted = Belt, wrist wraps, knee wraps (of any length), squat suit, bench shirt, deadlift suit, with maybe briefs.

Single-ply gear = Belt, wrist wraps, 2.0 meter knee wraps, single-ply polyester squat suit, single-ply polyester closed-back bench shirt, single-ply polyester deadlift suit.

Multi-ply gear = Belt, wrist wraps, 2.5 meter knee wraps, double-ply polyester or canvas squat suit, single- or double-ply polyester or denim briefs, double or triple-ply polyester or denim open-back bench shirt, double-ply polyester or canvas deadlift suit.

Generally speaking, these groupings of gear are what the rules allow in the respective federations. In other words, federations that only allow single-ply gear, generally only allow that gear to be made of polyester, for the bench shirts to be closed-back, do not allow briefs, and they generally only allow 2.0 meter knee wraps.

Meanwhile, federations that allow double-ply gear generally allow that gear to be made out of polyester, denim, or canvas and allow briefs, 2.5 meter wraps, and open-back shirts. Any deviations from these patterns will be noted.

The Federations

The information for the following federations is taken mostly from the federation's Web site, most especially their rulebook, contests schedule, and entry forms that were available for download at the time I checked their site. Some information is also taken from Powerlifting Watch (www.powerliftingwatch.com). The federations are being presented in alphabetical order.

Note that all federations hold weigh-ins the morning of the contest, usually starting 2-3 hours before the contest and lasting until half an hour before. But some also have "early weigh-ins" the day before the contest. The usual times for early weigh-ins (if any) will be noted.

100% Raw Powerlifting Federation (100% Raw):

Web site: www.rawpowerlifting.com
Contact information: Paul Bossi, President ~ 100% Raw Powerlifting Federation ~ 139 Marlas Way, Camden, NC 27921 ~ 252-336-4188 ~ pres@rawpowerlifting.com

100% Raw was founded in 1999. As its name implies, it is a strictly raw federation. Only a belt is allowed. Its motto is, "Where lifters compete, not technology." It is also a strictly drug free federation, utilizing urine testing for performance enhancing drugs.

There is a 24 hour weigh-in rule, although most contests only have weigh-ins starting around 5:00 pm the evening before the contest.

Along with regular powerlifting, 100% Raw also offers curls contests and bench for reps contests.

100% Raw is a rather large organization, claiming 2,000 registered lifters. It holds contests throughout the eastern USA.

American Drug-Free Powerlifting Federation (ADFPF):
World Drug-Free Powerlifting Federation. (WDFPF):

Web site: www.adfpf.org

Contact information: ADFPF, 27 Elmo Drive, Macomb, IL 61455 ~ president@adfpf.org

At one time, the federation now known as the USAPL was called the American Drug Free Powerlifting Association (ADFPA) and was associated with the WDFPF, which was founded in 1988. But when the ADFPA joined the IPF in 1997 and was renamed, the new ADFPF was formed as the US representative in the WDFPF.

The ADFPF has two divisions: an equipped division, which is single-ply, and an unequipped division. But the latter would be better called raw as it only allows a belt and wrist wraps.

As its name implies, the ADFPF is a drug tested federation, utilizing the Word Anti-Doping Agency (www.wada-ama.org/en/). Drug testing is via urine testing, although the rulebook does allow for the use of a lie detector.

There are no early weigh-ins.

With being based in Illinois, most contests are in that and adjoining states.

American Frantz Powerlifting Federation (AFPF):
Amateur American Frantz Powerlifting Federation (AAFPF)

Web site: www.frantzpowerlifting.com

Contact information: Ernie Frantz, Owner ~ American Frantz Powerlifting Federation ~ 630-546-3769 cell or Frantz Sports at 630-897-2582 ~ erniefrantz@aol.com

Scot Mendelson, President ~ 13752 Ventura Blvd, Sherman Oaks, CA 91423 ~ 818-399-0905 ~ mendy1000@sbcglobal.net

The AFPF/ AAFPF were formed in March 2008 when Ernie Frantz broke from the APF/ AAPF/ WPC, the federations he had originally founded.

The only difference between the AFPF and the AAFPF is the former is not drug tested while the latter is drug tested via urinalysis.

The AFPF/ AFAPF has two divisions: a raw division, allowing only a belt, and a multi-ply division, allowing any number of plies.

For the only entry form available on the site at this writing, early weigh-ins were from 9:00 am to 2:00 pm. The Web site lists state chairmen in a dozen states.

There is also a separate federation for children and teenagers called CREDO.

American Powerlifting Association (APA):
World Powerlifting Association (WPA):
Web site: www.apa-wpa.com
Contact information: Scott Taylor ~ 5833 First St #K-16 ~ Zephyrhills, FL 33542 ~ Phone: 941-697-7962

The APA was founded in 1987. It has three divisions: a "standard" gear division, which is double-ply, an unlimited gear division, and "raw' division. But the raw division would better be called unequipped as it allows a belt, wrist wraps, and knee wraps. But the APA is unique in being the only federations that allows 3.5 meter wraps in its equipped divisions.

The APA has both drug tested and non-tested divisions for each of its equipped and its raw divisions. The APA also holds curl contests.

There is a 24 hour weigh-in rule, which specifies that early weigh-ins have to occur at least 12 hours before the start of the contest. Most contests have early weigh-ins starting at 6:00 pm.

Most APA contests are held in the eastern USA.

American Powerlifting Committee (APC):
World United Amateur Powerlifting (WUAP).
Web site: www.americanpowerliftingcommittee.com
Contact information: L.B. Baker, President ~ APC, PO Box 40, Bogart, GA 30622 ~ lbbaker@irondawg.com or
lbbaker@americanpowerliftingcommittee.com

The APC was founded in 2003. It is a multi-ply federation, although a new raw division was added in January 2009. It has a 24 hour weigh-in rule. The one entry form I was able to check on the site had early weigh-ins from 12 noon – 2:00 pm and 6:00 – 8:00 pm.

With the president being in Georgia, there are several contest listed there, along with a few others throughout the USA.

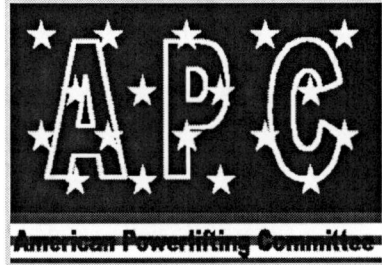

American Powerlifting Federation (APF):
Amateur American Powerlifting Federation (AAPF):
World Powerlifting Congress (WPC):
Amateur World Powerlifting Congress (AWPC)

Web site: http://worldpowerliftingcongress.com
Contact Information: WPC/APF, 505 Westgate Drive, Aurora, IL 60506 ~ 630-896-7309 ~ 1-866-389-4744 ~ Fax: 630-896-7309.

Quoting from their Web site:

World Powerlifting Congress was established by Ernie Frantz in 1986. The World Powerlifting Congress also known as the WPC, consists of 30 countries worldwide that participate in annual World Championships. We provide competitive and outstanding Powerlifting meets, and are successfully known as "a lifter's organization."

The APF was founded before the WPC, in 1982. The APF is the US representative of the WPC. The only difference between the APF/ WPC and the AAPF/ AWPC is the former are not drug tested while latter are drug tested via urinalysis.

All of these federations are multi-ply, allowing any number of plies, so you will sometimes see lifters with triple-ply shirts. There is also a raw division, which allows a belt and wrist wraps.

There is a 24 hour weigh-in rule, with weigh-ins starting as early as 9:00 am the day before the contest. With being based in Illinois, the APF is very active in states in the Central and Mountain Time Zones.

Amateur Athletic Union (AAU):
Web site: www.aausports.org/sprt_Powerlifting.asp
Contact information: National Powerlifting Chairman, Bill DePorter ~ 408-779-4208 or 408-289-0311 ~ william.deporter@baesystems.com

Quoting from the AAU Web site:

The first AAU Powerlifting meets began around 1963 under the auspices of the Weightlifting program, but Powerlifting was soon recognized as a separate sport. It remained so until Powerlifting officially left the AAU in 1981 as a result of restructuring in the AAU, promoted by the Amateur Sports Act of 1978. With the tremendous interest that this sport has generated over the past thirty-plus years, Powerlifting returned to the AAU in 1995.

So powerlifting actually began as an AAU sport, but it eventually left the AAU, but then later returned. Along with powerlifting, the AAU hosts over 30 other sports, from aquatics to wrestling.

For powerlifting, the AAU offers two divisions: a single-ply (called "assisted") division and a raw division, which allows only a belt. Early weigh-ins usually start at 6:00 pm the evening before. The AAU conducts drug testing via the National Center for Drug Free Sports (www.drugfreesport.com). The AAU hosts powerlifting contests throughout the USA.

Anti-Drug Athletes United (ADAU):
Web site: www.adaurawpower.com or www.pikitup.com
Contact information: Allan Siegel, President ~ ADAU, 304 Daisy Street, Clearfield PA 16830, phone or fax 814-768-9400 ~ al@pikitup.com

The ADAU was founded in 1999. It recently added the words "Raw Power" to its name, but not its acronym. The full name emphasizes that the ADAU is a strictly raw and drug free federation. Only a belt is allowed, and drug testing is usually performed via urinalysis, although

50

the rulebook allows for the use of a lie detector as well. Early weigh-ins are generally 6:00 pm the day before, but sometimes earlier.

Unique to the ADAU is its "single lift" contests. For these, all three powerlifts are contested. But they are separate contests; there is no total.

Most federations often allow lifters to enter just one lift or even just two lifts at a three lift contest, although sometimes you are only allowed to enter just benches or just benches and deadlifts. Many federations will also hold separate bench contests or separate bench and deadlift contests (called a "push/ pull" contest). But the ADAU is unique in holding contests in which all three powerlifters are contested as separate contests but without a total. They also keep separate records for lifts done in single lift contests and for lifts done in full power contests.

The ADAU holds many contests in Pennsylvania, but also some in adjoining states.

International Powerlifting Association (IPA):

Web site: www.ipapower.com
Contact information: Mark Chaillet, President ~ York Barbell Company ~ 330 Board Road, York, PA 17406 ~ 717-495-0024 ~ chailfit@yahoo.com or Ellen Chaillet: echaillet@aol.com.

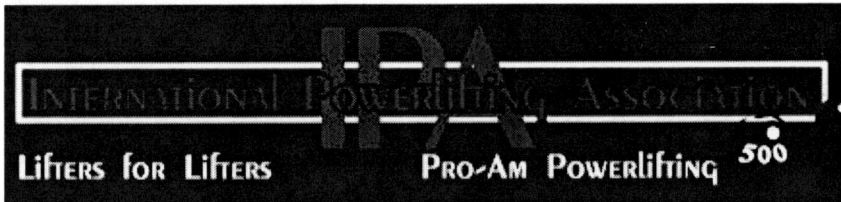

The IPA was founded in 1998. It has two divisions in regards to gear: an equipped division that allows double-ply gear and a raw division that allows a belt and wrist wraps.

The IPA also has three main divisions: Pro, Amateur, and Elite Amateur. But these terms do not necessarily refer to paid and non-paid divisions. There is sometimes a cash prize in the Pro division, but not always. The main difference is that the Pro division is not drug tested while the two Amateurs division are. However, once you reach a "Pro" total, you cannot lift in the Amateur division. You have to lift in either the Pro division or in the Elite Amateur division. Drug testing is done via urinalysis.

The IPA has a 24 hour weigh-in rule. Early weigh-ins are usually from 9:00 am – 12 noon, and again from 4-8:00 pm. However, some

IPA contests only have early weigh-ins from 6-8:00 pm. It is up to the meet director's discretion exactly when to hold early weigh-ins.

The president and vice-president of the IPA live in eastern Pennsylvania, so there are regularly contests in that area. In fact, the IPA now always holds its World Championships in June in York, PA and its National Championships in November, also in York. There are also often contests in New York, Ohio, and other northeastern states, and now occasionally contests in Texas and California.

Iron Boy Powerlifting (IBP):

Web site: www.ironboypowerlifting.com
Contact information: Keith Payne ~ Iron Boy Powerlifting, PO Box 1602, Clemmons, North Carolina 27012 ~ 336-766-3347 ~ keith@ironboypowerlifting.net

IBP was founded in 2001. It has an equipped and a raw division. The equipped division only allows preapproved gear, which looks to be all single-ply. The raw division would be better called unequipped as it allows a belt, wrist wraps, and knee wraps.

Unique to the IBP is it only allows 2.0 meter wraps for those competing at 198s or below but 2.5 meter knee wraps for those above 198.

Early weigh-ins are offered at some contests from 6-7:30 pm. Drug testing is mentioned in the rulebook, but there is no indication of the method.

Along with full powerlifting contests, the IBP also hosts bench and push/ pull contests, and at some meets, a curls contest.

IBP meets are held in North Carolina and South Carolina.

Natural Athlete Strength Association (NASA):

Web site: www.nasa-sports.com
Contact information: NASA - P.O. Box 735, Noble, OK. 73068 ~ 405-527-8513 ~ sqbpdl@aol.com

NASA was founded in 1990. It has two divisions: an equipped division that only allows single-ply gear and an unequipped division that allows a belt, wrist wraps, and knee wraps.

In addition, NASA has a separate "Power Sports" division. This is a raw division, allowing a belt only, but the lifts are curls + bench + deadlift = total. So basically, curls replace squats.

With being based in Oklahoma, NASA always holds its nationals contests in Oklahoma City. There are separate Equipped Nationals, Unequipped Nationals, and Power Sports Nationals. Again, with being based in Oklahoma, NASA is very active in the Midwest. There are also contests in West Virginia and Ohio, and elsewhere in the USA.

Early weigh-ins for NASA sometimes start at 6:00 pm, but for most contests they can start as late as 8:00 pm.

Pride Powerlifting (Pride):

Web site: www.pridepowerlifting.com
Contact information: 208-964-5066 ~ 509-868-2192 ~ Fax: 208-765-5827 ~ judysver@yahoo.com

Pride is a new federation, having started in 2003, with just a few contests being held in the northwest. It has three divisions: raw, equipped, and unlimited.

However, the raw division allows a belt, wrist wraps, and knee wraps, so it would be better called unequipped. Both the equipped and unlimited divisions allow double-ply gear. The main difference seems to be that only pre-approved gear is allowed in the equipped division. If your gear is not on the list, you will lift in the unlimited division. Also only the unlimited division allows open-back shirts. Only 2.0 meter knee wraps are allowed in all divisions.

Early weighs usually run from 1-8:00 pm the day before. There is no drug testing.

R.A.W. United (RAWU):

Web site: www.rawunited.org
Contact information: Dr. Spero S. Tshontikidis ~ 4353 Collinwood Drive, Melbourne, FL 32901 ~ 321-505-1194 ~ rawunited@cfl.rr.com

Quoting from the Web site:

Redeemed Among the World United, or R.A.W. United, is a Christian-based, powerlifting federation that hosts sanctioned competitions. Meets are open to lifters of all federations, and all current membership cards are honored.

RAWU is a brand new federation, having held its first contest in December 2008, although the president has been hosting contests for 25 years with other federations, most recently with 100% Raw.

RAWU has two divisions: an Ironman division that allows only a belt, and a Raw division that allows a belt, wrist wraps, and knee sleeves. It currently holds contests in Florida and Pennsylvania. Contest proceeds are donated to US military personal in Iraq and Afghanistan. RAWU even holds contests in Iraq.

Early weigh-ins are 5-8:00 pm. Drug testing is by urinalysis.

Son Light Power (SLP):

Web site: www.sonlightpower.com
Contact information: Son Light Power Gym ~ 122 West Sale Street ,
Tuscola, Illinois 61953 ~ 217-253-5429 ~ Fax 217-253-5429 ~ sonlightgym@verizon.net

"Son" in this organization's name refers to Jesus Christ, the Son of God, so it is another a Christian federation. There are separate raw and assisted divisions. The assisted division is single-ply. It is also a drug-free federation.

Most of its meets are bench/ deadlift meets, but its National Championship also has full powerlifting. There are also curl contests. Most contests are held in Illinois and surrounding states.

Southern Powerlifting Federation (SPF):
World Bench and Powerlifting Association (WBPA):
Web site: www.southernpowerlifting.com/
Contact Information: Jesse Rodgers, President ~ 1326 Koblan Drive.,
Hixson, TN 37343 ~ 423-876-8410 ~ rodgersmadmax@bellsouth.net

The SLP was founded in 2000 and the WBPA in 2004. It has two divisions: a multi-ply division and a raw division, which allows a belt, wrist wraps, and knee wraps. SLP contests offer full power meets, single-lift, bench for reps, and curls.

Much to this writer's dismay, the bottom weight class for men is 132s; there are no 114s or 123s. There is drug testing, but no mention about early weigh-ins. Contests are held in the southeastern USA.

Syndicated Strength Alliance (SSA):
Web site: www.strengthalliance.com
Contact information: Sandi & Zane McCaslin ~ Syndicated Strength Alliance (SSA) ~ PO Box 137, Fultonville, NY 12072 ~ (518) 829-7838 ~ admin@strengthalliance.com

The SSA was founded in 2007. It offers contests in New York and Oregon. There are three divisions: standard, single-ply, and multi-ply. The "standard" division allows a belt, wrist wraps, knee wraps, and something akin to a basic blast shirt. 2.5 meter knee wraps are allowed in all divisions. There is a 24 hour weigh-in rule.

United Powerlifting Association (UPA):
Web site: www.unitedpowerliftingassociation.com
Contact Information: Kenny Patterson ~ 4423 Gaffney Ct., Columbus, Ohio 43224 ~ (614) 335-5181 ~ kpatterson@unitedpowerliftingassociation.com

The UPA was founded in 2007. A handful of listed contests are scattered throughout several different states. The UPA allows double-ply gear. There is a 24 hour weigh-in rule.

United States Powerlifting Federation (USPF):

Web site: www.uspf.com or www.wvuspf.com.
Contact Information: David Jeffrey, President ~ P.O.Box 231 ~ Parkersburg, WV 26012 ~ (304) 489-2428 ~ matofficial@yahoo.com

At one time, the USPF was the USA representative in the International Powerlifting Federation (IPF). But it became inactive in the 1990s, but later reorganized.

When it reorganized, most of its contests were held on the west coast. But now, there are also contests in West Virginia and surrounding states.

When first reorganized, the USPF was a single-ply federation and a member of the World Powerlifting Federation (WPF). But more recently, a double-ply division was added. For that division only, it is part of the Global Powerlifting Committee (GPC). But for both divisions, 2.5 meter knee wraps are allowed and only closed-back bench shirts, but Velcro enclosed shirts area allowed for the latter.

The rulebook allows weigh-ins up to 24 hours before the start of the contest. But most entry forms I checked only had early weigh-ins from 6-8:00 pm the evening before.

USA Powerlifting (USAPL):
International Powerlifting Federation (IPF):

Web sites:
USAPL: www.usapowerlifting.com
IPF: www.powerlifting-ipf.com
Contact information: USAPL National Office: Dr. Larry Maile, Ph.D., President ~ PO Box 668, Columbia City, IN 46725 ~ (260) 248-4889 ~ Fax: (260) 248-4879

From the Web site:

USA Powerlifting (formerly American Drug Free Power-lifting Association, Inc.) is the leading powerlifting organization in the United States. USA Powerlifting is a member of the International Powerlifting Federation (IPF), the governing body of powerlifting internationally. The IPF is comprised of member federations from eighty-three countries on six continents.

When the USPF had its troubles, in 1997, the USAPL took over as the USA's repre-sentative in the IPF. Up until that time, the USAPL had been called the ADFPA and was as-sociated with the WDFPA.

The USAPL is the largest federation in the USA, and the IPF is the largest international federation.

The USPF has two divisions: a single-ply division and a newer raw division. The raw division allows a belt, wrist wraps, and knee sleeves (not wraps). But the latter has been the source of much contro-versy in regards to what kind of knee sleeves will be allowed. That debate is still ongoing as of this writing.

The USAPL has the reputation of being the "strictest" federation in terms of its judging on depth on squats, of enforcing the "one-minute" rules for starting your attempt and for giving your next at-tempt, and with regards to gear in general. All gear needs to be pre-approved by the manufacturer, and you can only use such pre-approved gear.

There are no early weigh-ins. Weigh-ins only occur the morning of the contest, usually starting at 7:00 am and the contest at 9:00 am.

Much to this writer's chagrin, in 2007, the IPF/ USAPL eliminated the 114 pound weight class for men.

For the above two reasons, I never have and probably never will enter an USAPL contest. But the USAPL is very widespread, claiming "chairs" (state directors) in 44 states.

World Association of Bench and Deadlifters (WABDL):
Web site: www.wabdl.org
Contact information: P.O. Box 27499 - Golden Valley, MN 55427 ~ (763) 545-8654 or (503) 901-1622 ~ FAX: (763) 544-3776 wabdl@bendbroadband.com

As the name implies, the WABDL only offers the bench and deadlift. These are single lift contests. In other words, there is no squat and no total. The bench and deadlift are separate contests.

The WABDL allows double-ply gear, but only closed-back shirts. Early weigh-ins are required to take place the afternoon or evening before the contest. Drug testing is done via urinalysis.

The squat is my best lift, so I am not thrilled with a federation only holding bench/ deadlift contests. But many must like the idea as the WABDL is a very popular federation, with well-attended contests held throughout the USA. Its 2008 Worlds had 545 participants.

World Natural Powerlifting Federation (WNPF):

Web site: www.wnpf.net
Contact information: Troy Ford, President ~ PO Box 142347, Fayette-ville, GA. 30214 ~ 770 668-4841 ~ wnpf@aol.com

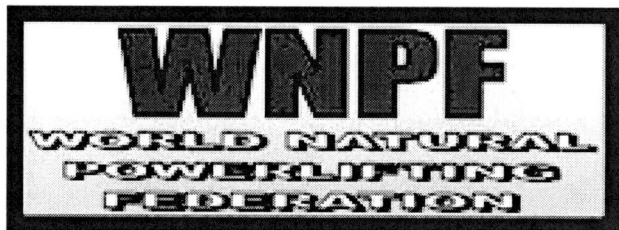

The WNPF has three divisions: raw, single-ply, and multi-ply. However, its raw division allows a belt, wrist wraps, and knee wraps, so it would better be called unequipped. Also at some WNPF contests, there will be a separate curl contest and even a separate bench for reps contest. The WNPF holds contests mainly in east coast and nearby states.

The "N" in WNPF stands for "natural" which means it is a strictly drug-tested federation. It uses a lie detector for its drug testing.

Eagerly weigh-ins usually start at 6:00 pm.

Note: In addition to the 21 discussed federations, there are also several smaller federations that only hold contests in a single state.

Chapter Four
My Federations Experiences

To date, including college, this writer has competed in five different powerlifting federations, with plans to compete in at least one more. In this chapter, I am going to present further details on these federations in the order in which I have competed in them. This will enable me to present the details in a "story" format and to draw upon my personal experiences in these federations.

United States Powerlifting Federation

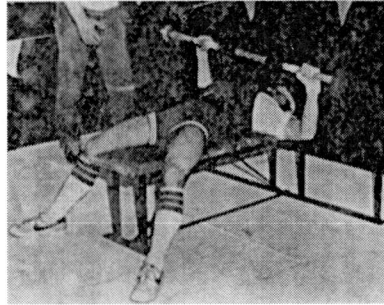

The USPF was the federation I competed in during college. The picture to the right is from USPF National Collegiates in 1981.

At that time, the USPF was basically the only federation around. A couple of other federations were just getting started, but just about all USA lifters competed in the USPF, which held contests in just about all states of the USA. It was truly a national organization.

At that time, the winners of the USPF Senior National Championships would represent the USA at the World Championships for the International Powerlifting Federation (IPF). And again, the IPF was the only worldwide powerlifting federation.

However, I remember that around the time I stopped powerlifting, the USPF was having some problems with the IPF in that the IPF began requiring testing for performance enhancing drugs, but the USPF was unwilling to conduct the testing.

At that time, the only allowed and available gear was single-ply, poly gear. Also at that time, weigh-ins were always the morning of the contest. Specifically, weigh-ins were usually held from 8-9:30 am, with the contest starting at 10:00 am.

Not being a morning person, I always found it very difficult to be there that early to weigh-in. Then after weighing in, it was even more difficult, especially if I had cut much weight, to eat and rehydrate, get dressed, warmed-up, and ready to lift all within two hours. No wonder I never had a 9/9 day in college.

However, something happened during the years that I wasn't powerlifting. As best as I've been able to reconstruct the history, at some point, the USPF did begin drug testing. But it began to have other problems related to a lawsuit and eventually went bankrupt. As a result, another federation took over as the USA's representative in the IPF. Eventually, the USPF reorganized and is now active again.

As stated in the previous chapter, the entry forms I checked on their Web site had early weigh-ins from 6-8:00 pm the evening before, although one had weigh-ins in the afternoon.

Weigh-ins are again held the morning of the contest, staring 2-3 hours before the start of the contest, with the contest itself not starting until 10:00 am or as late as 12 noon. I really wish the USPF had those weigh-in and contest start times back in college!

I live in western Pennsylvania. Since the USPF regularly holds contests at the Pittsburgh airport, along with in West Virginia and Ohio, it is possible that I could enter another USPF contest someday.

International Powerlifting Association

When I first started thinking about competing again in early 2003, I began looking around for a contest to enter. Much to my dismay, the first contests I looked at in my area only had weigh-ins the morning of the contest, starting at 7:00 am, with the contest starting at 9:00 am. That was even worse than in college!

But then I came across an IPA contest in Newark, Ohio, the Iron House Classic, on Saturday, April 12th. The IPA has a 24 hour weigh-

in rule. For this particular contest, there were weigh-ins on Friday, from 9:00 am – 12 noon, and again from 4-8:00 pm. That sounded so great to me, to be able to weigh-in the day before the contest.

Newark was about a 3½ hour drive from my home. But I figured I could drive out on Friday morning and be there in time to weigh-in right at 4:00 pm. That is the main reason I decided on an IPA contest to enter for my first contest in 21 years.

I have since entered several more IPA contests. The picture on the preceding page is from my second IPA contest, 2003 IPA Worlds. You can see the use of a monolift, mentioned in Chapter One. The massive back in the foreground is that of the head judge, Gene Rychlak, vice-president of the IPA and the first person to bench over 1,000 pounds.

For all of the IPA contests I have entered, there has been weigh-ins the day before the contest. For a couple of these, I went out a day early, on Thursday, so I could weigh-in first thing Friday morning. That way, I'd have all day for eating and rehydrating. It also gave me a chance to rest after the long drive the day before. However, one IPA contest only had weigh-ins from 6-8:00 pm on Friday.

For my first contest, I did not yet understand all of the differences between gear and especially about some gear being multi-ply. So for that first contest, I got new single-ply gear. But once I understood that the IPA allows double-ply gear, for my third IPA contest, I got a double-ply poly squat suit and bench shirt, along with 2.5 meter wraps.

But backing up, I very much enjoyed that first IPA contest. What I especially liked was it had a very "rowdy" atmosphere, with heavy metal music blaring, lots of screaming by the lifters (yours truly included), and cheering by the audience, and there actually was a decent sized audience, something I had never seen in college. That atmosphere helped me put in a great performance, going 9/9, while breaking six IPA records.

There has been the same atmosphere at every subsequent IPA contest I have entered. I have also found IPA lifters and officials to be very friendly and the contests very well run and enjoyable, and I have always gotten along well with Mark Chaillet, the president of the IPA, and his wife Ellen, who usually runs the scorer's table at major IPA contests.

There was one rule difference from college that struck me when I read over the IPA Rulebook before that first contest. In college, on squats, after you took the weight off of the racks and got set, you would need to nod to the head judge, and then wait until he gave you a verbal "Squat" signal, with a hand motion down, before starting your descent. But the IPA does not have a "Squat" signal. You just start when you are ready. I would later find out that this is unique to the IPA. All other federations still utilize a "Squat" signal.

This has led to some controversy about the IPA in that there will be lifters who do not have their legs straight, with the knees locked, at the start of the lift, even though the rules state that you need to do so. But I always do, and I would suggest the reader do so as well since it is required in all other federations.

There has also been some claims about the IPA being lax in its enforcement of the rules, most notably on squat depth. Many have the impression that the IPA regularly passes high squats. All I can say is, at my last IPA contest, I received two red lights for depth on my third attempt, and thus the lift did not pass. But afterwards just about every lifter who spoke to me said they thought the lift looked more than good enough, so the IPA is not that lax in that regard.

The IPA's motto is "Lifters for lifters." And its contests do provide an atmosphere that is very lifter friendly. For instance, a clock is generally not used to time lifters to be sure they start their lift within a minute of their name being called as "up" and to be sure they give their next attempts within a minute. In some federations, if you are so much as one second over, you will forfeit the lift.

The IPA is also not very picky in regards to unimportant things like having a pocket on your T-shirt. I know of cases in other federations where a lifter had to rip off a pocket to be allowed to lift, but the IPA couldn't care less about such things.

To date, I have entered a half dozen IPA contests and now hold 19 IPA records. I could easily have continued competing strictly in the IPA, and I might still enter further IPA contests in the future. But I have now entered other federations for two main reasons.

The first had to do gear rules. Along with its multi-ply division, the IPA eventually added a raw division. Initially, I always entered the equipped division, but when I got fed up with gear back in the winter of 2005-2006, I planned on entering the raw division. The IPAs' raw rules allow only a belt and wrist wraps but no knee support. But in training heavy raw, I got injured and thought it best to use knee wraps. So I looked for a federation that allowed knee wraps in its raw or better unequipped division.

Second, as stated previously, the IPA holds contests regularly in eastern PA and in Ohio, and I entered several of those contests. But they all required a 3-4 hour drive. Initially, I could handle such a drive, but eventually, my health deteriorated, so that on top of entering a contest, even that long of a drive was too much for me. As such, when possible, I try to enter contests within an hour or two from my home.

One time, the IPA held a contest in western PA, its PA State Championships in 2007, so I entered that contest. But there were only about a dozen lifters at that contest, so there has not been another IPA contest in western PA. As a result, I have been forced to look for other federations holding contests in my area. And that leads to the next federation I entered.

World Natural Powerlifting Federation

I entered one WNPF contest, in April 2006, about an hour from my home. The main reason I entered this WNPF contest was because the WNPF allows knee wraps in its "raw" division. That makes the name somewhat of a misnomer and the WNPF has caught some heat due to this. It would better be called an unequipped division.

The contest was well-run. The judging was strict but fair. But I did notice that the "Press" command on benches was slow coming, as was the "Down" command on deadlifts. So be prepared to hold the bar extra long if you enter a WNPF contest.

But what I really noticed was the atmosphere at the contest was completely different from what I had grown accustomed to in the IPA. There was no music, no screaming by lifters, and no cheering from the sparse audience. With the quiet atmosphere, I felt out of place being the only lifting screaming (as can be seen in the picture). I also found it hard to get psyched up for my lifts, and that could be why I missed my third squat and bench attempts.

0   I also made a mistake for the contest in that I did not cut to 114s. I lifted at 123s for the first and only time since I started competing again. The reason I did so is the WNPF does not have weigh-ins until 6:00 pm the evening before the contest. By this point, I had gotten used to weighing in at least by 4:00 pm, if not at 9:00 am the day before. As such, 6:00 pm seemed so late, and I was afraid I would not be able to adequately eat and rehydrate.

In fact, it was later that I entered the one IPA contest that also did not have weigh-ins until 6:00 pm. For that contest I cut to 114s, but I was not able to adequately rehydrate. That seriously affected my performance, especially since it was very hot on contest day, so I was severally dehydrated by deadlifts. But then, for a later contest, I refined my post-weigh-in procedure and did just fine with a 6:00 weigh-in. That procedure will be discussed in detail in Chapter 21.

But back to the WNPF contest, with lifting unequipped, I predictably totaled less than I had for my previous contests with gear, but going up a weight class really exaggerated the difference. That left me dissatisfied with my performance, even thought I went 7/9 and broke eight WNPF records.

I mention this as what weight class to enter and what gear to use are important decisions every powerlifter must make. Your decisions on these issues could very well affect your contest satisfaction. Both of these points will be addressed in detail later.

But on the WNPF, one point to note is it is now actually two federations in one. What is described in Chapter Two and what I entered was the "regular" WNPF. But there is now also a "WNPF Lifetime." The difference is, for the regular WNPF "lifters must be a minimum of 3 years drug free" while in the WNPF Lifetime, as the name implies, you can never have used performance enhancing drugs.

Also, the regular WNPF has the three divisions described in Chapter Two, while the WNPF Lifetime only has two divisions, "raw" and single-ply. If I were to enter another WNPF contest, it would probably be in the Lifetime WNPF and its raw division.

American Powerlifting Federation

I entered one APF contest, its Pennsylvania State Championships, held in the Pittsburgh area in September 2006. It reminded me of the IPA. It had the same rowdy atmosphere, with blaring music, screaming lifters, and a rather substantial and cheering audience.

The APF has a 24 hour weigh-in rule like the IPA. In fact, for that APF contest, I weighed in at 9:00 am on Friday, and that probably helped my performance.

However, this was the contest where I had to dip into my backup gear. Having to change suits during squat warm-ups left me very exhausted throughout the day. That is when I really began to get disgruntled about gear. This will be discussed in detail later in this book.

But on the APF contest, despite being exhausted from the gear problems, I went 7/9, broke four APF records, and won Best Lifter, and that performance is also why I enjoyed the contest. The only reason I have not entered another APF contest is they have not held another contest in the Pittsburgh area since then. That could be because there were again only about a dozen lifters at the contest, which is also how it was that I was able to win Best Lifter.

Natural Athlete Strength Association

With being disgruntled with gear, I tried once again to train raw to enter the IPA's raw division, but once again got injured. So I looked for another federation with an unequipped division. NASA has just such a division and was holding a contest in the Pittsburgh area, its Northeastern States, in June 2008, so I entered that contest.

But in training for the contest, my health was such now that even wrapping my knees was too exhausting, so instead of using knee wraps, I trained squats and competed wearing APT's heavy knee sleeves, and that worked out very well. For the first time since my first contest five years before, I went 9/9. I also broke eight NASA records.

There was music at the contest. It was not as blaring as at IPA contests. However, the meet director had told me beforehand that lifters could bring their own music to be played during their attempts. Being a Christian, I burned a CD with heavy metal Christian music (yes there is such a thing, better known as White Metal). Unfortunately, that CD did not work in their system, but I also took a store-bought CD with similar music.

As it turned out, Greg van Hoose, the meet director, and his wife Susan (who was the scorekeeper and played the music) were also Christians. She had already planned on playing Christian rock music at the contest, so she ended up playing my CD during the contest as well. That added to my enjoyment of the contest.

The lifters and meet officials were also very friendly. In addition, with lifting unequipped with just knee sleeves, I did not have gear distracting and tiring me out, so I very much enjoyed the contest.

But one thing I did not like was weigh-ins were not until 6:00 pm the evening before the contest. But this time, I was able to eat and re-hydrate in such a way that it did not adversely affect my performance. However, I later learned that for most NASA contests, weigh-ins are not until as late as 8:00 pm the evening before. That would be way too late for me, so I doubt I'd enter a NASA contest with such late "early" weigh-ins.

As mentioned in the previous chapter, NASA has a separate "Power Sports" division that basically replaces squats with curls.

This I find to be rather strange. Squats are a major, compound movement, utilizing large amounts of musculature. In fact, if all you did was to squat, you would end up with very good overall body strength. But curls are an isolation exercise, working just one small set of muscles. It is only vanity that makes them popular, not productivity.

Personally, squats are my best lift, while my biceps strength is weak. So you will never see me entering a power sports or curls contest. But the option is there in NASA, and the division is very popular

The NASA contest I entered was the first time I know of that NASA held a contest in the Pittsburgh area, but once again, there were only about a dozen lifters at the contest, and NASA has not held another contest in the Pittsburgh area since. However, NASA regularly holds contest in Ohio and West Virginia, so it is possible I could enter another NASA contest in the future.

Anti-Drug Athletes United

This writer remembers Al Siegel, the president of the ADAU, from my college lifting days. At that time, Al regularly held contests in Clearfield, PA, in central PA, not too far from Penn State Main Campus, so I remember entering a couple of his contests. Those contests were held under the auspices of the USPF. Later, Al hosted contests with the AAU, but then he founded the ADAU in 1999. He still holds contests in Clearfield.

I have not yet entered an ADAU contest, but I almost entered one in Pittsburgh held during the time I was working on this book, with plans of entering another one shortly after that. But I had to forgo those plans due to a hamstring injury and other heath setbacks.

Both of those contests were single lift contests. As mentioned in Chapter Two, in the ADAU, for such contests, there is no total. That sounded rather strange to me as I've always considered the total to be most important. Since all three lifts are being contested, I see no reason why the lifter who competes in all three lifts should not be given credit for a total.

But Al told me the single-lifts contests are mainly for new and master lifters. New lifters might not yet be doing all three lifts, while master lifters might have injuries that prevent performing one or two of the lifts, so these contests give such persons a chance to compete.

Moreover, to the ADAU's credit, there are separate records for lifts done in a full power contest and for lifts done in a single-lift contest. That actually makes a lot of sense. There is a world of difference between deadlifting after having already squatted and benched and just deadlifting or even deadlifting after only benching.

The main holdup with me entering the ADAU is it is a strictly raw federation, with only a belt being allowed. As mentioned, I have gotten injured when I have tried to train for a raw contest before.

But if I were to enter one of Al's contests in Clearfield, it will probably feel rather strange returning to the same town to enter a contest by the same meet director as for contests I entered in college so many years ago.

R.A.W. United

I also have not yet entered a RAWU contest. But RAWU regularly holds contests in Greenscastle, PA, which is near Harrisburg and a little over three hours from my home. That is farther away than I would prefer. However, the contest is held in a Sports Inn, which is adjacent to a Comfort Inn. That makes for a very convenient set-up and means there would be no additional driving once I get to the hotel.

RAWU's Raw division has my favored gear rules of allowing a belt, wrist wraps, and knee sleeves. Both APT's heavy and Convict knee sleeves are approved for use.

RAWU has early weigh-ins starting at 5:00 pm, with the contests themselves not starting until 10:00 am. Plus, RAWU is a Christian-based federation, with both Christian and secular rock being played at contests. All of these points make it an appealing federation, so as of this writing, I am training for a RAWU contest.

However, be sure not to get confused on the terminology for RAWU's two divisions. What this book has termed "raw" (belt only), RAWU calls "Ironman." What this book has termed "unequipped" (belt, wrist wraps, knee support), RAWU calls "Raw."

Also, in RAWU, for two-session or two-day events, heavyweights compete first then lightweights and females. This is the reverse from every contest I've ever entered and from what was described in Chapter One. But according to the president, Spero Tshontikidis, this is so the loaders and spotters are "fresh" when handling the heavier weights.

Pittsburgh Contests

Before closing this chapter, I want to include a short discussion on contests in my area. As mentioned, I have entered three different contests in the Pittsburgh area by three different federations. There was also an ADAU contest in my area that I thought of entering. In all four contests, only about a dozen lifters competed, and all of these federations have not held another contest in this area since.

However, I do not believe this sparse participation is due to there not being much interest in powerlifting here in the Pittsburgh area. Each year, there is an unsanctioned bench/ deadlift contest at the Pittsburgh airport that is very well attended. I've never entered it, but it does show there is support for powerlifting here.

I think what happened for each of the three contests I entered is they were not advertised until a month or two before in *Powerlifting USA* magazine. I found out about them from the Internet, but many lifters still rely on *Powerlifting USA* for their contest information, and most lifters need more than a month or two to prepare for a contest.

The airport contest is usually advertised as much as a year in advance. So meet directors take note, be sure to advertise your contest in *Powerlifting USA* at least several months in advance.

Chapter Five
Raw versus Equipped Debate

This chapter will take an in-depth look at the debates over supportive gear in powerlifting by presenting the pro and con arguments on all sides. It is hoped this information will help the reader to make the very difficult decision of whether to lift raw, unequipped, or equipped.

Definitions of "Raw"

There are at least three federations that are strictly raw, meaning they do not have a division that allows supportive suits, shirts, or briefs. But there are also many federations that have a separate raw or unequipped division in addition to its equipped division. There is also a national "Raw Unity Meet" held each January in Florida. However, the definition of raw varies among all of these.

There are four possible definitions of the word "raw" among these federations and contests.

1. A belt
2. A belt and wrist wraps
3. A belt, wrist wraps, and knee sleeves
4. A belt, wrist wraps, and knee wraps

Chapter Three proposed that to clear up some of the confusion, it would be helpful to use the term "raw" to refer to the first two, and the term "unequipped" to refer to the second two. But, unfortunately, such a distinction is not generally followed.

But whether raw or unequipped, the main point of having such lifting as opposed to equipped powerlifting is that raw/ unequipped advocates believe that lifts done with a suit and shirt are not "real."

By that is meant, it is felt that when using such gear, it is the gear that is lifting the weight, or at least, greatly assisting in doing so, and thus you do not have a true test of strength. In fact, the slogan of the 100% Raw Federation is, "Where Lifters Compete, Not Technology!"

The point is, such lifters believe the gear has evolved to the point where powerlifting is no longer a test of pure strength but a test of who can find the best gear. There is something to be said for this opinion, as will be discussed shortly. However, such attitudes really only apply to suits and shirts, not to wraps. The important distinction between these two very different types of gear will be outlined shortly.

But here it will be said there are far less differences between any of these definitions of raw or unequipped lifting than there is between any of them and lifting with a suit and shirt. So frankly, it would be prudent if raw advocates would quit fighting amongst themselves and band together.

Belt and Wraps Comments

All federations allow a belt in its raw or unequipped division. The reason for this is it felt prudent to allow some lower back support for those who feel it is necessary. Moreover, a belt adds little to how much a lifter can lift in any of the three powerlifts, so arguments against gear would not apply to a belt.

But the same could be said for wrist wraps. They are purely supportive, not adding anything to one's lift. So this writer has always found it rather strange for raw federations or divisions to not allow wrist wraps.

This was in fact one reason I decided not to try raw powerlifting when I first started powerlifting again. I remembered from my college lifting days that I often felt strain in my wrists, and thus always wore wrist wraps.

As things turned out, I was correct in my concern. About a month before my second contest, I hurt my right wrist during training when I wasn't wearing wrist wraps. In order to keep training, I wore wrist wraps in training until and at that contest. If I had not been able to do so, I would have had to cancel my plans to enter that contest.

I was also concerned about doing heavy squats without knee support. Back in college, I remember that in 1981, I hurt my knees at Pennsylvania State Collegiates in February. But I was able to keep training for National Collegiates the next month by wearing knee wraps, and of course, I wore them at that contest. If I had not been able to do so, I would have missed out on winning National Collegiates.

After that, I always wore knee wraps when doing heavy squats (less than four reps). I never had knee problems after that in college. But ironically, after I stopped powerlifting, I injured both knees in separate accidents, and thus experienced chronic knee pain for years.

After I started using free weights and thus squatting again, the knee pain cleared up and has only rarely been a problem since. However, almost always I have worn knee support when doing heavy squats. The only times I've had problems is when I have tried training for a raw contest without knee support.

That is why, the two times I have competed without gear, I competed in divisions that allowed knee support. The first time I used knee wraps; the second time, I used knee sleeves. I know I am not alone in such a situation. There are many lifters who have knee problems who would not be able to do squats let alone compete without some kind of knee support.

These reasons are also why I recommended in Chapter One that for your first contest to wear a belt, wrist wraps, and knee sleeves or knee wraps. It would not be good to get injured at your first contest.

However, the reason why many raw federations and divisions do not allow knee support is that knee wraps can add significantly to how much a lifter can squat, and with continuing improvements in gear technology, how much they add continues to increase. That is a legitimate concern, but so is the health of lifters' knees, and that is why many raw/ unequipped divisions allow knee support.

However, I have long thought a good compromise between those who believe raw should mean no knee wraps and those who believe that wraps should be allowed would be to allow knee sleeves. In fact, the aforementioned Raw Unity Meet contest allows knee sleeves.

The knee sleeves I wore for my second unequipped contest were APT"s heavy knee sleeves. Those provided plenty of support for my knees, but they did not add much of anything to my squat.

But I can see why some would be hesitant to allow knee sleeves. As with all other gear, very quickly, gear manufacturers would come out with improved knee sleeves that do add significantly to one's squat. In Chapter Two, it was mentioned that APT also has Convict knee sleeves that are heavier and longer that their heavy knee sleeves and these conceivably could add slightly to one's squat. Much more dramatically increases could be had from the Inzer's knee sleeves with Velcro straps that were mentioned in that chapter.

In any case, it would require some very specific writing of the rules to delineate what kind of knee sleeves are allowed and what kind are not. It might even require pre-approving all knee sleeves. It is much easier to just outlaw all knee support.

In fact, two of the raw-only federations, ADAU Raw Power and 100% Raw, allow only a belt. At its national committee meeting in 2007, the ADAU voted on whether wrist wraps should be allowed. The idea was voted down 8-1. If the ADAU so strongly rejected allowing wrist wraps, it is very doubtful they would even consider allowing knee sleeves.

Meanwhile, 100% Raw is just as dogmatic in its rejection of gear, as its name indicates, so I doubt they would ever consider allowing wrist wraps and knee sleeves.

However, with the largest powerlifting federation, the USAPL, now having a raw division that allows wrist wraps and knee sleeves, I suspect that kind of lifting will become more popular. In fact, the newest raw-only federation, RAWU, has two divisions, one allowing knee sleeves and wrist wraps and one that does not.

If I were to set the rules, I would allow something akin to APT's heavy and Convict knee sleeves. They provide plenty of protection for the knees but without adding significantly to the lift. But I would not allow Inzer's knee sleeves. The Velcro straps are unnecessary for knee protection. Their only purpose is so the sleeves are able to be worn unnaturally tight and thus can add significantly to one's squat.

Costs and Sponsorships

Before leaving the subject of whether wraps should be allowed in raw competition, two final points need to be addressed that will become even more significant when raw versus equipped lifting is considered. They are the cost of the gear and the sponsorship by gear companies of contests and federations.

In regards to the first, there is no doubt it is less expensive to lift raw without wraps than to lift unequipped with wraps. The raw lifter would only at best need to purchase a belt, along with maybe specialty shoes for squats and deadlifts. But, as mentioned in Chapter Two, a belt can last a lifetime, and squat and deadlift shoes will last a long time as well. So once those are purchased, that will be the extent of the raw lifter's investment in gear.

But wraps of all sorts tend to wear out rather quickly, so they need to be purchased regularly, and that will constitute an ongoing and added expense for the unequipped lifter. But wraps are not really that expensive, so it is not that great of an expense.

However, these same reasons are why it easier to find sponsorship for a contest or federation that allows wraps than one that does not. A gear company has little reason to sponsor a federation or contest that allows only raw lifting. The company simply will not get much return on its investment.

But if the contest allows wraps, then a gear company will know that promotion of its products at the contest could lead to ongoing sales of its wraps in the future and thus will be more likely to offer sponsorship.

Such sponsorships are absolutely essential for the continuing existence of powerlifting. Without sponsorships, it can be very difficult for it to be financially viable for a meet director to put on a meet. At the very least, without sponsorship, the meet director will be forced to charge the lifters a much higher entry fee.

Of course, it is possible to find other types of companies to sponsor powerlifting contests, but powerlifting gear companies are the most likely candidates as they are the type of companies that will most directly profit from sponsoring a contest.

Belt and Wraps vs. Suits, Briefs, and Shirts

The controversy over knee wraps pales in comparison to the controversy over the other kinds of powerlifting gear, namely, squat and deadlifts suits, briefs, and bench press shirts. The reason for this is several-fold.

First off, wraps, along belts, are rather "basic" support gear, worn even by many who are not powerlifters to provide support for the given body parts. But supportive suits, briefs, and shirts are unique to powerlifting.

Second, suits, briefs, and shirts have the potential to add much more to one's lift than even extra long knee wraps.

Third, belt and wraps are relatively inexpensive, but suits, briefs, and shirts can be quite costly, and this leads to the feeling that those who cannot afford top of the line gear are at a distinct disadvantage.

Fourth, belts and wraps are easy to put on and take off, while suits, briefs, and shirts can be quite a struggle. You can easily expend as much energy on gear as in the actual execution of the lift

Fifth, it is very easy to find a belt and wraps that fit properly, and the different brands all work basically the same. In fact, knee wraps are a "one size fits all" type of gear. But much time, effort, and money can be spent finding the type of suits, briefs, and shirts that work best for a given individual, in finding the right size, and in getting it all altered so it fits just right.

Pros of Raw Lifting/
Cons of Equipped Lifting

It is now time to look at the pros and cons of raw versus equipped lifting. Some of these points have been touched on previously, but it will be good to list them all out in one place. The arguments put forth by each side to support its position will also be presented.

First to be looked at are the pros of raw lifting and thus the cons of equipped lifting.

1. Raw lifting is "real" – using gear is "cheating":

This has been mentioned previously and is epitomized by 100% Raw's slogan, "Where lifters compete, not technology." Again, the idea is, when using gear, it is felt it is the gear that is lifting the weight, not the lifter. Many raw advocates will even refer to equipped lifting as "cheating." Moreover, comparisons to other sports that utilize ever-improving gear are said not to be valid as gear is not needed to power-lift, as compared to some other sports where gear is necessary.

This attitude isn't unique to raw powerlifters. When I have tried to explain what a bench press shirt is to a non-powerlifter and how it can help the lifter lift the weight, the non-powerlifter always has responded, "Isn't that cheating?" I then have to explain that such shirts are allowed by the rules. But the non-powerlifter will then often shake his head and walk away.

2. Raw lifting is cheaper:

There is no doubt this is true, as previously discussed. Belt and wraps are not very expensive, but suits and shirts can be very expensive, especially multi-ply gear. That expense can potentially scare many away from powerlifting. It can also lead to the feeling that having the money to purchase the latest and greatest gear can become the determining factor in who wins a contest, not the lifters' ability.

3. Getting gear can be a hassle:

When ordering gear, you either have to figure out the size to order based on a "sizing chart" or take measurements and let the company pick the size for you. Either way, it can often take weeks for the gear to come, and when it does, you will often have gotten the wrong size. You then need to ship it back and get a different size, again waiting several weeks. Then when you get the replacement gear, it might still not fit quite right, so you need to ship it back to get altered.

After waiting several more weeks, you might finally have gotten gear that fits right, but you still won't know how well it works until you try it out in a workout. After all of that, you might find the new gear doesn't work quite as well as you had hoped, and you're already looking for new gear.

The many problems this writer has had in this regard will be discussed later in this book. But here, it will be said that all of these hassles and potential nightmares are avoided when lifting raw.

4. Raw workouts and contests are shorter:

Again, there is no doubt this is true. It can easily take 10-20 minutes to get a tight squat suit on, and about the same time for tight briefs if those are worn. It then takes time to wraps one's knees, to tighten wrist wraps, to pull up the suit straps, and to tighten the belt. And then after the lift, it takes further time to loosen all of that gear and to roll up the wraps for the next lift. And then more time to get the suit and briefs off.

Later in this book, it will be asserted that the ideal workout time is an hour to an hour and a half. But there is almost no way to get in a squat workout with full gear done within that time period.

As for contests, with the one minute rule for starting your attempts, you would think it would not make a difference. However, at raw contests, lifters are usually ready to go as soon as their name is called. But at equipped contests, lifters will often use that full minute to get started. Moreover, not all federations actually use a clock. As such, there is often 2-3 minutes after a lifter's name is called and when the lift is actually started. Those extra seconds and minutes add up over the course of a contest.

5. Equipped lifting can be dangerous:

The gear enables lifters to lift far more weight than they would be able to without it. With that greater weight comes a greater chance of an accident occurring.

For instance, one time when squatting alone in a power rack with full gear, I started going down but then realized I would not be able to make the lift, so I started back up again. When I did, the weight slipped off of my back. The bar slammed onto the safety bars in the power rack, bounced up off of the bars and out of the power rack, and then almost went through a wall. Fortunately, I was not injured and no on was near the rack. But if someone had been, it could have been disastrous.

That accident of course could have happened if I were lifting raw. But the greater weight I was using due to the gear increased the likelihood of the problem and the force of the dropped and bounced weight and thus the potential danger.

If I were using spotters as is the smarter method of training, things might have actually been worse. If the spotters did not catch the weight initially, then they would have been in the way of the bouncing weight. And it is spotters who are put most in danger from gear.

The lifter might have his body supported with gear, but the spotters do not. Yet, they will be called on to lift that extra poundage, and with the greater the poundage, the greater is the chance of injury.

As for the lifter, the gear does protect the body parts that are supported, as will be discussed more shortly. However, not all body parts are so protected. Most especially, as discussed in Chapter Two, elbow support of any sort is not allowed when benching. However, a shirt will artificially increase the amount of weight a lifter can lift. This could conceivably increase the risk to the elbows.

Moreover, a scary phenomenon has been on the rise in powerlifting, that of powerlifters spontaneously breaking a forearm bone while benching. In every case I have heard of this happening, the lifter was wearing a bench shirt. As such, it seems apparent the shirt is increasing what the lifter can lift beyond what the muscles would be able to do by themselves. As a result, the poundage being lifted is beyond the stress point of the bones. This simply does not happen with raw lifting as the bones are always effectively stronger than the muscles.

6. Blowouts are very dangerous:

This was touched on in Chapter Two. A "blowout" is when a suit or shirt rips. Usually, a suit will rip in the "seat of the pants" when descending into the hole, while a shirt will rip at the seam between the sleeve and the body of the shirt, again, when bringing the bar down.

When such a rip occurs, all of the support the suit or shirt provides will immediately disappear. As such, the weight will in essence become much heavier all at once. The lifter could very easily lose control of the bar. If the spotters are not paying attention, the lifter could get crushed underneath. Or the spotters could get caught under the bar. Either way, the results could be traumatic.

Fortunately, will today's gear, such blowouts are very rare. But they do still happen.

7. Gear is unpredictable:

Exactly how you put on gear (such as how well you have your shirt pulled down), how tight you wrap your knees, how tight you pull the straps if they have Velcro, and how worn-out the gear is can all affect the effectiveness of the gear. As a result, the gear might help more one time and less the next.

Another variable is bodyweight. If you cut weight for a contest, gear that fit just right in training might now be loose and not help as much as expected.

This all can easily lead to missed lifts at a contest and often bomb outs. With raw lifting, the only variable is your own body.

8. Powerlifting should be about getting the bar up:

Squat gear can make it difficult to squat down below parallel, and a bench press shirt can make it difficult to touch your chest with the bar as is required by the rules. Many bomb outs have occurred at contests as a result of lifters not being able to do so.

This is also why you will often see in meet reports that a lifter missed his first attempt, but then increased the weight for his second attempt and got it. Normally, that would not make any sense. If a lifter could not bench say 400 pounds, then how is it that he was able to make 440?

The answer is that he did not miss the first attempt because he was not strong enough to press the weight up. He missed it because the weight was not heavy enough to "push" the bar down to the chest against the shirt. But by adding 40 pounds, the lifter was able to touch and thus get the lift.

But all of this is contrary to what powerlifting should be about. Powerlifting should be about who can lift the most weight, not about who is able to overcome their gear and get the bar down. And this leads to the next point.

9. Gear can make powerlifting a joke:

The feeling that the use of gear is "cheating" and the inability to get the bar down can make powerlifting a joke among non-powerlifters. Think for instance what the audience must be thinking when they see lifter after lifter missing a bench attempt because they cannot get the bar down to their chest. "What are those shirts made of?" is probably a common thought. The audience could very well walk away thinking that the sport is just about shirts and not lifting.

That type of reputation hurts the popularity of the sport and its ability to attain sponsorships and media exposure. There are also many who believe the "joke" made of powerlifting due to gear is why powerlifting has never made it into the Olympics.

10. Gear is distracting:

With worries about getting the gear on in time for your lift, with getting it adjusted properly, and with how very uncomfortable the gear is, your focus throughout a contest can easily be on the gear rather than what a powerlifting contest is really about—lifting heavy weights.

11. Gear is exhausting:

Much effort can be expended getting gear on and off. On top of the grueling day that is a powerlifting contest, this can leave the lifter very exhausted by day's end. Many lifters find their deadlift suffers much more when having previously squatted and benched with gear as opposed to having done those lifts raw.

12. Raw lifting is more fun:

With all of the difficulties of gear, with it being so distracting and tiring, using gear can take all of the "fun" out of powerlifting.

This has definitely been this writer's experience. At my last couple of contests using gear, I simply was not able to enjoy myself due to being so concerned and exhausted from the gear. But at my NASA contest in 2008 where I lifted unequipped, I very much enjoyed myself as I was able to focus on the contest and not so much on gear.

Pros of Equipped Lifting/ Cons of Raw Lifting

Next to be looked at are the pros of equipped lifting and thus the cons of raw lifting.

1. Equipped lifting is safer:

Freak accidents aside, with gear, the most vulnerable body parts are protected. The wrists, knees, shoulders, hips, and groin areas are all protected with full gear. These are all areas where many lifters have sustained injuries. The gear can prevent these injuries.

This is without a doubt the most important and strongest argument in the favor of gear. Many injuries can easily occur in raw lifting that would have been prevented with the use of gear.

However, it must be added that all that is needed for injury prevention is single-ply gear. Multi-ply gear is simply not necessary for this purpose.

2. Gear prevents chronic pain:

Sooner or later, many lifters develop chronic pain in one or more joints, but this is even more likely among raw lifters than among equipped lifters. Many older raw lifters even regret having lifted raw throughout their careers due to the problems they now experience.

3. Equipped lifting enables lifters to keep competing:

Related to the previous points, many lifters over time develop chronic pain due to injuries or simply long-term use and abuse of the joints. But gear can allow such lifters to continue to lift and compete.

I already mentioned my experiences where wrist and knee pain would have kept me from contests if I had not been able to wear wraps to support those body parts. And again, there are many lifters with knee problems which would prevent them from doing heavy squats without knee support.

There are also many lifters who could not bench heavy due to shoulder pain without a bench shirt or who could not squat and deadlift heavy due to hip pain without a suit.

As for myself, I have had a chronic problem with my left pec for about three years as of this writing. The pain is only minor and occasional. But if it were to get much worse, the only way I'd be able to perform heavy benches would be with a shirt.

Such problems are especially the case among master lifters, but even younger lifters can sustain injuries or chronic abuse problems that require the use of gear to keep lifting and competing.

If the reader has any such problems, then you will have no choice but to lift with the gear that is required to support the injured or chronic pain area. But again, all that is needed in this regard is single-ply gear.

4. Equipped lifting encourages sponsorships:

This was mentioned previously in regards to wraps, but it is even more meaningful in regards to suits, briefs, and shirts for the simple reason that such gear is much more expensive and thus more profitable for gear companies.

Gear companies like APT, Crain, Inzer, and Titan regularly sponsor contests. Without their sponsorships, many contests simply would not happen. And such companies would not sponsor contests if the gear they make is not allowed to be used by the lifters at those contests.

5. Equipped lifting increases bragging rights:

Gear enables powerlifters to lift more weight, even more so if it is multi-ply gear, and this extra weight enables lifters to brag that much more about how much they can lift. This is especially the case when bragging to non-powerlifters who don't have a clue about gear. This is of course pure ego, but it is not an unimportant point. Many people only powerlift for those bragging rights.

For myself, when people ask me how much I can lift, when I was using gear, I would respond by saying I can squat and deadlift over 400 pounds, and it felt so good to be able to say that. But my best raw squat is less than 400, so I am no longer able to make that claim. I can still brag about being able to deadlift over 400, but it's not quite the same. And my raw bench sounds so pitiful as compared to my equipped bench that I now tend to avoid saying what I can bench.

6. Equipped lifting makes powerlifting more popular:

Contrary to previous claims, non-powerlifters really do not care whether a lifter is wearing gear or not. They are simply impressed by seeing huge amounts of weight lifted. And the gear enables those weights to be even greater, especially so if it is multi-ply gear. Such massive amounts of weights being lifted will make powerlifting more popular among the general population and thus more likely to attain media exposure and sponsorships by even non-gear companies.

7. Gear improvements are normal in many sports:

In almost all sports, there have been improvements in gear that have enabled the respective athletes to better previous competitors, so there is no reason why the same should not occur in powerlifting.

Consider, for instance, the 2008 Beijing Summer Olympics. More swimming world records were broken at that Olympics than in the two previous Olympics combined. Part of the reason for this was the new and improved swimming suits the swimmers were wearing.

This relates back to the previous point. The "star" of the Beijing Olympics was Michael Phelps with his eight gold medals and world records. Viewers did not care that all of those world records would not have been possible without the new suits. They just enjoyed watching Phelps swim fast, win gold, and break records, and the higher than ever before viewership ratings for that Olympics proves that point.

Phelps has become so popular that he is now a multi-millionaire due to all of the endorsement deals he has received. Wouldn't it be great if the same could be said for the "stars" of powerlifting?

Relationships of the Lifts

Before closing this chapter, one final point will be addressed. Generally speaking, when lifting raw, people can deadlift more than they can squat, and they can squat more than they can bench. However, when using gear, a different situation often occurs. With gear, people can often out-squat their deadlift. With double-ply gear, some lifters can even out-bench their deadlift. The reason for this is that gear helps much on squats and benches but very little on deadlifts.

There are several implications to this phenomenon. First, it is for this reason that many lifters believe the deadlift is the only "unvarnished" lift. By that is meant only the deadlift is still a true test of strength while the other two lifts are more tests of who can utilize gear the best.

Second, it is only on deadlifts that you can compare lifts done between federations. As such, only the deadlift list in *Powerlifting USA* Top 100 and Top 20 charts is truly meaningful. These charts will be discussed in the next chapter.

Third, it is only on deadlifts that you can compare lifts done today with lifts performed years ago before today's advancements in gear.

Finally, when reading contest reports, you can often tell if the contest allowed gear or not by checking the relationships of the lifts. If by and large, lifters are out-deadlifting their squats, then it is probably a raw contest. If most lifters are out-squatting their deadlifts, then it is probably an equipped contest. If there are lifters out-benching their deadlifts, it is probably a multi-ply equipped contest.

The only exception to this rule is if "little people" (a.k.a. midgets or dwarfs) are involved. Even when lifting raw, little people very often out-squat and even out-bench their deadlifts. This is due to the arms and legs of some types of little people being rather short as compared to the trunks of their bodies. This gives them very good leverage and a short stroke on squats and benches. However, their fingers are so short that they have a hard time holding onto the bar on deadlifts, so their deadlifts suffers.

I first noticed this at National Collegiates in 1981. Another lifter at 114s was a little person. He squatted and benched about the same as me, but his deadlift was far below mine. I watched him warming up on deadlifts, and the bar kept slipping out of his hands even with very light weights.

Conclusion

This writer is somewhat biased against suits and shirts given the many problems I've had with such gear, as will be detailed in Chapter 23. I am also somewhat biased against raw lifting given the injuries I have suffered when training raw, as mentioned previously and as will be discussed in detail in Chapter 24.

I am bias for unequipped lifting—using a belt, wrist wraps, and knee sleeves or knee wraps. That limited amount of gear will prevent many injuries but not cause a whole lot of hassles or expense.

That is why I recommended utilizing that limited gear for your first contest in Chapter One. But after that, the reader will have to decide for yourself whether to use gear or not. Hopefully, this chapter and other information in this book will help you in making that decision. Of course, what the rules are for contests held in your area can also be a determining factor in that decision.

But I will say it is prudent to make a decision one way or the other and to stick with it. Going back and forth between using gear and not using gear will hurt your long-term progress and even worse, could lead to injury.

Moreover, if you have been lifting with gear for an extended period, it would not be wise to try all at once to lift raw. After much time having various body parts supported with gear, they will not be able to handle heavy lifting without the gear.

The reverse is also true. If you have been lifting raw for an extended period of time, it will take quite some time to get used to gear and the "extra" weight it enables you to handle.

As such, when going either way, give yourself at least several months to make the transition.

Chapter Six
Fixing Powerlifting

As mentioned previously, there are over 20 different powerlifting federations in the USA. There are also debates over the type of supportive gear that should be allowed in powerlifting. Another major issue of debate is testing for performance enhancing drugs. There are also differences between federations in regards to weigh-in times, the use of a monolift, and other issues.

With all of these differences of opinion, the sport of powerlifting is in a real mess today. Before offering some possible solutions, this chapter will first outline the problems this mess causes.

Too Many Champions

In most sports, to be called a state champion means you are the best athlete or team in that state for that calendar year. To be called a national champion means you are the best athlete or team in the USA for that year. To be called a world champion means you are the best athlete or team in the world that year. But what about powerlifting?

Back when I powerlifted in college, there was just one federation, the USPF. So when I "brag" about being a two-time Pennsylvania State Collegiate champion, it means I was the best collegiate powerlifter in Pennsylvania for the 114 and 123 pound weights classes in 1981 and 1982, respectively.

When I say I was National Collegiate Champion in 1981 and runner-up in 1982, I was the best collegiate lifter in the country at 114s in 1981 and the second best at 123s in 1982.

Moreover, back then, I always had competition at every contest I entered. For instance, the year I won National Collegiates there were nine lifters in my weight class, so I beat eight other lifters for the title.

However, the situation is far different today. Most all of the 20+ federations hold its own state, national, and even world championships each year. That means, in a given weight and age class, there are potentially over twenty different respective champions in a given year.

But it gets even worse. Many federations have two or even three different divisions just in regards to what kind of gear is allowed. Some federations even further subdivide these divisions into drug-tested and non-drug-tested divisions. Each of those different divisions and subdivision has their own "champion."

As a result, for a given weight and age class, there are potentially dozens of state, national, and world champions. What that means is that there is no longer much meaning to being such a champion. That is why I have not mentioned in this book about the state, regional, national, and even world "championships" that I have won since I started powerlifting again in 2003, as they are all rather meaningless titles.

Making them even more meaningless is that in every contest I have entered since I started competing again I was the only person in my weight class. So all I had to do was to enter and not bomb out and I was automatically a "champion." This is often the case for many others who "win" championships. They win by default of being the only person in their weight and age class.

The reason for this is, with so many federations to choose from, the talent is diluted across the various federations. Remember this when someone starts bragging about having won so many championships.

One final point worth mentioning is that some federations have qualifying totals that have to be met before entering their Nationals contest, but for others, anyone can enter Nationals. Similarly, in some federations, you have to enter and at least place if not win their Nationals to enter Worlds. But in other federations anyone can enter Worlds.

What this means is that in the federations without qualifying standards, it is meaningless to say you competed in Nationals or Worlds. But for those with qualifying standards, there is at least some pride that you were able to qualify to enter those contests.

Too Many Records

I mentioned earlier in this book that in college I held seven different Pennsylvania collegiate records (three at 114s and four at 123s) and one national collegiate record (the squat at 123s). Again, with only one federation, these records were meaningful. They meant I had lifted more weight than any other collegiate lifter had previously lifted in my state or in the country for my weight class.

But since 2003, I now hold 39 different records. How is that possible given there are only four different records in powerlifting (squat, bench press, deadlift, total)? The answer in part is because for most contests I enter both the open and the masters divisions, so that gives me up to eight records to shoot for. In fact, that is the reason I enter both divisions, to give me more records to break.

But still, that's only eight records. But I have broken records in four different federations in both divisions, and in one federation, the IPA, I have broken records in both the drug tested (Am) and non-drug-tested (Pro) divisions. That is how I have accumulated so many different records.

In this case, those records are somewhat meaningful. When I was breaking someone else's records, at least I was in essence competing against and defeating that person. And that is why I go after records, to give me some competition.

However, in a few cases, I was the first person in that federation to compete in the masters division in my weight class, so I *set* rather than *broke* those records and thus did not "beat" anyone.

But more to the point, none of my records are true records in the sense of having lifted more weight than anyone before in my weight and age class. For every one of them, you can find someone else that has lifted more in a federation I have not yet competed in.

That is why I will generally talk about breaking say an "IPA record" not a "world record" even though all of the records I have broken in the IPA have been that federation's "world" records.

Remember all of this when someone begins bragging about holding a "national" or even "world" record. That record does not mean he or she has lifted more weight than anyone else ever has before in the country or world in that weight class. It simply means he or she has lifted more than anyone else who has ever entered that particular federation. It is even possible that he or she was the first one to lift in that class in that federation and thus set the record simply by entering a contest and not bombing out.

Ranking Lists

Each month, *Powerlifting USA* magazine publishes a "Top 100 Ranking" list for a different weight class, so in the course of a year each weight class gets its listings.

These ratings list the top 100 lifts performed in the USA in the previous year for the squat, bench press, deadlift, and total. The idea is to give lifters an idea of how their performances compare to all of the other lifters in their weight class in the country.

This sounds like a great idea and one that would help fix the problem of so many different federations. Lifters in all federations are listed together, so you can compare your lifts to those done in other federations.

However, there are many flaws with the lists. First off, all lifters are listed together regardless of gender or age. But this problem is offset by once a year *Powerlifting USA* publishing separate Top 20 lists for women, teenagers, and master lifters. So those classes of lifters can see how they compare against just those in the same class.

But the real problem with both the Top 100 lists and the Top 20 lists is there is no distinction made for the type of gear the lifter used, if there was drug testing at the contest, if there was a monolift, different weigh-in times, etc. The lists do not even indicate what federation each lifter's lifts were performed in, so there is no way of investigating things to figure such different factors out.

Back in my college lifting days, this was not a problem as just about all lifters competed in the same federation and under the same rules, so there was an even playing field.

My best ranking back then was in 1982 when I placed #5 in the squat at 123s. I was rather proud of that placing, especially when you considered that I was only 21 years old, so I was in essence competing against lifters who were older than I was, but there still were only four lifters in the country that could out-squat me.

On the ranking list released in October 2008 for 114s, I was also ranked #5 in the squat. That was for a squat performed at a contest I entered a year before. However, my squat from a contest in June 2008 would only place me at #36.

What happened? Did my squat get that much worse in one year that I fell so far in the rankings? Not really. The difference is due to in 2007 I competed using multi-ply gear, while in 2008 I competed unequipped, wearing just knee sleeves for squats.

That is the fundamental flaw in the ranking lists. Those who compete with multi-ply gear have a distinct advantage over those who compete with single-ply gear and especially over those who compete raw or unequipped.

In fact, one reason I was using multi-ply gear at that time was to aid my performance in the ranking lists. My best placement was in 2006. I placed #4 for squats and in the top 10 for deadlifts and total. On the masters list, I was #1 in squat, bench, deadlift, and total.

With those rankings I reached my initial goals I had set for myself when I began to compete again. With those goals reached, I began to compete unequipped and have ceased to concern myself as much with *Powerlifting USA's* ranking lists as I know that I will never do that well again in them.

Fixing the Champions Problem

When I competed in the APF Pennsylvania State Championships in 2006, the meet director lamented that there were only a dozen lifters at what was supposed to be a state championship. He mentioned that what really needed to be done was for all of the multi-ply federations to get together and hold a "unified" state championship.

That is a great idea, and in fact, there has been on occasion joint contests held by two or more federations. Such contests are a step in the right direction. Federations and divisions with similar rules could easily combine together for unified contests.

Basically, every lifter knows that there really are three main divisions in powerlifting in regards to gear: raw, single-ply, and multi-ply. A distinction has been made in this book between raw and unequipped lifting, but it was also mentioned this distinction is minor compared to the difference between raw/ unequipped lifting and equipped lifting.

There are also some multi-ply federations and divisions that allow just double-ply gear while others allow triple-ply or even an unlimited number of plies. But once you get to double-ply, further plies do not make that great of a difference due to diminishing returns. But the big difference is between single-ply and more than single-ply.

The point is, if the federations or divisions with similar gear rules could just quit their bickering and at least get together for an occasional contest with other federations with the same gear rules there could be state and even national contests with decent turnouts and with their champions being true champions.

Another idea is to hold state or national championships that are independent of any federation but to which each federation sends its best lifters. This is the idea behind the Raw Unity Meet.

By allowing wrist wraps and knee sleeves, the contest is trying to strike a compromise between raw and unequipped lifters, and it is hoped that the best lifters from the various raw and unequipped federations and divisions will attend.

Unfortunately, this ideal has not yet been fully realized, so the contest actually adds yet one more set of "national champions" to the already blotted number of "champions." But it is nevertheless an attempted step in the right direction.

Finally, I think it is best if some kind of standard must be met to compete in a contest that is labeled as a Nationals or Worlds contest. That way, the meets will be truly for the best lifters, and it will be meaningful to just qualify.

Fixing the Records Problem

You will sometimes hear of someone breaking an "all-time, all-federation" record. This means the record is a "true" record in the sense of being the most weight ever lifted in that weight and age class. However, such all-time records normally do not make a distinction between what type of gear was used to set the record. So again, those using multi-ply gear have a distinct advantage in setting such records.

One solution would again be to hold a "combined" contest, with several different federations with similar rules being involved. Records could then be set in all of the participating federations. This would have the effect of bringing those records together. With more such contests, then the records in a given weight and age class for a given type of gear would be the same across several different federations.

Another solution would be have a "clearinghouse" of some sort to keep track of records set in all the different federations performed with the same type of gear. In other words, what is needed is for there to be separate "all-time" records for raw, single-ply, and multi-ply lifters. Lists of state, national, and world all-time records would be helpful.

This is not to say there is a problem with federation records. The distinctions between gear is only one of the many differences between federations, so it is prudent for each federation to keep track of its own records. This also gives lifters something to shoot for in situations like mine when there is only one lifter in a given age and weight class at a contest.

Personal Records

It would be good to interject here a very important point. Do not get discouraged over all of this talk about records, championships, and the like if you are not lifting at such a level. The most important person to compete against is yourself, and the most important records for anyone to break are your own personal records (PRs). In fact, this is one thing that makes powerlifting so great.

Even if you are the only person in your weight class, or you are not able to win or even place at a contest or to break federation records, you will always have the goal of improving upon your previous performances at each contest. The lifter who can continually set new PRs is a successful lifter, regardless of how many contests have been won or federation records have been broken.

Fixing the Ranking List Problem

A serious step has already been taken to fix the ranking list problem by Powerlifting Watch Web site (www.PowerliftingWatch.com). Starting in 2006, it began to publish its own Top 50 lists.

Like Powerlifting USA's Top 100 lists, these lists combine lifters of all ages. However, there are separate lists for male and female lifters. But most importantly, there are separate lists for raw, single-ply, and multi-ply lifters. These lists can only be viewed by making a payment to the Web site. But the cost is minimal.

These lists are a great step in leveling the playing field by enabling lifters to see how they fare against lifters using the same type of gear as they do.

But there are some problems with the lists. First, the raw lists include both raw and unequipped lifters together. So you effectively have lifters competing without knee wraps against those who use knee wraps. That can put raw lifters at a disadvantage in the squat and total.

Second, no distinction is made for drug-tested versus non-drug tested, differing weigh-in times, and other minor differences between federations.

But in defense of the lists, to account for all of these differences would require many more than three lists, and you'd be back to the same problem of too many "champions." Moreover, Powerlifting Watch's lists indicate which federation each lifter's lifts were performed in, so it is possible to figure out these other factors if they are important to you to know.

However, the biggest flaw as far as this writer is concerned is that the bottom list for men is 132s. In other words, lifts done in the 114, 123, and 132 pound weight classes are all combined together.

It was for this reason that when the lists first came out, I didn't bother subscribing to them. But after my unequipped contest in June of 2008, I did so. Much to my surprise, I was ranked #2 for squat and total to that date for 2008.

That was the only contest I entered in 2008, so for the final list for 2008, I had moved down to #5 for squat and #7 for the total. But I was still thrilled with that ranking given that I was effectively competing against lifters as much as two weight classes above me and against lifters potentially half my age. I also only wore knee sleeves at that contest, but many of the lifters in the raw list were probably wearing knee wraps.

Not a Problem

As mentioned previously in this book, at most any contest, there are separate divisions for male and female lifters, about a dozen different weight classes for each gender, separate divisions for teenager lifters (usually by two-year increments), and separate divisions for master lifters (usually by five year increments). There is also sometimes a separate division for "Special Olympics" competitors.

What this means is that in a given federation, there are potentially dozens of national champions and dozens of national record holders. But these distinctions are not a problem. In fact, I would say having so many divisions is another thing that makes powerlifting so great.

Powerlifting in one of the few sports in which both men and women of all sizes and ages can successfully compete. At some contests, you will see both teenagers and senior citizens competing side by side. It goes without saying, you wouldn't expect a teenager or a senior citizen to compete successfully against someone in their 20s or 30s, and you wouldn't expect someone my size to compete successfully against someone weighing over 300 pounds. But by having all of the different age and weight classes, powerlifting offers something for everyone.

However, I do think the ADAU has a good idea. At some of its contests, all lifters regardless of age must enter the "Open" division. Then for an extra fee, teenagers and master lifters can enter their age-appropriate division.

In this way, you have the best of both worlds. It increases the likelihood there will actually be some competition in each weight class in the Open division, even if it is a teenager, a 30 year old, and a senior citizen competing against each other. But then, the teen and the senior citizen can enter their appropriate age divisions so as not to have to compete against someone twice or half their age.

One Last Problem

As mentioned earlier in this chapter, when I competed in National Collegiates in 1981, there were nine lifters in my 114 pound weight class. That was the greatest number of lifters in any weight class at that contest. And again, I always had competition at every contest I entered in college, at both 114s and 123s.

But now, both of these weight classes have sparse competition, so much so that I have never had competition at any contest I have competed in so far. As a result, some federations have eliminated the 114 and even 123 pound weight class for men, while Powerlifting Watch does not feel there are enough lifters in these classes to keep track of separate ranking lists for them.

So what has happened? Part of the reason for the change could be the very real problem of the ever-growing waistlines of Americans. As a result, even short men like myself now tend to weigh more than 123 pounds. It is also possible the average height of Americans has gone up in the past 25 years.

There is also the very real fact that powerlifters tend to gain weight the longer they lift and compete. This happened to me back in college. For a while, I competed at 114s, but eventually, I moved up to 123s. I'm guessing that if I had continued to lift throughout my 20s and 30s, by today, I would be up to 132s or even 148s.

I say this as at my first contest in 2003, I met a lifter who remembered me from my college lifting days. At that time, we were both in the 123 pound weight class and about the same height. When I checked the Top 100 ranking list from 1982 mentioned previously, we were side-by-side in all four categories. But now, he was competing at 148s and lifting far more than me, while I was down to 114s. Of course, the reason for this is he had continued to lift and compete through all of those years when I had stopped lifting.

In any case, it is obviously much to this writer's chagrin that the 114 and even 123 pound weight classes have been eliminated in some federations. But I think a much better solution would be to in essence combine and average together 114s and 123s and come up with a new 119 pound weight class.

I say this as part of the problem is that the bottom three weight classes are too close together. There is only a nine pound difference between 114s and 123s, and another nine pounds between 123s and 132s, but then there are 16 pounds between 132s and 148s. However, a 119 pound class would be 13 pounds less than 132s and thus give more of an even difference between the bottom weight classes.

This new 119 pound weight class would still have fewer lifters than the heavier weight classes, but it would be more competitive than either 114s or 123s, with all of the lifters from the former 114s and probably the lighter half of the former 123s competing in it. The heavier half of the 123s would probably move up to 132s, thus increasing the number of lifters in that class. But the new 119s would still be light enough to give shorter lifters like myself a weight class to compete in.

Unfortunately, given the mess that is powerlifting, I doubt such a change could ever be effectively made. It would require all of the different federations to get together to adopt the new weight class and for

Powerlifting USA and Powerlifting Watch to include the new class in their ranking lists. But I figured I'd throw the idea out.

This is a much better solution than eliminating the bottom weight classes. To me, doing so is discrimination against short people. I have even heard of some people saying that if someone cannot carry at least 132 pounds of bodyweight then he shouldn't be powerlifting. Such an attitude is deplorable.

A few facts: an average weight for someone my height (5'1") would be about 111 pounds. I base this on a "formula" I learned back in college that to get a rough estimate of the average weight for a male is to allot 105 pounds for the first five feet then add six pounds for each additional inch. (For women, the formula is 100 pounds for the first five feet and five pounds for each additional inch). This means that the 114 pound weight class is already three pounds over the average weight for a male my height. And yes there are men even shorter than me and thus whose average weight would be even lower.

Moreover, my "normal" weight is over 120 pounds, so I am actually over ten pounds above average already. I am just skilled at cutting weight, and I should not be penalized for my ability to do so.

More to the point, back in the spring of 2002, due to health problems, my weight had fallen to a low of 106 pounds. So from then to date, I have gained over 15 pounds, almost all of it muscle. But at my age (48 at this writing), I doubt I will be gaining much more, at least in the form of muscle. The only way I could "bulk up" to 132s would be to gain fat, which would be injurious to my health.

My point is, as mentioned previously, one thing that makes powerlifting so great is that people of all ages and sizes can compete successfully. But to eliminate the bottom weight classes is to defy this statement.

Section Two

Training Basics

Chapter Seven
Designing a Training Routine

This chapter will look at various factors to consider in designing a powerlifting training routine.

But first it needs to be mentioned, this chapter, and the rest of this book for that matter, assumes the reader possesses a reasonable degree of general fitness and has been training with weights for at least several months and has made enough progress to be thinking about entering a powerlifting contest or is already competing.

If you are someone who is completely out of shape or are brand new to weight training, then I would suggest you check out the chapter "Starting and Progressing in an Exercise Program" in my book *God-given Foods Eating Plan* (see Appendix #2). That chapter assumes the reader is not exercising at all and thus details how to start to get back into shape and then to gradually ease into a weight training program.

Warm-Ups

It is imperative to warm-up before working out. Many suggest starting with 5-10 minutes of light aerobics. I used to do that but found it to be a waste of time.

When I was working out at a commercial gym, I would instead gather together all of the weights I would need for my first exercise, placing them by the station I would be using. I found all that walking around and carrying of weights provided sufficient general warm-up.

Now, with my home, gym I store all of my equipment inside of my power rack. So I need to clear all of that out and set up the rack for my first exercise. That setting up provides sufficient general warm-up.

Once the general warm-up/ set-up are finished, the best way to warm-up for the first exercise of the day is to do that exercise using very light weights for high reps.

Specifically, I always do the first set with just the bar for 15 reps. I then use a decreasing reps approach for the rest of my warm-ups. How many warm-up sets I do depends on how many reps I will be doing for my first work set. The higher the weight and the lower the reps the greater number of warm-up sets needed.

If the first work set is to be for 5-8 reps, then I will use the following rep scheme: 15, 8, 5, 3. If the first set is for 3-4 reps, then a set of a single is also needed (15, 8, 5, 3, 1). If the first set is for 1-2 reps, then yet another single might be needed (15, 8, 5, 3, 1, 1). The final set is done with about 10% less weight than is to be used for the first work set. The rest of the sets are then spaced out evenly in-between.

These warm-up sets are based on a one rep max (1RM) of at most 450 pounds, and proportionally less for reps. Those using greater weights will need additional warm-ups. Generally, you do not want to jump more than 90 pounds between sets, or a pair of 45s for each set.

This means a basic warm-up scheme for a first work set of 450 would be: 45/15, 135/8, 225/5, 315/3, 405/1. If the first work set is for less than this, then reduce the weights as needed. If it is greater, then add triples or singles as needed.

How many warm-ups sets need to be done for subsequent exercises depends again on the number of reps to be done and how closely the next exercise resembles the previous one in terms of the muscles utilized.

If deadlifts are being done after squats then a fewer number of warm-up sets will be needed as the muscles being worked are similar. You could skip the first set with the bar and maybe even the set of eight. But if benches are following squats, then a similar warm-up scheme as for squats will be needed since different muscle groups are being used.

For subsequent minor exercises, then 1-3 warm-ups will suffice, again, depending on the number of reps to be done and how closely that exercise resembles the previous one.

Number of Work Sets

Opinions vary widely on the best number of work sets to do. Some advocate doing only one work set per lift, usually done to failure, while others advocate four or more sets, done to less than failure.

But many find that one set is not enough. Progress can be made with one set, but usually only for a while. Eventually the progress stalls. But going the other way, more than four sets is just too much. That many sets can easily lead to overtraining. Also, it is hard to keep up a high intensity for that many sets. As such, I generally recommend 2-3 work sets, four sets at the most.

Number of Reps

Opinions also vary widely on how many reps a powerlifter should perform for each set. Since at a contest only one rep is performed, then some advocate doing mostly singles and maybe doubles in training. "Train as you compete" is the mantra. Such one rep advocates often recommend doing singles not just on the actual powerlifts but on a variety of major assistance exercises.

However, those who advocate such training methods often seem to be injured. This makes sense as doing singles and doubles is rather dangerous. The amount of weight being handled and the lack of a "warm-up" within the set itself open the door to potential injury.

Moreover, in this writer opinion, singles and doubles are not really that effective for building strength. They are great for testing strength, hence why singles are done at a contest, but the "time under tension" when doing singles and doubles in not sufficient to foster muscular strength development. By this is meant, the amount of time that the muscle fibers are being stressed when doing singles and doubles is not sufficient to stimulate growth and thus strengthening of the fibers.

However, since powerlifting *is* about who can lift the most weight for one rep, then yes, heavy singles and doubles do need to be done on a regular basis in training. But I believe singles should only be done on the powerlifts, not on assistance work. But I will go as low as triples on major assistance work, maybe a double with proper precautions.

In this writer opinion, 3-8 reps are the best rep range for building strength for powerlifting. With this rep range, heavy weights can still be utilized, while the time under tension is sufficient for muscle fiber stimulation. But the weights are not so heavy as to incur a high risk of injury. Also, there is sufficient warm-up within the set to lower the risk of injury. As such, most of the sets in my training routine utilize this rep range.

However, there is no point for a powerlifter to do more than eight reps. Once you get that high in reps, the amount of weight is way too low to condition the powerlifter for a heavy single. Moreover, the type of muscle fibers and the energy system being utilized when doing say a set of 12 reps are completely different than when doing a single. A discussion of those points is beyond the scope of this book, but it should be rather obvious that a set of 12 reps is very different than a heavy single.

How to go about incorporating these different reps ranges within a powerlifting routine will be discussed in-depth in the next chapter. But it should be mentioned here that these recommendations are for the actual powerlifts and other "compound movements." By this term is meant exercises that work more than one muscle group at a time, most especially "look-alike" lifts to the powerlifts like front squats and dumbbell benches. For such exercises, 3-8 reps work great.

However, isolation exercises generally need higher reps, in the 8-15 range. The term "isolation" refers to exercises that only work one muscle at a time, like arms, calves, and ab work.

When to Use Gear

At what point should supportive gear be utilized in one's routine? This again is an issue that will be addressed in more depth in the next chapter. But here it will be said that when doing five or more reps, there is no reason to use any gear.

Meanwhile, when doing heavy singles and doubles, it is best to use whatever gear you will be using at your next contest. This is for safety's sake and to get you used to handling the heavier weights that gear enables.

What gear to use with 3-4 reps will depend on what level of gear will be used for the next contest. Full gear can be utilized, if the lifter is able to get the bar down with a lighter weight. If not, then some sort of "partial gear" should be used.

Partial gear might refer to using single-ply gear when at the contest you will be using double-ply gear. Or it could refer to using just knee wraps and a belt when at the contest you will also be wearing a squat suit.

But it should be noted that these recommendations only apply to the actual powerlifts. I think it is best to do most assistance exercises completely raw, unless the lifter has an injury that requires support. But again, I believe singles should not be done on assistance work. But if you are going to do singles on assistance, then it would be prudent to wear at least a belt and wraps.

Rest between Sets

How long of a rest should a powerlifter take between sets? The shorter the rest time, the greater the general conditioning, which is good, so some recommend taking only 1-2 minutes rest between sets. However, with such a short rest time, there will be less strength and energy for the next set. As a result, the amount of weight that can be handled will gradually decrease with each set. But a powerlifter needs to be prepared to handle heavy weights. As such, some recommend taking 5-10 minutes rest between sets, but that will provide little conditioning and will make for long workouts.

As a compromise between the two, I generally take about 3-4 minutes rest between heavy sets of the actual powerlifts and major assistance work. That is sufficient time for recovery to allow a full effort to be exerted on the next set. But it is short enough to provide conditioning and to keep the workouts from getting too lengthy.

But that is only for the actual work sets. Warm-up sets only need about half that time, about 1-2 minutes rest. The same goes for rest times between sets of minor exercises.

The exception to this rule would be "speed work." This specialty type of training will be discussed later in Chapter 13.

Exercise Selection

It should go without saying that powerlifters need to do the actual powerlifts: squats, bench presses, and deadlifts. But beyond these three core lifts are many possible assistance exercises. The best ones for the powerlifter will be detailed in Section Three.

But here it will be said that the vast bulk of power training should be done utilizing free weights, not machines. Machines simply do not provide the same degree of muscular involvement as free weight exercises do, and the difference the powerlifts and similar movements on machines is too vast.

Take, for instance, bench presses. When doing benches with a barbell, your own muscles must keep the weight from veering upwards, downwards, to the sides, twisting, or from coming up uneven. Dumbbells provide even greater muscular involvement, as dumbbells can move in even greater ways than a barbell, hence why dumbbell benches are a great assistance exercise for benches.

However, all such movements are prevented with a machine. The machine is in essence doing the work of stabilizing the lift not your muscles. As a result, your stabilizer muscles will not be strengthened, and thus you would not be prepared for actual benches.

The only exceptions to this are cable machines. The reason for this is that with cable machines your range of motion is not restricted as it is with most other machines. So lat pulldown and cable pulls are very good exercises.

Workout Frequency and a Warning

How often should a powerlifter work out? There is again great variety of opinions in this regard. Some find they can make progress with as little as two workouts a week, while others will work out as much as 5-6 days a week.

Looking at the bottom end of this range, some lifters might only have time to work out twice a week. If that is the case, don't fret. It is possible to work out just twice a week and make really good progress.

A basic two day a week program is outlined on the next page.

Day One:
Squat
Bench
Upper Back Exercise
Abs

Day Two:
Deadlift
Bench Assistance Exercise
Arms
Abs

Short and simple, but such a plan can be effective. However, a twice a week program can have a couple of drawbacks. First off, I have found that working out only twice a week is not often enough to keep me in "lifting shape." Even with some aerobic exercise on in-between days, I end up dragging on the lifting days. Second, twice a week does not leave much time for a variety of exercises to be done.

On the other extreme, back in college I used to work out as much as 5-6 days a week and made good progress doing so. But in retrospect, I only "got away" with lifting that often as I was young, and thus my recuperative abilities were very high. But if I were to try that today, I would quickly end up overtrained. Moreover, even back then, I think I would have been better off working out just four days a week.

The problem with 5-6 days a week is no matter how much you spilt up the body parts, there is always some overlapping. As a result, the various body parts never have time to fully recover, but most of all, the body as a whole does not have sufficient recovery time. Over time, you will end up overtrained or even injured. As I think back, probably some of my injuries in college were due to working out too often.

But the main reason I lifted that often back then is worth investigating. It was not because I felt I needed that much work to progress. I had also used a four days a week routine back then with good success. But I "needed" to lift 5-6 times a week not for physical but for psychological reasons.

Basically, it was from my lifting prowess that I attained my sense of self-worth. As such, the only time I felt truly "alive" was when in the gym. Moreover, most of my friends, both male and female, were powerlifters, bodybuilders, or at least lifted weights. I simply had little life outside of the gym.

If this is you, be forewarned, it is a sad state of affairs. You need to have a life and to find your self-worth outside of the gym. Depending on your lifting abilities is fragile ground. Career ending injuries can and do happen. If your whole life is wrapped up in your lifting, then if your lifting falls apart, so will you. I know; I've been there.

After my lifting fall apart back in college, I fell apart emotionally, and my life was a real mess. But by trusting in Jesus Christ as my Lord and Savior, I found self-worth and inner strength in Him that enabled me to get my act together and to go on with my life. But it is much better to recognize your need for something beyond lifting before everything comes crashing down.

Preaching aside, the point of this story is that the best workout frequency is three or four times a week. Of these two options, four times a week is probably your best option and is probably the most common lifting frequency among powerlifters. The training routines to be detailed in this book are mostly based on lifting four times a week, but two or three days a week programs will also be touched on.

The basic format for a four days a week program is as follows:

Day One: Squats
Day Two: Benches
Day Three: Deadlifts
Day Four: Bench Assistance

Best Four Day a Week Schedule

When lifting four days a week, two basic schedules can be used. The first would be to lift Monday, Wednesday, Friday, Saturday. With this schedule, you would only have to lift two days in a row one time a week.

The other basic schedule would be: Monday, Tuesday, Thursday, Friday. With this schedule, you would lift two days in a row twice. However, you would also get a two day break (Saturday and Sunday).

The most important factor as to which is best would be which fits into your own personal schedule best. But if both are doable, then it would be good to experiment and see which works best for you.

In college, I usually used the latter format. But when I first started powerlifting again, I used the former. I figured that only lifting two days in a row once a week would be the most important point. But then I tried the latter and found it worked better.

I think the reason is that the two day break really is a break. In other words, after the two days off, on the first day back, it just seems like it has been a while since I have lifted. That psychological break can be as important as the physical break. But on the physical level, two days off in a row gives the body time to recover. With the first schedule, there is never that sense of having taken a break, and the body never has a chance to get caught up on recovery. At least, that's been my experience.

Of course, the exact days a week can vary, as long as the pattern is the same. Most importantly, never lift three days in a row. Personally, I lift Sunday, Monday, Wednesday, and Thursday. This way, I have Friday and Saturday off.

Workout Breaks and Another Warning

No matter how many days a week you work out, it can be beneficial to skip a workout every once in a while. This might sound counter-productive, but taking an "extra" day off can give your body a chance to "catch up" in terms of recovery. It will give your psych a break as well. As a result, you'll probably feel refreshed for your next workout.

With the second of the above four day a week plans (M, Tu, Th, F), the best workout to skip would be Monday or Friday (Day One or Day Four). That way, you'll have three days off in a row.

But it should be noted, when skipping a workout, it is best for your next workout to do the workout you skipped, and then rotate the workouts from there. In other words, if you have been squatting on Mondays but then skip Monday's workout, then squat on Tuesday. This means the exact days you perform each lift will change after each workout break. But this is better than just skipping squats for that week, and thus going two weeks without squatting.

There also might be times when you are really dragging and simply don't feel "up" to lifting. This is when you really need to "know" your body. Are you simply not in the mood to lift? If so, then get your act together and get your butt into the gym! However, your body could be telling you that you are overtrained and need a break. If so, then don't be stubborn and take the day off.

This can be hard to do and takes us back to the previous point about having a "life" outside of the gym. Some lifters find it hard to skip a workout no matter how terrible they feel because then are "obsessed" with lifting. But lifting when you are overtrained can easily lead to injury, as this writer recently found out the hard way.

For quite some time, I had it written into my workout plan to skip a workout every four weeks. That pattern worked well. But after one such skipped workout when I felt like I didn't need the break, I decided it wasn't really necessary to skip a workout every four weeks, so I lifted for the next five weeks straight.

Meanwhile, that fifth week, my health problems had been flaring up, and I lost a quite a bit of sleep as a result. I thought of taking a day off at the beginning of that week, but stubbornly stuck to my new plan of not skipping workouts. The night before the last workout of the fifth week, I barely slept a wink. As a result, I felt terrible the next day. But despite the problems, I went ahead and worked out anyway.

On my second work set of the day, I felt a "pop" in my left hamstring that really hurt. I stupidly tried one more rep, which caused even more pain. And that was the end of that workout and of workouts for the next several days. This was the worst injury I had sustained since I started lifting weights again over six years before. The worse part about it was I should not even have been lifting that day!

The real irony of this whole situation is that injury occurred the day before I wrote this section! Maybe if had gotten to working on this section before that workout, it would have woken me up and I would have skipped the workout. Or maybe, I would have written this section differently, saying it wasn't necessary to skip a workout on occasion.

That hamstring injury will be discussed more later in this book. But here, take the warning and take an "extra" day off once in a while and especially if you are really dragging and feeling overtrained. Trust me; if you get injured on a day you should not even have been lifting, you will really be kicking yourself afterwards.

However, don't take this advice the wrong way. This is not an excuse to be missing workouts all the time. Consistency in training is vital to making steady progress. If you are missing more than one workout a month due to just not feeling like it or not having the time, you need to re-evaluate your schedule and priorities. You simply cannot be missing workouts that often and expect to make progress.

If you feel you need to take more than one workout off a month due to being overtrained, then you need to re-evaluate your training program. You are probably doing too much on a regular basis and need to cut back.

It can also be beneficial to take an extended break from lifting of a couple of weeks up to a full month once a year. Yes, you will lose some strength and have to cut back on the weights some when you return, but not as much as you might think. It will probably only a take a few weeks to get back to where you were before the break, and within a couple of weeks after that you'll probably find that you're stronger than ever.

A good time for such a break is while on vacation. Rather than trying to be "dedicated" and finding a gym while on vacation, just relax and enjoy your vacation. In the long run, you'll be better off for it.

Another good time would be at the end of the contest year, which for many would coincide with the Christmas holiday season.

However, during this extended time off, do not become a couch potato. Engage in some other kind of physical activity. Go for walks, ride a bicycle, go swimming, or maybe just get caught up on projects around your home.

But again, I am only talking about at most a month off once a year. More than that and it will take too long to get your lifts back up or to make progress. This is especially the case for older lifters.

This might sound counter-intuitive, but the older you are the less you can afford extended breaks from lifting. The reason for this is once you get past 40, your body will naturally go into "catabolic mode" (losing muscle) very quickly when you stop lifting, so more than a month off and you will experience a significant loss of strength.

It is also good to take short break is at the end of each training cycle and after a contest. More about that will be said later in this book.

Cardiovascular Work

Despite popular thoughts to the contrary, powerlifting workouts do provide cardiovascular (aerobic) benefits. This is especially the case if you keep up a decent pace through your workouts. But it would still be prudent to do some specific cardio work for the additional heart benefits and to develop the general conditioning that is needed to make it through the grueling day that is a powerlifting contest. That is why some powerlifters refer to cardio work as "general physical preparedness" (GPP). However, too much cardio work can detract from the body's ability to recover from powerlifting workouts. As such, cardio work should be kept to a minimum.

If you are doing cardio like bicycling or running on a day separate from your powerlifting workouts, it should be kept to 30-60 minutes, two or three times a week. Such cardio should be done at a moderate not high intensity. Also, do not do the lifting workouts and the cardio at the same time, making for a two hour workout. That is simply too long. If you need to do both on the same day, then do one in the morning then the other in the afternoon or evening.

However, an even better approach is to do what I call "short, very intense cardio" immediately after your powerlifting workouts. Since you are already tired out from the lifting, it will take less time to produce the same results. Doing cardio after lifting also increases the amount of calories and fat calories burned during the cardio work as the glycogen stores are already depleted from the lifting.

Moreover, by doing the cardio at a high intensity, it does not take much time to produce cardiovascular benefits. I saw a study a while back that found that just *six minutes* of cardio done at a very high intensity provides the same cardiovascular benefits as *two hours* of cardio done at a moderate intensity. And doing the cardio after the powerlifting workouts only adds to the benefits.

Personally, I hit a heavy bag on bench days as it works the same muscles as benches do. I feel it mainly in the pressing muscles, namely the chest (pecs), shoulders (anterior delts to be exact), and triceps. I do step-ups on my squat box on squat days as they work the quadriceps (thighs) like squats, and on deadlift days I jump rope as I mainly feel that in my upper back, forearms, hamstrings, and calves, again, muscles worked in deadlifts.

I tried hitting the heavy bag on bench assistance days as well as on bench days, but that proved to be too much. But many would probably be able to handle the heavy bag twice a week. A better option would be to do something completely different on Day Four. A speed bag would be a good option. I just don't have any place to hang one up in my home gym.

Another option that is popular with many powerlifters is sled dragging. APT's sled is picture to the right. The idea here is the same as pulling a child on a sled in the winter. Only instead of a child, weights are placed on the post in the middle. This way, you can control and gradually increase the resistance. Instead of pulling across snow, a parking lot or similar surface is generally used. But this of course assumes you have such an open space for dragging the sled. Sled dragging would best be done on squat and/ or deadlift days.

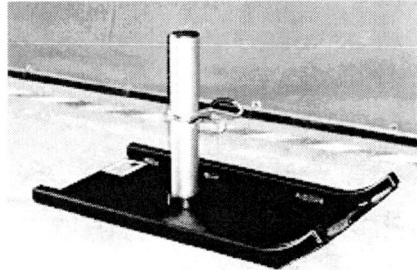

Whatever method is used, the basic plan is to start with just a couple of minutes then gradually work up to six minutes. The first and last 30 seconds should be done at a slower pace for warm-up and cool-down. Once you get to six minutes, work on increasing the intensity rather than the time.

I know this program works for cardiovascular fitness as my blood pressure and resting heart rate are both below normal. When I last checked it, my numbers were: BP – 116/ 78; RHR – 50.

Normal blood pressure is 120/80 and a normal RHR is 60-80 bpm. But it is even better for the blood pressure to be below 120/80, and the lower the RHR is the stronger the heart is. The reason is, a stronger

105

heart is able to pump more blood with each pump, so it doesn't have to pump as often. I heard that when Lance Armstrong was in shape for his Tour de France wins, his RHR was 16.

Stretching

Long before I had started lifting again, I had been stretching on a regular basis, and continued to do so when I started lifting, usually stretching for about 10-15 minutes after each workout. However, due to my fibromyalgia, that extra 10-15 minutes was proving too tiring on top of an hour or so of lifting. So I dropped off stretching and had not done any stretching for almost a year. But it was then that I sustained the hamstring injury mentioned earlier. It could be that without stretching, my hamstring had tightened up, thus contributing to the injury. I then went back to stretching, even though it is difficult for me to do so.

I mention this as there are some who believe that stretching is not necessary and does not prevent injuries. That's easy to claim, but if you omit stretching and get injured, then like me, you'll be kicking yourself. But a few points are worth noting.

Stretching is *not* a form of warm-up. Stretching when you are "cold" could lead to injury. Also, some studies have shown that stretching before a weightlifting workout reduces one's strength for the workout. This means stretching should be done either after the workout or on off days. If it is done on off days, then you should do at least a few minutes of aerobics before stretching to warm the body up. Another possibility is to stretch after a hot bath or shower.

The stretching should be done in a slow, controlled manner (no bouncing!). Slowly stretch as far as you can do so comfortably, without straining, and hold that position. If you pay attention, after about ten seconds or so, you should notice your muscles relaxing some, and you'll be able to stretch just a little bit farther. Do so, and then hold that new position for another ten seconds or so. Then release the stretch. Altogether, each stretch should be held for 20-30 seconds.

Be sure to include enough stretches to work the entire body. But if you're using a split routine, concentrate on stretching the muscles that were worked in that workout. Books and Web sites are available that provide detailed instructions and illustrations on how to perform various stretches.

Cool Down

It is generally a good idea to "cool down" after a workout. This can involve doing a few light sets or a few minutes of light aerobics or stretching. This helps to reduce lactic acid buildup in the muscles and lessen post-workout soreness. As for myself, my 10-15 minutes of stretching and the time I spend cleaning up and putting everything back inside my power rack serves as my cool-down.

Workout Length

How long should a workout last? Opinions vary in this regard. Some claim a workout should always last less than an hour while other powerlifters will work out for two hours or longer.

But a point to note is how the workout is timed. Those who claim to work out for less than an hour are probably only including the time they actually spend lifting. In other words, they are timing the workout from the start of the first warm-up set to the finish of the last work set. However, that is not all that is done in a workout.

Time is always spent at the beginning of a workout setting things up. Then there might be a general warm-up, then the actual lifting. After lifting, many will do some kind of cardio, such as the intense cardio mentioned previously, and then stretching, then maybe a cool-down, and finally, clean up. If you are working out in a public gym, always take all of the weights off of any bars or equipment you used and put them away. It takes time, but it is the courteous thing to do.

The point is, if you include all of these steps—set up, warm-up, lifting, cardio, stretching, cool-down, clean-up—then most likely those powerlifters who claim to lift for less than an hour are probably spending more like an hour and a half in the gym. However, they are correct in that the time spent in actual hard lifting and cardio should last less than an hour.

The reason for this is hormone levels; specifically testosterone and growth hormone begin to decline within an hour or so of starting an intense workout. But elevated levels of both of these hormones are vital for progress in lifting, and in fact, power training should elevate the levels of these hormones, as long as you do not overdo it.

Given that the levels of both of these hormones naturally decline as a person ages, this is point has even greater importance for the older lifter, but it cannot be ignored by younger lifters. The latter might get away with two hour workouts, but they would still be better off with shorter workouts.

It would be ideal but impractical to test your hormone levels on a regular basis to be sure you are not overdoing it. But as a rough guide, watch your sex drive. If it is declining, most likely you are overdoing it in the gym as both testosterone and growth hormone are intimately involved in a man's sex drive and even in the sex drive of a woman.

On the other hand, it is difficult to get in a quality workout in less than an hour, again, assuming all aspects of the workout are included in the timing.

All of that said, the total workout time including all of the above aspects should be between an hour and an hour and a half. If workouts are taking much longer than this, then you are probably doing too many exercises, too many sets, and/ or taking too long of rests between sets. But all of these can be counter-productive. Of course, it is also possible you are spending too much time talking! Socializing is nice, but you are in the gym to work out. Save extended socializing for afterwards.

But one exception to all of this is when full gear is used. As mentioned previously, it can take quite some time to get in and out of a tight squat suit or bench press shirt. In fact, I would say it would be almost impossible to get a full gear squat workout done in an hour. That problem has been cited previously as one serious argument against the use of gear. Again, this becomes even more important for the older lifter who cannot afford to have his hormone levels suppressed by spending an extended period of time in the gym.

Individual Variability and Adaptation

There is no such thing as a "perfect" routine. No workout will work for everyone. Just because some top-level lifter uses a particular routine, it doesn't mean it will be right for you. Everyone has to experiment to see what works best. This book will try to provide some suggestions to narrow down the experimentation period. But as the saying goes, YMMV ("your mileage may vary").

Also, no matter how well a routine seems to be working, if you follow it for too long the body will adapt to it. When this happens, progress will slow or come to a halt altogether. As such, it is important to periodically change something in your routine. You can change most any of the previously discussed factors. Suggestions on how to change things around will be detailed in the next chapter.

However, a routine should not be changed too often. Constantly changing a routine could cause you to end up always being sore from doing something "new." It is also difficult and even unwise to put full effort into a new exercise or routine. Some degree of adaptation is needed to be comfortable with it and for it to be safe to put in an all out effort. Also some consistency is needed to gauge one's progress.

But how often should a routine be changed? Most obviously, if you're stagnating, it's time to change something. And if you're getting bored with a current routine, change it. But it would be good to change a routine before such things happen. Again, suggestions on how to do so will be presented shortly.

Training and Other Logs

One final point is worth mentioning; it is very important to keep a training log. Record every rep, every set, every exercise, for every workout. It also helps if you record your bodyweight, at least on occasion. You might also want to include notes about how you were feeling during each workout, and any other pertinent data.

Having a record of what you have been doing is the only way to be able to track what works and what doesn't work. You might think you are making progress, but by checking the log you might see that you are not doing as well as you think you are. Moreover, if you have a complicated routine or do many different exercises each week, it can be difficult simply to remember what exercises are to be done on a given day. Even more difficult is remembering exactly what weights were used and how many reps you got with that weight in your last workout and thus what weights should be used for that day's workout.

As for myself, after each set, I immediately write down exactly how many reps I got for the set. After my workout, I sit down and write out what weights I plan on using the next time I do that particular workout. I base my weights for my next workout on how many reps I got for the weights used in that day's workout.

Back in college, I wrote down my workouts in a spiral 3" x 5" notepad. I eventually had a whole stack of them. But now, I print out charts I have prepared in my word processing program. I then store them in a file cabinet. Each day's chart has 25 rows and seven columns. I write the exercises in the far left column, leaving a line between each exercise for each planned set. Then each successive column is for a different day, with the date in the top row. I have enough room for two such charts on each printed page.

You can also purchase specialty workout logs. Pictured on the next page is APT's "Powerlifting Exercise Fitness Journal."

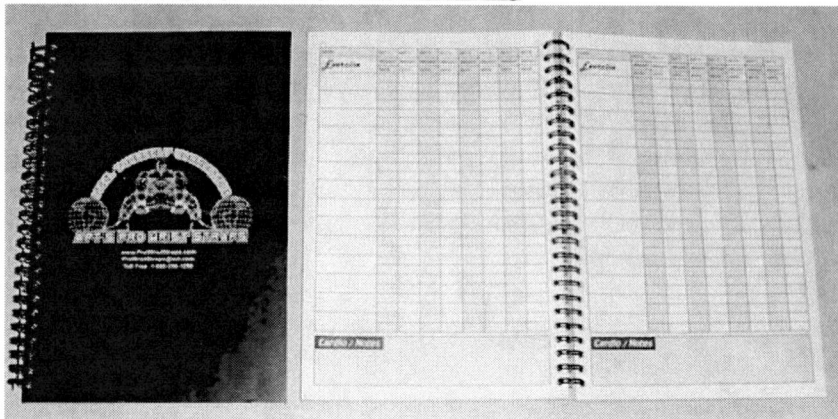

I would also suggest keeping a food log, a supplements log, a bodyweight log, and a body measurements log. For the food log, it would be wise on occasion to evaluate your diet for levels of protein, fat, carbs, and other nutrients. An easy way to do so is with a software program like *DietPower* (see Appendix #1).

Keeping track of what supplements you are currently taking and what supplements you tried in the past, including when you started and stopped them and what amounts you used, can also be helpful. A bodyweight log would be a record of your weight changes over time.

If it is possible to evaluate your body fat percentage, this would be useful as well. It's also a good idea to keep track of other body measurements, like chest, biceps, thighs, calves, etc. By comparing all of these logs, you can get a very good idea of the progress you are making, and again, what is working and what is not working.

As for myself, I have separate files on my computer for all of these types of logs. Each week, I post my workout logs on my fitness Web site, on my MySpace page, and in the Weight Trainer's United forum (see Appendix #3). Samples of these logs will be presented in Chapter 15. The final chapter of my book *God-given Foods Eating Plan* presents a week's log of my eating plan (see Appendix #2).

Chapter Eight
Training Intensity, Cycles, and Miscellaneous Training Tips

This chapter will look in more detail at some important issues that were touched on in the previous chapter.

Training Intensity

There are different philosophies on hard you should work when training. Should you continue doing a set to failure, stop at a specific number of reps, or something in-between? The first part of this chapter will discuss these different options.

Training to Failure:

By training to failure is meant to use an all out effort, continuing a set until you are unable to complete the final rep. This means that you always "miss" the last rep of the set. Some claim one such all out set is all that is needed for ultimate strength development.

When working to failure, a range of reps is needed for the goal rep rather than a specific number of reps as you can never be sure of just how many reps it will take to reach failure. Once the top number of reps is reached the weight is increased for the next workout.

The range for the reps usually needs to be wider the higher the reps. A common rep range for the average lifter is 8-12 reps, but powerlifters should train with lower reps, so something like 5-8 or 1-4 would be better.

To comment, there is no doubt you will get stronger training in this fashion. But personally I have found that after a period of time I cease to make progress doing one set to failure. Of course, you could do two sets to failure. In such a case the lifter will probably not be able to do as many reps for the second set as for the first set.

However, regardless of the number of sets, working to failure on all sets all of the time can easily lead to overtraining. It is also taxing psychologically. You can "burn-out" trying to push that hard on each and every set.

Moreover, it can be draining emotionally to always miss the last rep of a set. Missing a rep is an emotional "downer" while completing the full number of reps in a set can give you a sense of satisfaction. It just feels good to complete the full number of reps you planned on doing. So there are several potential problems with the working to failure philosophy.

Specific Number of Reps:

The next philosophy is to use multiple sets and go for a specific number of reps, like 3 sets of 5 reps. Again, there is no doubt you will gain strength with this method. But again, there are potential drawbacks.

It is possible that in going for a specific number of reps the lifter might not work hard enough. Sometimes it can be hard to know beforehand exactly how much weight to use for a given number of planned reps. If you planned on doing five reps, you will probably stop at five even if the fifth rep is not that difficult.

As a result, what usually happens is you start adding additional sets to get in some real work. But once you start doing more than four sets, you do not push very hard on the first couple of sets, so they are often just glorified warm-ups and not real work sets. But even with the lower intensity, such a volume of sets can lead to overtraining. At the very least, it makes for very long workouts.

Training to *Almost* Failure:

What is needed in training is a balance between working hard enough without working too hard or too much. To accomplish this, my approach is as follows.

I use a range for my reps rather than a specific number, but I use a smaller range than the one set to failure range. I usually use a range like 4-5 or 3-5. Also, I usually do two or three sets rather than just one.

For the first set I will work very hard, but I will hold back from going "all out." For instance, if my goal range is 4-5, if it would take an all out effort to get the fifth rep I will stop at four. The reason for this is I want to be sure I have enough strength left to get at least four reps on the second set.

For the second set I will work as hard as I am able, but I will stop the set when I would probably not be able to complete the next rep. But if there is a reasonable chance that I can get the next rep, then I will go for it. Ideally, even if it requires an all out effort, I should always be able to complete the last rep I attempt. As a result, I am not really working to failure. My method would best be described as training to *almost* failure.

When I can complete the top number of reps for each set for any given exercise I will increase the weight for the next workout to stay within the prescribed range for the next workout. If for some reason

I'm unable to complete the bottom number of reps for both sets I would drop the weight for the next workout.

Final Points on Intensity:

Training to almost failure is very effective. But you need to be prepared to work very hard for it to be effective. If you just go through the motions then it won't work.

It also takes an experienced lifter to do properly. You need to "just know" if you will be able to complete the next rep or not, and thus when to stop a set. It also takes some experimentation to discover how large of a rep range is required for various exercises and how much to increase the weight when the top number of reps is achieved for all sets. Different exercises will require different rep ranges and weight increases.

But once such parameters are figured out, you should be able to make slow but continual progress using this training method. Patience is required as results will not be quick. But over time, slow but steady increases will produce significant strength improvements.

Training Cycles for the Powerlifts

It is now time to put the information from the previous and this chapter into a training cycle. All of these cycles assume each powerlift is done once a week, such as with the two days a week and four days a week programs outlined in the previous chapter. It is also assumed that two or three work sets are being done for the powerlifts.

Basic Cycle (a.k.a. Periodization):

First to be looked at is the most basic type of cycle. This is the type of cycle I used when I first thought about competing again, and it is the cycle I would recommend for the new powerlifter, especially for the person looking to enter his or her first contest.

Most people when they first start lifting weights usually do something like 2-3 sets of 8-12 reps on most exercises. And this is a good rep range to use when starting out. But to enter a powerlifting contest, you need to gradually prepare your body for a one rep max (1RM).

The best way to do so is to gradually decrease the reps and increase the weights over a period of weeks. Gear also needs to be added in to get used to it for the contest. The following is a basic framework for a twelve week cycle.

Weeks	Reps Range	Gear
1-3	7-8	Completely Raw
4-6	5-6	Completely Raw
7-9	3-4	Partial Gear
10-12	1-2	Full Gear

This type of cycle is also called "periodization" as a "period" of time is spent at each rep range.

What is meant by "partial gear" depends on what and how much gear you are planning on using at the contest. For example, if you are planning on using single-ply gear, you will probably want to use a belt and wraps for the partial gear. Then for the final three weeks, use whatever gear you will be using at the contest.

If using multi-ply gear, then you might want to start adding gear at the 5-6 rep range. In that case, for those workouts use a belt and wraps. For the 3-4 reps range, use single-ply gear, then use full, multi-ply gear for the 1-2 rep range.

If you are competing raw or unequipped, then add the belt (and wraps) at the 3-4 reps range.

After the contest, you should take a short break from lifting, and then this same type of cycle can be repeated. Of course, the exact number of weeks for each rep range needs to be adjusted so as to "peak" for the contest. But generally, you want 2-4 weeks at each rep range, so this cycle can be adjusted to last from 8-16 weeks. But it is best if you know a few months ahead when your next contest will be so you can plan on each phase lasting about an even amount of time.

This is a very effective type of cycle. Many powerlifters will use something like this throughout their lifting careers. There are many points in its favor.

First, the higher, completely raw reps in the first half of the routine provide conditioning and muscular endurance. Also, by lifting completely raw, the body parts that are protected when using gear are strengthened. Higher reps are also better for building the strength of tendons and ligaments. This writer has found that doing higher, completely raw reps can be very helpful for these reasons.

Also, the higher reps provide a break from the heavier weights that lower reps entail. Doing low reps all of the time can lead to physical and mental burnout.

This cycle enables the lifter to gradually get used to handling heavier weights and to using gear. Enough time is then spent at the lower reps with gear to get fully conditioned for the heavier weights and to get used to the gear for the contest.

Finally, after the contest, going back to higher, completely raw reps provides a significant change and thus prevents stagnation from doing the same thing over and over again.

However, there are some problems with this type of cycle as well. The main problem is one of the claimed benefits, the change it provides. When using this cycle, I found I never really got used to any of the rep ranges and thus was always sore and tired.

In other words, it seemed just as I was getting used to the higher reps, the reps would drop, and the low reps would be very fatiguing. The heavier weights also felt like a ton. This is especially the case when going from lifting completely raw to lifting with multi-ply gear.

Then the same thing would happen when starting a new cycle. After weeks of doing low reps, the higher reps would be extremely fatiguing. So basically, there was too much time between the extremes of reps. It was for this reason that I began to use routines that incorporate both higher, completely raw reps and lower, equipped reps without long breaks between the two.

Mini-Cycles:

The idea behind a mini-cycle is pretty straightforward. The same rep progression as for the basic cycle is used, except only one week is spent at each rep range. As such, a mini-cycle will only last four weeks. However, the mini-cycle will be repeated 3-5 times, so the total time for the routine will be 12-20 weeks.

In this way, there is only four weeks between the highest and lowest reps, so you never really get out of shape for either. But it provides greater change than the basic cycle as the reps and gear usage is always changing. But gradual progress can be made for the same rep range, mini-cycle to mini-cycle.

Again, it helps to know ahead of time when you next contest will be so you can lay out your plans on how long each mini-cycle will last and how many to plan on.

However, the drawback is again that things can be changing too often. With four weeks between the same rep range it can be hard to pick out the proper weights to hit the target rep range.

Alternate High/ Low Reps with Drop Reps:

This routine shortens the mini-cycle even further into just two weeks. The first week, high reps are done, the second week, low reps. In this way, I found I can stay conditioned for both basic rep ranges.

The rep range for the first week is 5-8, while the second is 1-4. Lifting is done completely raw the first week and equipped the second week, using full gear.

But it is here that it would be good to utilize what is called a "drop reps" approach to lifting. By this is meant, the weights are increased and thus the number of reps dropped from the first to the second set, and from the second to the third set if a third set is done.

For the high rep week and two work sets, the rep ranges would be 7-8, 5-6. If three sets are done, things are a little more complicated. I will write the first week up as 3 x 8-5. By this is meant, three sets are done, with the weight increasing and dropping by one rep each set. But one "extra" rep is included in the range to allot for a missed rep. This means a workout could go 8,7,6 or 8,7,5, or 8,6,5.

For the low rep week and two work sets, the rep ranges would be 3-4, 1-2. For three sets, it would be written as 3 x 4-1. Again, start with four reps and add weight and drop one or two reps for each set.

I have found this type of routine to be very effective. It enables you to stay used to doing both higher, completely raw reps and lower, equipped reps. With only two weeks between doing the same rep range, a gradual increase can be made for the duration of the routine.

As for how long to run this routine, it can theoretically be use indefinitely. However, stagnation will eventually set in. As such, it is best to only use it for about 12 weeks, or six weeks for each rep range then a change needs to be made. After that time period, change to another type of routine, or start a new "High/ Low Reps" routine, but with dropping the weights some for the first two weeks then gradually work back up. This concept will be discussed more fully later.

But here, it is important to note that this routine provides flexibility if you're not sure ahead of time when your next contest will be. You can just continue it until you decide on a contest.

Note also that ideally the final week of hard training before a contest should be a low rep week. If it works out that it is a high rep week, then do the low reps week two weeks in a row. You want to go into a contest having handled heavy weights for your last hard workouts.

Changing Exercises:

In addition to changing reps, there is another way to provide variety in a training cycle, namely, by changing exercises.

First in this regard, it will be said that it is recommended that all assistance exercises should be changed each time you start a new routine. In this way, you will not stagnate doing the same assistance exercises routine after routine. A wide variety of assistance exercises will be described in Section Three.

However, as powerlifters, the actual powerlifts have to be done for the bulk of any routine. Now, there are some who would disagree. They will advocate only doing major assistance exercises for the ma-

116

jority of a routine, and then only switching to the actual powerlifts shortly before a contest.

By "major assistance exercises" is meant mainly "look-alike" lifts, meaning lifts that are similar but not identical to the actual powerlifts. Again, many such lifts will be described later. But for example here, close stance squats with the bar high on the neck would be a "look-alike" lift to power squats, where the stance is usually at least shoulder width and the bar is held lower on the back.

For the cycles already presented, as stated, it is assumed that the actual powerlifts are being done each week. But many would want to do one major assistance exercise after each powerlift. For example, power squats would be done first, then close stance squats. In this case, it would probably be best to only do two work sets for each. More specific routines of this type will be presented later.

However, one way to really mix things up would be to in some way alternate between power squats and close stance squats. In this way, "change" will come from the change from the assistance exercise to the actual powerlift.

Alternate Weeks Routine:

The first method for alternating assistance exercises and the powerlifts is to alternate weeks, doing assistance work the first week (Week A), then the actual powerlifts the next week (Week B).

This would be similar to the "alternate high/ low reps" cycle mentioned previously, except now it is the exercises that are being alternated rather than the reps. Again, probably about twelve weeks would be the limit for a routine, but again, it provides flexibility if you're not sure when your next contest will be.

It would still be advisable to change the reps some through the course of the cycle. You could start with sets of eight reps done completely raw on the powerlifts, but then gradually drop the reps and add gear as with the basic cycle, ending with 1-2 reps with full gear at the end. Another plan will be detailed shortly.

For the assistance work, I recommend doing all assistance work completely raw. I have never seen the point of using gear on assistance work. As stated previously, when you support a body part with gear the body part is not strengthened as well as without gear. But then for safety's sake, I would not recommend dropping lower than a triple.

For further variety, be sure to change the assistance exercises routine to routine.

Similar to the High/ Low Reps routine, ideally the final week of hard training before a contest should be the week with the actual powerlifts. If it works out that it is the assistance week (Week A), then instead do Week B two weeks in a row. You want to go into a contest having performed the actual powerlifts for your last hard workouts.

Four Week Rotation:

This routine takes things a step farther than the previous one. Rather than just alternating two different sets of workouts, here you alternate four different sets of workouts. This means you will only be doing each exercise once a month.

For instance, on squats, the first week would be front squats, the second week close stance-high bar squats, the third week chain squats, and the fourth week power squats. The idea here is that by alternating so many different exercises it prevents stagnation and enables you to put forth maximal effort on each exercise without getting burned out.

I have used such a routine with some success, but also ran into some problems. The first problem is that with only doing a given exercise once a month, it is difficult to estimate how much weight to use the next time that exercise is done. If the routine is carried out for 12 weeks, the actual powerlifts are only done three times. As such, to make any progress requires making large jumps from one time the exercise is done to the next. The routine simply does not lend itself to gradual increases. But such slow and steady increases are the best way to make progress.

Moreover, there simply is too much change to get used to a given exercise, so constant soreness can be a problem. Also, there is no natural place to end the routine and start a new one.

But most of all, it is very difficult to perfect your form on a given exercise. Although all four exercises are variations of squats, they are considerably different exercises. Most importantly, the proper form for each assistance exercise differs somewhat from proper form on power squats. So you are constantly adjusting your form and never are able to perfect your form on what matters most, actual power squats.

Off-Season/ In-Season Routine:

The idea here is to have a distinct "off-season" and "in-season." The main distinction between the two "seasons" is during the off-season, major assistance exercises are done *instead of* the actual powerlifts. Then during the in-season, the actual powerlifts are done almost exclusively. In this way, the off-season provides an extended break from doing the actual powerlifts and provides time for doing a wide variety of different exercises. Then the focus on the powerlifts during the in-season enables a gradual increase to be had on the lifts.

Ideally, each season should last 8-12 weeks, so the whole routine will run for 16-24 weeks. Needless to day, this system is for the person who only competes in 2-3 contests a year, with the contests spaced more or less evenly apart. But that really is an ideal number of contests to enter a year, as will be discussed later.

The idea behind an off-season is that after focusing exclusively on the powerlifts before and of course during a contest, it is good to then focus on different exercises for a break from the powerlifts.

Variety can be provided during the off-season by utilizing an alternating weeks system of doing one set of assistance exercise one week, then a different set the next week. For those who compete equipped, one set of these exercises should entail the use of chains and bands.

The use of chains and bands will be discussed in-depth later, but here, it will just be said, they mimic the effect that gear provides and enables higher weights to be handled, just as with gear. In this way, the lifter stays used to handling heavier weights during the off-season.

It is also recommended as before that different assistance exercises be utilized for each new routine. A variety of rep ranges can also be utilized during the off-season.

For the in-season, any of the previously discussed cycles can be utilized. So you could run a basic cycle for 12 weeks or three, four-week mini-cycles or an alternating high/ low reps routine. This will provide variety during the in-season. Another plan will be discussed shortly.

One possible difficulty with this routine is the long break between doing the same exercises. There will be at least eight weeks between when the actual powerlifts are done, while with changing the assistance exercises during each off-season, you might only do the same set of exercises for one routine a year.

With such long breaks between doing the same exercises, it can be difficult to pick the appropriate weights for each exercise at the start of a routine. It might also take some time to remember how best to perform an exercise and thus to perfect your form on the lift. But this is actually an advantage as it provides a natural beginning and end to the routine and a natural place to "deload" before lifting heavy again, as will be discussed shortly

The other difficulty is you need to know several months in advance when your next contest will be. That is the only way to know how long each season should last and when to make the transition from the off to the in-season.

Remember when counting out the weeks to allot for an occasional day off and for time off the week before the contest. So basically, for 20 weeks of actual training, you will probably need to start the off-season about 23 weeks before the contest and transition to the in-season about 11-12 weeks before.

Miscellaneous Training Tips

Some final training tips will be presented to close out this chapter.

Starting Weights:

It has been mentioned that generally speaking, eight reps is the highest a powerlifter will want to go. It is also good to have included what is called "deload" weeks in your routine. A deload week is when you do not work as hard as usual during your workouts in order to provide a break from hard lifting.

It is especially important to take it easy the first couple of weeks after a contest. In fact, it is best to take about a week off after a contest, then a couple of relatively easy weeks of workouts before getting back into really hard training. If you are starting with an alternating weeks type of routine, then the first two weeks will all be "new" exercise and thus a very good time to not work as hard as usual. This will also give you time to figure out your form on each lift before pushing hard on them.

You'll probably find that if you do try to lift heavy right after a contest your strength levels will be down, and you won't be able to lift as much as you did right before the contest. That is because, if you trained properly, you "peaked" for the contest. There is also a physiological letdown after a contest that makes it hard to get as psyched up for a workout right after a contest

That said, there are two ways to figure out your "starting weights" for a new routine. The first requires what was recommended previously, keeping a detailed training log.

By looking back at your log, you can see what weights you used the last time you did a particular exercise. You would then begin the new routine with about 10 percent less weight than you ended with the last time you did that exercise for the same number of reps. This should ensure you get the full number of reps for your first workout without having to use full effort.

However, if you are doing a completely new exercise or if it has been a long time since you last did a particular exercise, then this approach will not work. It also might not work after an extended break from lifting as it is difficult to gauge how much strength might have been lost during that break.

In these cases, another approach is needed. What I will do is start with my normal warm-up sets of 15 and 8 reps. But then I will do sets of whatever my top rep will be for the next few workouts. So if I am planning on using a 3 x 6-3 plan, then I will start by doing sets of six, starting very light, but then gradually adding weight and increasing reps until I hit one relatively hard set. I will stop at that point. That weight will then be my starter weight for subsequent workouts.

By only doing one relatively hard set, these initial workouts will not be very fatiguing, but then once you get to the third week, it will be time to start pushing harder for the remainder of the routine or for the duration of the off-season, if following that routine.

Either of these approaches should then be followed for the start of the next routine or for the in-season. In this way, the first couple of weeks of each new routine or "season" will be deload weeks. It will also give you time to re-familiarize yourself with the proper form on the lifts to be done before pushing hard on them. You can then ease into the harder lifting.

Additional Rep Ranges:

After the initial week or two of a new routine, it will be time to cycle down to heavier weights. The previously discussed cycles can be utilized here on the powerlifts, but another plan is as follows.

Using the first start approach, just gradually increase the weights each workout until you are back to working very hard on each set.

Using the second start approach, continue doing sets of six after the first week, adding weight each set, until you hit a weight that only allows you do get five reps. You have now gradually moved into the drop reps range of 6-3 reps. Follow that for a few of weeks.

For instance, after I took a four week break over Christmas 2008, I did sets of six for the first two workouts for each lift, but then dropped to 3 x 6-3 for the next two workouts. My deadlift workouts went as follows (warm-ups in brackets):

[45/15, 135/8, 185/6, 225/6] 245/6, 265/6
[45/15, 135/8, 190/5, 245/3] 275/6, 290/6, 305/6
[45/15, 135/8, 210/5, 285/3] 315/6, 330/5, 345/3
[45/15, 135/8, 210/5, 285/3] 320/6, 335/5, 350/3

It will then be necessary to get lower on reps and to add in gear. The next range could be 3 x 5-6, 3-4, 1-2. Here, you will start adding twice as much weight from set to set as before. The first set should be done completely raw, but some will want to add gear for the next two sets.

121

When using minimal gear, this scheme works fine. However, for those utilizing multi-ply gear, the jump would be too much. A better approach for such lifters might be to do 3 x 5-8 completely raw the first few weeks then drop to 3 x 4-1 for the rest of the weeks, all sets done with gear. This way, you'll get in three heavy sets with full gear.

For major assistance work, the 3 x 6-3 scheme also works well, so you could use the same approach of starting with sets of six. But you could also spread things out more by doing 3 x 7-8, 5-6, 3-4. This way, you'll get in both higher and lower rep work on assistance. In this case, you could start with sets of eight the first week. Or you could still do sets of six the first week, but then use your top weight for your first set of eight the next week. That way, you'd be increasing the reps rather than the weights to move into harder training.

If doing two sets on major assistance work, you could start at 2 x 7-8 and drop to 2 x 3-4 by the end of a routine. Or you could use a drop reps approach and do 2 x 7-8, 5-6 for the first half and drop to 2 x 5-6, 3-4 for the second half. You might want to go as low as 2 x 4-5, 2-3, but be careful doing a heavy double if you are not using any gear.

Drop Reps with Back-off Set:

Another approach deserves special mention. I like to call it "drop reps with back-off set." Here, the rep ranges are: 3-4, 1-2, 7-8. The first two sets are done with whatever gear you will be using at your next contest; the last set is done completely raw. This scheme works well for both raw and equipped lifters.

The first two sets provide the needed low rep work with contest gear while you are fresh. The back-off set is then done for higher rep, completely raw work, but after the lower rep equipped work so as not to tire you out for the more important heavy sets.

This scheme works well with the Alternating Weeks routine. Since both low reps and high reps are done each actual powerlift workout, you get in both types of work at once and thus stay conditioned for both throughout the routine.

This rep scheme can also be done every week, at least for a short while. It would thus be a good plan to use for the in-season portion of the Off-Season/ In-Season routine. You can very things some by going back and forth between doing 3 x 4, 2, 8 for a workout or two, then 3 x 3, 1, 7 the next workout or two.

Another option would be to use any of the preceding cycles for the bulk of a routine, but to end that routine about a month before the contest and then switch to the drop reps with back-off set plan and doing the actual powerlifts every week for that final month.

In this way, the focus will be one the actual powerlifts with contest gear for the final month before a contest. But the back-off set will maintain your conditioning and keep the joints strong.

If you have been following the powerlift with a major assistance exercise during the routine, both for two sets, when you switch to the drop reps with back-off set, it would be best to drop off the major assistance exercise so as not to overtrain. But you could substitute a minor assistance exercise. In that case, do that exercise each week.

I have found the drop reps with back-off set scheme to work very well. It incorporates in one workout the rep ranges and gear usage I have found to work best on the powerlifts.

If you use this approach on major assistance work, it would be best to go a little higher on the reps: 4-5, 2-3, 7-8.

This approach makes perfect sense given the following quote I came across in a bodybuilding magazine, "Finishing off heavy sets with a lighter set that enables you to get higher reps doubles the GH [growth hormone] release" (*Iron Man*, June 2008, p.114).

Deloading and Peaking for a Contest:

This will be a good place to interject an important point about powerlifting progress that many only learn the hard way.

When you first start lifting weights and competing, most likely, you will make rather steady progress for the first several months or even couple of years. But eventually, the progress will slow down and often halt altogether. It is then that many lifters like myself will begin to experiment with many different routines.

However, the problem is often not with the routine but with the simple fact that you cannot continually progress ever upward. It seems that way at the start, but such long-term steady progress is not realistic.

What is needed is to back-off or "deload" on occasion, dropping the weights and intensity down for a period of time and then working back up. This is something that is difficult for many lifters to do and takes us back to the discussion about a lifter's self-worth being tied up in lifting. Many simply cannot ease off without emotional turmoil, as if not lifting heavy for a period of time makes them less than a person.

As a result, what often happens is the lifter keeps pushing until he or she gets injured and thus is forced to drop the weights and intensity way down and to work slowly back up. And when that happens, with time, the lifter might eventually progress past their previous personal bests. They are then often hailed for their determination and progress.

However, what really happened is the injury forced the lifter to back-off on intensity for a period of time. It was that "deloading" that enabled the greater gains after the injury had healed.

But it would have been much better to have backed off before the injury. In that way, much anguish could have been avoided. This is why it is recommended that at the start of each new routine you spend a week or two working at a lower intensity before getting back into full intensity.

Moreover, you should plan on it taking a few weeks to get back to where you were at the end of your last routine. In this way, your steady progress will be realized not so much workout to workout as from the end of one routine to the end of the next routine. And if you think about it, that is what matters.

It is what you are doing at the end of a routine and most of all at the contest that matters. What you do at the start or even middle of the routine is irrelevant.

To put it another way, you cannot stay at your peak performance year-round. What is important is to peak for a contest, and for that peak to be ever increasing. And that is what most of the routines presented in this chapter are geared towards, peaking for one day at the end of the routine. But to realize this, you also need to back-off on the intensity at the beginning of each routine.

The off-season/ in-season routine especially is helpful in this regard as it has two built-in places for backing off, at the start of each season. And with the complete change of exercises season to season, it is very natural to start relatively easy at the beginning of each new season while you are learning (or re-learning) how to perform the lifts and thus avoid any possible emotional turmoil over not pushing hard enough. But then plenty of time is still allotted for progress over the remainder of each season.

But similar to that would be to plan on two different routines when preparing for a contest, each lasting 8-12 weeks. The start of each routine would be the deload period, with harder training for the duration of each routine.

Picking Weights

One last point needs to be addressed further before closing this chapter, that of when and how much to increase the weights you utilize workout to workout and set to set.

If your reps for all sets are within the prescribed rep range, then increase the weights for the next workout. But by how much will have to be determined by trial and error. Also to be determined by trial and error is how much to increase the weights set to set for the "drop reps" approach described previously.

First, on the drop reps sets approach, on say the 3 x 6-3 rep range, as stated, the reason for having a four rep range for only three sets is to allow some leeway when increasing the weight and a "missed" rep.

But how much to increase the weight to force a drop of one rep from set to set? This will depend on how much you are lifting. But a basic guideline will be a five pound increase for every hundred pounds lifted. For example, if you lift 200/6, then increase to 210 for the second set. If you lift 300/6, then increase to 315, etc.

If you are using a rep scheme like 5-6, 3-4, 1-2, then you will want to drop two reps from set to set. In that case, of course, you would increase by twice as much. In the above cases, that would be to 220 and 330 respectively.

Things are a little more difficult for a weights in-between the hundreds. If you do 150/6, then to drop one rep the ideal would be to increase by 7.5 pounds to 157.5 for the next set; if you do 250/6, then the increase would be 12.5 pounds to 262.5. This can easily be done using a pair of 1¼ pound plates. These are available from New York Barbell (see Appendix #1). They are light and small enough to be carried in one's gym bag back and forth to a gym.

Dumbbell exercises are more difficult. If you are using changeable dumbbells, then you will need two pairs of 1¼s for exercises that use two dumbbells, like dumbbell benches. If you use a pair of 50s, that is a total of 100 pounds. Add a 1¼ to each side of each dumbbell, and you'll have your increase of five pounds total.

But things get more difficult for the in-between the hundreds weights. If you're using a pair of 25s, that is a total of 50 pounds, so the needed increase would be only 2.5 pounds. This can be accomplished by using "fractional plates." These usually come in a set of pairs of 1.0, 0.75, 0.5, and 0.25 pound plates. They are available from APT Pro Gear.

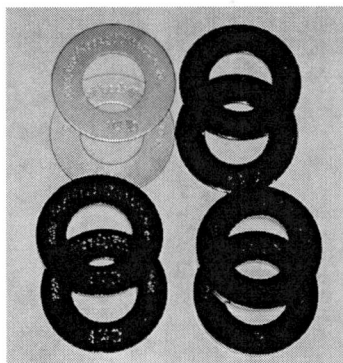

Even for exercises that require two dumbbells, you still only need one set of fractional plates. Add a 0.75 on one side of each dumbbell and a 0.5 + 0.25 on the other sides. That will have you increasing by 1.5 pounds on each dumbbell for a total of a 3.0 pound increase to a total of 53 pounds. For exercises that require very light weights and only one dumbbell, like rotator cuff work, you can increase by as little as 0.5 pounds using the pair of 0.25s.

Starting and Progressing in Powerlifting

If you are using pre-set dumbbells like those found in most gyms, then you will be forced to increase by a minimum of five pounds for exercises that use only one dumbbell and by ten pounds when doing exercises that use two dumbbells. In this case, you probably won't be able to use a drop reps approach. Just do the two or three work sets with the same weights. You will also have to increase the rep ranges, so you are doing more reps before increasing the weights for the next workout. So instead of 3-6 for dumbbell benches, you might need to do at least eight reps before increasing the weights.

Of course, how difficult the first set is will also affect how much to increase the weight for the second set. If the first set was especially difficult, then increase by a little less than the guideline; if it was rather easy, then increase by a little more.

If the reps for all sets are within the prescribed range, then you will want to increase the weights for the next workout. How much weight you are using for an exercise and how difficult the sets were will again affect how much to increase by. But probably half of the previous amounts would be a starting guideline. In other words, about 2½ pounds for each hundred pounds lifted. But that small of an increase will definitely require using 1¼s and fractional plates.

It is also best to be conservative in increasing weight as it is better if the first set is a little too light than too heavy. If it is too light then you can increase by that much more for the second set. But if it is too heavy, then you will have to use the same weight or even drop it for the second set, but that is opposite of the drop reps plan.

If you are stagnating and use the same weight and reps for an exercise two workouts in a row, then it would be wise to decrease the weight for the next workout enough that you can get the highest number of reps on all sets without a full effort. This will give that exercise somewhat of a "deload" week. Then increase the weight back for the next workout. This should break you out of the sticking point.

Finally, the drop reps with back-off set scheme presents some difficulties when picking weights. You will need to increase the weight so as to drop by two reps from the first to the second set, but then you need to drop the weight so as to increase by six reps from the second to third set. But an easier way to look at it is you need to drop the weight so as to increase by four reps from the first to the third set.

In this case, you drop the weight from set one to set three by twice as much as you increased it from set one to set two. But you also need to estimate how much your gear adds and add that to how much you drop the weight for the final set. For example, if you did 300/4, 330/2 for the first two sets, and your gear adds 40 pounds, then your final set will be 200/8 (30 x 2 + 40 = 100 pounds to drop from set one to three).

Chapter Nine
Proper Performance
of the Powerlifts

This chapter describes how to properly perform squats, bench presses, and deadlifts.

Proper Performance of Squats

Squats are one of the best exercises there is for overall strength development. Squats work the entire lower body, including the quadriceps, glutes, hamstrings, and calves. Due to the training effect of utilizing such large muscles groups, the entire body receives benefit.

To perform squats, be sure to use a power bar (with knurling in the middle) to prevent slippage. It is helpful in this regard to chalk your upper back where the bar rests. It is best not to use any type of padding. Get used to using just the bar without padding as the pad can cause slippage, and a pad most definitely will not be used at a contest.

Set the racks so that the bar is a little below shoulder level, duck under the bar. It should then rest on the upper back (on the traps, just above the scapula). It should not be placed high on the neck. Powerlifters will want to carry the bar as low as possible. However, by rule, the top of the bar cannot be more than two inches below the top of the deltoids, or in some federations, more than the thickness of the bar.

Initially, the amount of weight is not important; what is important is being sure to use correct form.

Foot spacing will affect which muscles are emphasized in the lift. A narrow (closer than shoulder width) stance emphasizes the quads and outer thighs. A wide (greater than shoulder width) stance will emphasize the glutes and inner things. A medium (shoulder width stance) will put equal emphasis on all of these muscle groups. Powerlifters generally use a shoulder width or wider stance as greater weights can be utilized than with a close stance. But you need to experiment to see what type of stance works best for you.

For beginners, it is recommended that a shoulder width stance be utilized as it is easiest to perform. The toes should be facing somewhat outward, about 20-45 degrees, but again, you need to experiment as different foot angles can change the feel of the lift.

Keep the head looking forward or slightly upward throughout the performance of the lift. The elbows should be elevated so as to be bet-

127

ter able to hold onto the bar and to keep it from slipping. There should be a slight arch in the back, with the lower part of the pelvis rotated backwards. This position should be maintained throughout.

Once the bar is raised off of the squat racks, if the contest is using hydraulic racks (or if in a gym with such racks or in a power rack), the lifter needs to walk back with the weight. This is called the "walkout." However, it is neither necessary nor desirable to take several steps. Instead, take one step back first with the right foot, then one step back with the left foot. Then step out to the side with the right foot and then with the left to get into the proper foot position. So that's right back, left back, right out, left out. And that is all that should be needed. If the lifter hits the racks with the bar, this means he/she is bending too far forward during the performance of the lift.

If you are using a monolift, then the scenario is different as no walkout is needed. However, if you are not used to a monolift, you need to be careful. The tendency is to stand too close to the bar. This can then cause the lifter to lose balance and to stumble backwards and for the bar to slide off backwards. I know, this happened to me once and cost me my third attempt.

The problem is, if you are used to walking the weight out, you tend to get in close to the bar, then when you step backwards, your momentum keeps the bar on your back. But with a monolift, there is no backward momentum. So you need to take your initial stance further back than you would with walkout racks.

If you are not used to a monolift, be sure to practice in the warm-up room. If you are still unsure, then you are allowed to walk the weight out even if a monolift is being used. Just be sure to tell the head judge and spotters ahead of time that you will be doing so.

That said, the lifter should look straight ahead and continue to do so throughout the lift. This will help prevent the lifter from bending too far forward. A slight forward bend is okay, but the lift should not be turned into a "good morning" exercise. The upper back should remain arched and the shoulders back.

At a contest, wait for the head referee's "Squat" command before starting the descent. The lifter should then sit down and back into the squatting position, with the buttocks going back some so as to keep the knees from coming too far forward. They should not go past the toes.

There should be a controlled descent. Do not "drop" down quickly and "bounce" back up. That can wreck havoc on the knees. A slight drop and bounce when you are almost to parallel is okay, but anything more than that is flirting with disaster.

The feet should remain flat on the floor. The heels should not come up, and nothing should be placed under the heels. If the lifter has difficulty with this, then flexibility exercises for the Achilles should be performed. However, it is okay and even helpful to use shoes with a slight heel. But the heel should be less than an inch thick. Such a heel will help to prevent loss of balance backwards that some experience when doing squats.

The knees should stay in line with the lower leg and foot throughout. There should be no inward or outward turning of the knees.

By rule, powerlifters *must* break parallel. By parallel is meant when the top of the knees are below the top of the thighs at the "cease" where the thighs connect to the torso. Also by rule, powerlifters must have the knees locked at the start and completion of the lift.

As for breathing, the lifter should inhale during the descent and exhale during the ascent.

At the completion of the lift, the weight needs to be walked back in. But at a contest, wait for the head referee's "Rack" command before starting to do so. If a monolift is being used, then wait for the rack to be swung back into place to lower the bar back down onto it.

One final issue, if one person is spotting, the spotter should watch closely throughout the performance of the lift. The spotter should stand behind the lifter as close as possible without interfering with the lifter. The spotter's hands should be kept below the chest (male) or under the arms (female). The spotter should be in position to lift the lifter up and backwards as need be. The spotter should squat with the lifter. In this way, the spotter's legs will be bent so they can be used if the lifter needs assistance.

If two people are spotting, they should stand on either side of the lifter, with the hands cupped together directly below the end of the bar. But sure to not let your hands actually touch the bar, but follow it closely down and then back up, then help the lifter re-rack the weight.

Many of the preceding points can be seen in the pictures on the next page (taken at 2006 APF PA States).

In the first picture, I have just lifted the bar off the monolift racks. Notice how far back the bar is from the racks (seen on the left side of the picture). That is due to being a small step back from the bar when I lifted it up. My legs are locked. I am looking forward. The bar is in a low location on my back. But later I changed my form and brought my hand grip in and now hold the bar a little higher on my back. This helps keep me from leaning forward too much.

However, in the second picture, the amount of forward lean is appropriate. I am sitting back so that my knees are not going past my toes. I am still looking forward. But I am not quite below parallel in this picture. But the lift was passed, so the picture was probably taken while I was still descending.

In these pictures, there are three spotters, so you have both scenarios described previously. One spotter behind me and two spotters at either side, with their hands ready to catch the bar.

Proper Performance of Bench Presses

The bench press is a great exercise for developing upper body strength. It utilizes the chest (pectrolis major and minor), shoulders (anterior delts), and triceps.

To perform bench presses, the lifter should lie flat on the bench. Beginners should not arch. However, powerlifters and more advanced lifters will find that arching enables greater weights to be handled.

The shoulders, head, and buttocks should be flat on the bench, and the feet flat on the floor. None of these should move throughout the movement. Any such movement could be cause for disqualification at a powerlifting meet, except some federations allow the head to come up. Otherwise, only the arms should move. To help prevent slippage, chalk your upper back and buttocks.

The bar should be grasped with an overhand grip, thumbs around the bar, and slightly wider than shoulder width. Do not use a thumbless grip. It is very dangerous and not legal in some federations. An underhand grip is also not legal in some federations.

Lift the bar off of the uprights to arm's length, elbows locked. Lower the weight to the chest, and then pause momentarily at the bottom. At a contest, wait for the head referee's "Press" command. The bar must not bounce at the chest nor sink into the chest after the command. Then press it upwards until the arms are straight and elbows locked, being sure to come up and especially to lockout evenly. Then wait for the referee's "Rack" command before re-racking the weight.

Some authorities recommend that at the start of the lift to hold the bar so that it is above the chin. The bar would then be lowed in an arch until it touches on the lower part of the chest. But other authorities believe it is best to press the bar up in a straight line rather than in an arch. In this case, the starting position would be directly above the "target" location on the chest. But some authorities recommend pressing the bar slightly towards the feet. So the three options are: pressing the bar in an arch towards the chin, pressing it in a straight line up, or pressing it in a straight line slightly towards the feet. It would be advisable to experiment with each form to see which works best for you.

Exactly where to touch the chest is also a matter of experimentation. Personally, I touch the chest about an inch below the nipple line. When lifting raw, the elbows should flare out somewhat during the descent but not excessively as this could cause rotator cuff damage. When lifting with a shirt, keeping the elbows tucked in can make it easier to touch the bar to the chest.

During the ascent it is helpful to bring the elbows in slightly so as to more fully utilize triceps strength. The lifter should inhale during the downward motion and exhale during the upward motion.

If there is one spotter, he should stand behind the head of the lifter, behind the bar and uprights. The spotter should squat down as needed so as to be ready to grab the bar at any time. In this way, the spotter's legs can be used to lift the weight if needed. However, the spotter should not grab the bar too early. Do not touch the bar unless the lifter asks for help or if the bar starts to go back down.

The spotter should hand-off the weight to the lifter using a three count. If you're using your own hand-off person at a contest, be sure he knows to get completely off of the platform afterwards so as not to block the view of the head judge. If he doesn't get out of the way, you could get red-lighted. The contest spotters will take it from there. If there are two spotters, the performance is the same as for squats.

Many of the preceding points can be seen in the picture below (taken at 2005 IPA Iron House Classic). My head, shoulders, and butt are firmly on the bench. You can see from the bar location that I had touched my chest a little below nipple level and am coming straight up and evenly. My grip is a little wider than shoulder width. Note also the two spotters' with cupped hands under but not touching the bar.

There are four common variations of the bench press. The first is wide grip benches. The purpose of using a wide grip is to put emphasis on the outer chest (lateral pectoralis major). It also helps with the push off of the chest when doing regular grip benches, so wide grip benches are better suited for those who compete raw. About one hand width wider than your regular bench grip would be a good width to begin with. But be careful as this exercise can be very taxing to the wrists and pecs and is best avoided by some lifters.

The second variation is a narrow grip bench. The purpose of using a narrow grip is to put emphasis on the inner chest (medial pectoralis major) and the triceps. The hands should be at least one hand width narrower than for one's regular bench. To emphasize the inner pecs, the elbows should flare out comfortably to the sides. To emphasize the triceps, keep the elbows in.

The third variation is incline benches. The purpose of doing incline benches is to emphasize the upper chest. The incline of the bench should be 30-45 degrees. Large volumes of incline work should not be done so as to not overtax the rotator cuff.

The path of the bar on inclines should be basically straight down and up, to and from the middle of the chest (halfway between the clavicle and nipple line).

The fourth common variation is decline benches. These emphasize the lower pecs. The angle of decline should be about 30 degrees. The path of the bar should be basically straight down and up from the bottom of the chest. Declines are especially helpful if you have a pronounced arch as an arched flat bench is basically a decline bench.

Inclines and declines can be varied by doing them with a normal, narrow, or wide grip. And flat, incline and declines benches can all be varied by using dumbbells.

Proper Performance of Deadlifts

Deadlifts are the best exercise there is for developing overall body strength. Almost every major muscle group is utilized while performing deadlifts. Deadlifts utilize the entire lower body (hips, buttocks, quads, hamstrings, and calves), the entire mid-section (low back, abs, and obliques), the upper back (lats and traps), and the forearms.

There are two ways to perform deadlifts: with a "conventional" (close) stance and with a "sumo" (wide) stance. For the former, the hands grasp the bar with the arms outside of the legs, but for the latter, the arms are inside of the legs.

The difference between these stances is that conventional stance deadlifts emphasize the lower back and hamstrings while sumo stance deadlifts emphasize the hips and quadriceps. But all of these muscles are worked to some degree with either stance. I would recommend that beginners start with the conventional stance, but then sometime later the lifter might want to experiment with the sumo stance.

When deadlifting, it is important to use a bar with knurling on it; otherwise, the lifter might lose his/ her grip. Start with the bar lying on the floor, and the lifter standing in the middle. Bend at the knees and grasp the bar on the knurling, with the arms outside of the legs (conventional) stance or inside of the legs (sumo stance).

The heels should be about 6-10" apart (conventional) and the arms as straight down as possible. The grip is a little wider with a conventional stance than with a sumo stance. For the former, all of the fingers should be completely on the knurling. For a sumo stance, one or two fingers can be on the smooth part of the bar. Don't worry, if your gripping strength is good, you'll have no problems holding onto the bar.

Most find that a mixed grip (a.k.a. reverse grip) works best. Grasp the bar with one palm facing forward (underhand grip) and with the other palm facing toward the body (overhand grip). Usually, the dominant hand should be in the overhand position.

At the start of the lift, the bar should be a couple of inches in front of the shins (conventional) or right against the shins (sumo). This bar placement is an important difference between the start of the two lifts.

The lifter should look forward the entire time. The back should be arched so that there is no rounding of the shoulders. Look forward or slightly upward the whole time. Do not look down.

The legs should be bent so that the buttocks are a little higher than the knees. The beginning position should be such that the lifter can push with the legs with about the same force as pulling with the back. It is a matter of how much the legs should be bent and how high the buttocks should be at the start. If the lifter starts with the buttocks too low and the legs bent too much, then the initial drive will be mostly with the legs. Conversely, if the buttocks are too high and the legs are too straight, the low back will do most of the work. It will take some experimentation to find the best balance between these two extremes.

The lift is started by simultaneously pushing with the legs and pulling with the back. The lifter should picture driving the heels into the ground and pulling back with the back. It is helpful for some to quickly drop the buttocks down some before starting the pull. As the buttocks are raised begin pushing with the legs when the buttocks are in the correct start position.

Keep pulling upward until the body is in an erect position. The shoulders should be straight, not rounded forward at the end of the lift. However, it is neither necessary nor desirable to round the shoulders backwards. Simply be sure that the body is straight.

Pause at the top, and then slowly lower the weight back to the floor, bending the legs and lowering the buttocks. Do not drop the bar nor bang it onto the floor. At a contest, wait for the head referee's "Down" command before starting to lower the weight.

In workouts, always pause at the floor before starting the second rep. Do not bounce the bar off of the floor. If the bar is bounced between reps, then the bottom part of the lift will not be strengthened.

As for breathing, inhale, taking a deep breath before starting the lift. If the lifter uses the method of dropping the buttocks before beginning the pull, then this is when a breath should be taken. Then exhale as the bar is raised. Inhale again as the bar is lowered. During the pause at the floor between reps, the lifter might want to take a breath or two in and out before inhaling to begin the second rep.

If the lifter has problems holding onto the bar, do not resort to using wrist straps. If the lifter does, then the forearms will not be strengthened and grip strength will not be improved, and wrist straps are not allowed at a contest, so learn to pull without them. It is preferable to do some forearm work to improve grip strength than to resort to lifting straps. Reverse curls done with a straight bar are a very effective exercise for this purpose.

The two pictures on the next page are of the start and completion of sumo deadlifts (taken at 2006 WNPF Western PA Championships. But note that the date is wrong, this contest was in April).

Note that my sumo stance is not near as wide as some. But you can see in these pictures how at the start of the lift, the bar is right against my shins. I am looking slightly up. My butt is down back, so the initial drive is from the legs.

136

At the end of the lift, I am standing erect but not leaning back excessively nor rounding my shoulders back as neither is necessary. I am still looking forward, but slightly upward.

Note also my mixed hand grip. But note that most lifters put their dominant hand in the overhand position and the opposite hand in the underhand position. I am right handed, but I put my left in the overhand position as a childhood injury makes it hard for me to turn my left hand into a full underhand position.

This final picture was taken in my home gym. It shows the starting position for conventional stance deadlifts. The differences from the sumo stance are the hands are outside of the legs and the bar is an inch or two in front of the shins rather than right up against them.

Videos of yours truly performing the powerlifts can be found on my fitness Web site (see Appendix #3).

Section Three

Powerlift
Assistance Exercises

Chapter Ten
Introduction and Squat Assistance Exercises

This section will describe different possible powerlift assistance exercises, but first, a general introduction to such exercises.

General Introduction

There are many quality powerlift assistance exercises that can be utilized to help your performance in the actual powerlifts, and some exercise that are not so helpful.

Exercises marked with an asterisk are "major" assistance exercises. By this is meant that these lifts can be done in place of the actual powerlift, as described in Chapter Eight.

It should go without saying that you should not do all of the exercises listed. Limit yourself to two of the major assistance exercises if performed on a day different from the powerlift or one major exercise if done after the powerlift. Then do at best a couple of the minor ones.

Choose assistance exercises that focus on where your sticking point or hardest part of the lift is. You should then reevaluate and change the exercises with every new routine. An especially good time for re-evaluation is right after a contest. Where you miss a lift or where the hardest part of the lift is at a contest is most important. So note where that is, and after the contest pick assistance exercise(s) that work that part of the lift.

Periodically changing assistance exercises will keep the lifter from adapting to a particular exercise and thus causing it to lose its effectiveness. It will also enable the lifter to be continually working on his/her sticking point. This will change periodically, and thus assistance exercises need to be changed accordingly.

But generally speaking, those who compete raw will need to emphasize assistance exercises that aid the bottom part or all aspects of each powerlift, while those who compete equipped should emphasize assistance exercises that work the top part of each powerlift. But there is overlap here. If you are a raw lifter but are missing near the top of the lift, then one or more of the exercises that help the top half of the lift might be helpful, and vice–a–versa.

But for both types of lifters, it can be helpful to pick one exercise that works the top part of the lift and one that works the bottom part or all aspects of the lift. However, equipped lifters should perform the top end lift first and raw lifters the bottom end or all aspects lift first.

For the most part, supportive gear should not be worn while doing assistance work, not even a belt. By lifting without gear, the lifter will strengthen the parts of the body normally supported by gear.

However, if you are going to work up to a heavy single or double, then it would be prudent to wear at least a belt and wraps. And if you have any injuries or chronic pain areas that require the use of supportive gear, then of course, utilize it. Additional possible exceptions to the no gear rule are noted in the exercise descriptions.

Squat Assistance Exercises

These squat assistance exercises are divided by which part of the squat they most benefit.

Helps All Aspects of Squats

Front Squats* – Front squats are performed by holding the bar on the top of the chest. The bar can be held by crossing the arms across the bar and holding it with the palms facing the body. Or the bar can be held with the palms facing away from the body, using the same grip one would have if you had had just done the "clean" part of a clean and jerk. Either way, when you squat down, be sure to break parallel.

Front squats can be performed using your regular squat stance or using a close stance, which would put more emphasis on the quads.

Either way, front squats are a very effective exercise. They force you to stay in an upright position, strengthening the core and helping to perfect form on regular squats.

But, unfortunately, holding the bar is very awkward, no matter how one holds it. The cross-over grip is not very stable and is very uncomfortable on the shoulders, while the "clean" type of grip puts great strain on the wrists. Wrist wraps might help in this regard.

The best way to do front squats would be with a "Sting Ray" (pictured on the next page and available at APT). These are two plastic "cups" that attach to the bar. They are then placed on the shoulders, and the bar held in the cross-over fashion. The Sting Ray reduces the strain on the shoulders and helps to hold the bar in place.

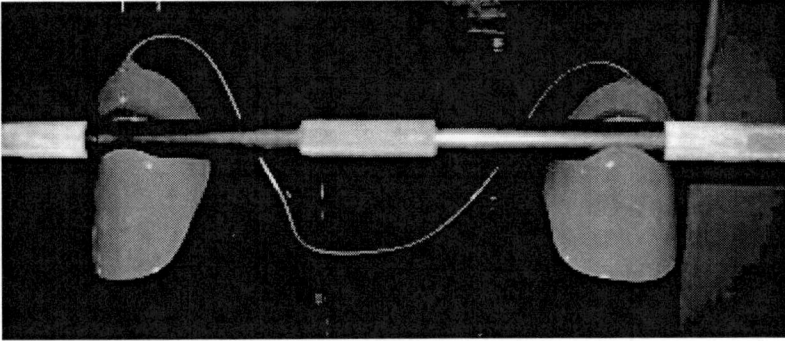

Close Stance, High Bar Squats* – As mentioned in the previous chapter, power squats are usually performed with a shoulder width or wider stance and the bar somewhat low on the back. This stance puts more emphasis on the larger gluteus and hip muscles. But more work can be provided to the quadriceps by using a close stance and putting the bar higher on the back, more on the neck.

The stance should be at least three inches closer on each side (or 6" total) than your regular stance. Again, be sure to break parallel.

To prevent undo strain on the neck, these can be done using a "Manta Ray" (pictured below and available from APT). Like the Sting Ray, this plastic device snaps onto the bar in the middle. It is then placed on the back as with regular squats. The Manta Ray takes the strain off of the neck and raises the bar up even higher, thus putting even more emphasis on the quads.

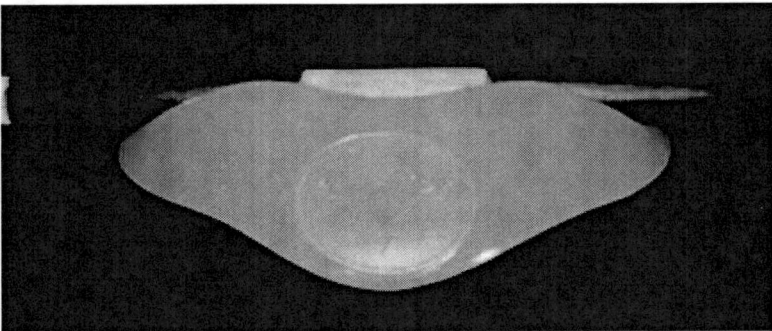

Wide Stance Squats* – These are basically the opposite of the above exercise. The feet are placed a few inches wider than your normal stance. This stance emphasizes the hips. The bar should be held in the lower, power squat position. But be careful as this stance can cause undo strain on the hips. If they bother you, then avoid them.

Box Squats* – Use a sturdy wooden or metal box. You squat down and sit on the box. The box should be at the height of your bottom position or maybe a little lower. Pause on the box and then come back up. Don't relax completely at the bottom (e.g. do not put all of the weight on the box). Stay tight and hold the weight.

Pictured is my box. It is 11.5" high. When sitting on it, I'm about 1" below parallel. But I am 5'1", so adjust the height for your height.

Some lifters swear by box squats, especially those who use a canvas suit. The reason is that a canvas suit functions similar to the box in that it "stops" the lifter at the bottom. But personally, I have not found them to be particularly helpful.

Helps the Bottom Part of Squats

Low Squats* – These are done in the power rack. You insert two sets of safety bars in the rack, one set of bars so you're 2-3" below parallel and the other set a few inches below lockout. You then place the bar on the bottom set of bars, squeeze down under it, then squat rapidly up and down tapping each set of bars.

The idea of using the top set of bars is so the lifter can keep moving rapidly without locking out the knees. This exercise helps one get out of the bottom on the squat and can even help with a sticking point near the middle of the lift. It also really pumps up the legs and glutes. The pictures to the right are of the set-up and performance.

Dead Stop Squats* – These are basically deadlifts, but with the bar on the back rather than in the hands. The set-up is similar to that as for low squats, but without the second set of safety bars. Set the safety bars so that with the bar placed on them you'll be 2–3" below parallel. Squeeze underneath, and starting from this dead stop, squat all the way up. Then come back down and rest the bar fully on the safeties. Then start again from the dead stop. This exercise helps the lifter get out of the bottom on the squat.

Pause Squats* – You do a regular squat, but at the bottom you pause for a slow three count ("1,001—1,002—1,003"), then come back up. But unlike the preceding exercise, for these you cannot relax your muscles while holding the pause. You must keep your muscles tight at all times. This exercise helps the lifter get out of the bottom on the squat and also really pumps up the quads.

Helps the Top Part of Squats

Chain, Band, and Reverse Band Squats* – These three exercises will be dealt with in Chapter Thirteen.

Partial Squats* – The idea here is to start from just below your sticking point and work from there. So exactly how far to go down will depend on the lifter's particular sticking point. Working from a couple of inches below this point will help the lifter to overcome the sticking point.

Since you can handle more weight than for regular squats, this exercise will also will get your body used to handling heavy weights. But the problem is, given the heavy weights utilized, partial squats can be very tasking on the lower back, so you have to be very careful when doing this exercise. It might also be prudent to wear a belt and wraps when performing this exercise.

For safety reasons, I would recommend doing these in a power rack with the safety bars set at the appropriate height. You can do them a couple of ways. The first is to walk the weight out and get set as usual. Then squat down until the bar just taps the safeties, then squat back up, then walk back in after the last rep. This will condition you to walking out and in and handling a heavier than normal weight.

An alternative would be to set the weight on the safety bars and to lift up straight from the safeties. Then set the bar back on the safety bars at the completion of the set. This avoids the possible danger of walking out with the extra heavy weight, but you lose the benefit of overloading the walkout and walkin.

The former approach would be best for those who have to walk the weight out at a contest, while the latter would be best for those using a monolift at a contest.

Bench Squats* – This is a form of partial but almost full squats. You squat until your butt touches a free bench. They should be done in a touch and go fashion of touching your butt on the bench. The height of the bench should be such that at the bottom you're a few inches above parallel. This will help those whose sticking point is just above parallel. But be careful that you don't get in the "habit" of squatting high and get called for depth come contest time.

These also should be done in a power rack, with the safety bars set just below where the bar is in the bottom. That way, if you get stuck you can easily set the bar down on the safeties and squeeze out.

Miscellaneous Exercises

Walkouts – You load about 10% more than your 1RM on the bar. You then lift the weight, step back, and get set as if you were going to squat the weight, but don't bend your knees. Just get set, and then return the weight to the racks. This is thus another exercise that will get your body used to handling heavier weights. It also should be done in a power rack for safety reasons. Set the safety bars high up in a power rack just below where the bar will be once you are set.

Walkouts should only be done occasionally, namely in the last couple of workouts pre-contest, not as a regular part of a routine. Given the heavy weights utilized, it would also be prudent to wear a belt and wraps when performing this exercise.

Rack Lift Ups – These are the same idea as walkouts, except they are for those who will be competing using a monolift but don't have one for training. You won't need to walk out with a monolift, so instead, put the safety bars high up in a power rack and practice lifting the bar up off of the bars in your squat stance. Load on about 10% more than your contest attempts so the weight will feel "light" at the meet. Again, these should only be done pre-contest, and given the heavy weights utilized, it would be prudent to wear a belt and wraps.

Lunges – You either hold a barbell on your shoulders as if doing squats or a dumbbell in each hand. You then step forward with one leg, bending it until your knee almost touches the ground. Then step back and repeat with the other leg. Alternatively, after stepping forward with one leg, you then step forward with the other leg and keep "walking" in this fashion across the floor.

However one does them, these really pump up the quads, but they would not have that great of a carry-over to squats given how different they are from squats and that only very light weights can be used. In fact, it is probably best to start with light dumbbells before even trying the 45 pounds of an unloaded Olympic bar.

Step-ups – As with lunges, you place a bar on the shoulders or hold a dumbbell in each hand. You then step up onto some kind of step, and then step down, and repeat with the other leg. Ideally, the step should be high enough that your thighs are parallel to the ground in the stepping up position. A squat box as pictured previously would work great, but even a lower step would be effective. Just be sure the step is very stable so you don't fall. These are similar to lunges in their effectiveness in pumping up the quads.

This exercise can also be done without weights or only very light weights as a cardio exercise. Using a squat box as pictured to the left provides a high step and thus a high intensity. Such an exercise would be great for the "very intense cardio" described in Chapter Seven.

Hack Squats/ Leg Presses – These are done on the respective machines. They are good exercises for working the legs, but they are not as effective as free weight exercises. The carry-over to regular squats would also not be as great as with the previously discussed major assistance exercises. As such, their use by the powerlifter should be very limited.

Leg Extensions – These are a favorite exercise of many non-powerlifters, but why is beyond me. I can only guess that they are easy to do as compared to real size and strength builders like squats. Moreover, personally I find leg extensions to be more taxing on the knees than squats. But leg extensions could have a place to help pump up the quads after doing one or more of the previous squat exercises. Just be sure to do them in a slow, controlled manner. Do not "swing" the weights. Their main value would probably be in rehabbing a knee injury (under the direction of a qualified physical therapist).

Calves Raises – The calves help to stabilize the lifter during the walkout, set up, and walkin for squats. I've found just a couple of sets of standing calves raises a week is sufficient to prevent any problems in this regard. The calves also help somewhat in the actual performance of squats and deadlifts.

Standing calves raises would be more beneficial than sitting ones. They can be done with a barbell if one has the balance to do so. Otherwise, they can also be done one leg at a time, holding a dumbbell in one hand (on the same side as the leg being worked) and holding onto a support with the other hand for balance. Also, various kinds of calf machines are generally found in most gyms.

Ab Exercises – The abdominal and oblique muscles are very important in stabilizing the trunk of the body when doing squats and deadlifts. And they get quite a bit of work when doing these lifts, especially if they're done without a belt or suit. However, some direct abdominal and oblique work would be prudent as well.

For each training routine, I would recommend doing at least one ab exercise where the chest is moved towards the hips (for the upper abs, e.g., crunches, sit-ups), one where the hips are moved towards the chest (for the lower abs, e.g., reverse crunches, leg raises), and one twisting motion (for the obliques, e.g., twisting versions of the preceding exercises).

In-depth descriptions of all of the various possible ab exercises is beyond the scope of this book. But a couple of points will be noted.

First, a very effective ab exercise is "Bicycle Abs" (pictured). This exercise incorporates all three of the mentioned motions. They are done lying on the floor and are a combination of twisting crunches and reverse crunches, touching left elbow to right knee, and vice-a-versa. The legs move as if peddling a bike.

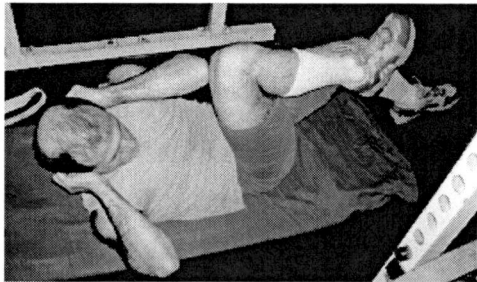

Second, when doing any kind of ab work, be sure to pause momentarily at the top and bottom of each rep so as to prevent momentum. This is especially important on various forms of leg raises so as to prevent swinging the legs. However, do not relax entirely at the top and bottom; try to maintain some tension in the abs throughout the movement.

Third, yes, leg raises (and sit-ups) should be done. At a doctor's appointment a while back, I was sitting on the exam table when the doctor asked me to lie down, so I just lay back without twisting around or using my hands. Then again, when she told me to sit up, I just sat straight up, again, without twisting or using my hands. The doctor commented that I must have strong abs and said something about doing a lot of crunches.

I didn't bother to correct her and tell her that it is because I usually do full sit-ups and leg raises, not wimpy crunches and reverse crunches that I am able to lay down and sit up without twisting or using my hands.

I know most personal trainers would be horrified at recommending sit-ups and leg raises. But really, when in the real world do you just bend forward a couple of inches? A physically active person should have no problems with sitting up and lying down without twisting or using their hands, and it is real sit-ups and leg raises that develop that ability.

This is not to say there is not a place for crunches and reverse crunches. They should be done for variety's sake, but also do full sit-ups and leg raises.

Chapter Eleven
Bench Press
Assistance Exercises

This chapter will discuss assistance exercise for the bench press, but first one general point.

It is recommended that raw lifters pause all of their reps on regular benches and on any "pressing" type of assistance work. Meanwhile, shirted benchers would probably be better of using a touch 'n go method when not using a shirt. Just be sure you are not bouncing the bar off of the chest. However, practice using a pause anytime the shirt is used in training and when using chains and bands.

Helps All Aspects of Benches

Weighted Dips* – These are very taxing to all three major muscles groups used in the bench press, the pecs (especially the lower pecs), anterior delts, and triceps.

If you are unable to do dips with your bodyweight, then you have a couple of options. The first is to only do partial dips, gradually going deeper with each workout as you are able. A second option would be to have a spotter hold your legs and give you as much assistance as necessary to complete a full dip. There are also machines available for performing assisted dips.

Once you are able to do a number of reps with your bodyweight, you need to add weight. To do so, you need to use a dip belt. I got mine from Crain.ws, but they are also available from APT and elsewhere (see Appendix #1). You hang weights from the chain on the belt, as can be seen in the picture.

If you look closely, you'll see I added a couple of clasps, one to connect the two ends of the belt together, and another connecting the chain back to the belt. The clasps are the kind seen on cable machines at most gyms. They are available from any hardware store.

To target the anterior delts and

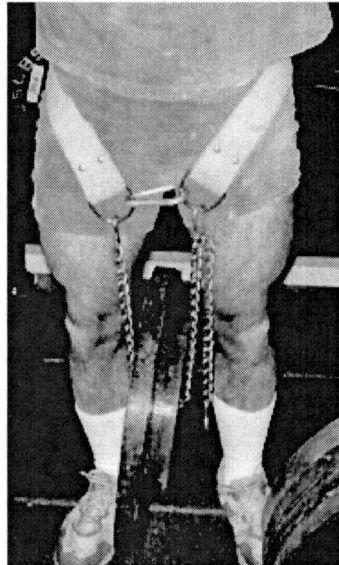

lower pecs you need to lean forward about 15 degrees. Done in this fashion, dips help mainly the bottom two-thirds of the bench. If you do them straight up and down then your triceps will get most of the work, and the exercise will help mainly the top third of the bench.

But it needs to be noted, dips are an "advanced" exercise; beginners should not do them, and even experienced lifters must take much care in doing them. Use proper form and concentrate so as not to lose control. If they bother your shoulders, stop them immediately.

But when you do them, you need to actually "dip." I say this as too often in gyms I've seen guys barely bend their arms and call it a dip. That does no good whatsoever, except to stroke the ego with the amount of weight than can be used.

On the other hand, you do not want to dip down too far as that puts too much strain on the shoulders. I think it is best if you come down until the upper arms are about parallel to the ground, as seen in the above picture.

Be sure you are thoroughly warmed-up before attempting weighted dips. Always perform a warm-up set with no weight before adding weight. Be sure to do them in a slow, controlled manner so as not to hurt your shoulders.

For a very challenging alternative to regular dips, try doing them using gymnastics rings. Having to keep your arms from flaring out along with dipping is very taxing to the chest, shoulders, and arms.

Feet on Bench Benches* – Rather than putting your feet on the floor, for this exercise, you put them up on the bench. This eliminates all leg drive from the lift. It also makes it impossible to arch. As a result, the training effective is different from regular benches but also very effective. But be careful you do not roll off of the bench!

Incline Bench Presses* – A very good exercise for working the upper pecs and anterior delts. The higher the angle of the bench, the more the delts will be worked and the less the pecs. An angle of about 45 degrees is generally recommended.

Decline Bench Presses* – These work the lower pecs and anterior delts. But they are very awkward to do. You are almost hanging upside down, which can cause a headache for some. And it can be difficult to press the weight up without "wobbling" as you do. But if you can get the hang of them, declines are an effective exercise. They work the lower pecs, which are involved in regular benches, especially if you arch when benching.

Below are pictures of my FID (Flat, Incline, Decline) Bench in the incline and decline positions. The incline angle could be a little higher than in the picture.

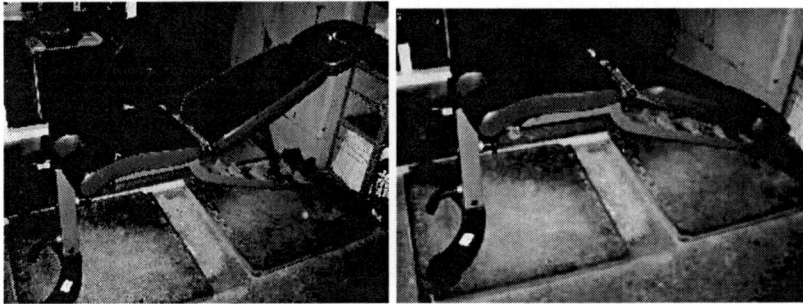

Reverse Grip Bench Presses* – For this exercise, the lifter holds the bar with a palms up (curl) grip. Using a reverse grip forces the elbows to stay in to the sides and thus emphasizes the triceps.

A few powerlifters even use this grip for their competitive grip. However, some federations do not allow a reverse grip to be used in competition, so be sure to check beforehand.

Dumbbell Bench Presses* – Doing benches with dumbbells works more musculature than barbell benches. This is because more stabilizer muscles are needed to keep control of the dumbbells. However, it is because of the unwieldy nature of dumbbells that they can be more dangerous. If a dumbbell "gets way from you" while performing a lift, you could pull something trying to pull it back in place. To avoid this, be sure to concentrate at all times while using dumbbells. Of course, that's good advice when lifting in general, but even more so with dumbbells.

The biggest difficulty with dumbbells is getting them into place. I would suggest the following: Set the weights on the floor at the foot of the bench and sit on the end of the bench. Pick up the weights and swing them onto your thighs, plates against your thighs. Then lean backwards keeping your legs bent. When you are lying on the bench, lower your legs to the floor, and then rotate the weights into place.

Keeping the legs bent while going back will help prevent straining the back. Just be careful you don't roll off the bench before you put your legs down.

An even better alternative is to use "Power Hooks." These wrap onto the dumbbells and then are hooked onto a bar placed in a power rack. The lifter then racks and un-racks the dumbbells as you would a barbell. Power hooks can be purchased from APT. The picture is of my Olympic-sized dumbbells hanging on Power Hooks from the bar.

Dumbbells can also be used for doing incline and decline benches. The same comments as above would apply for these exercises as well. However, for declines you would have to have someone hand the weights to you after getting set, as they're no way to safely get in position while holding the weights, unless you are using the above mentioned Power Hooks.

Helps the Bottom Part of Benches

Wide Grip Benches* – This exercise works the anterior delts and pecs to a greater degree than regular benches, and they basically take the triceps out of the movement. As such, they help the bottom and middle part of the lift.

However, wide grip benches place quite a bit of strain on the wrists. Wrist wraps might help in this regard. But if wide grip benches still cause undo discomfort, then it would be best to avoid them. They are also very stressful on the pecs. Again, if they cause undo discomfort, then avoid them. Personally, I am unable to do wide grip benches due to having a tender left pec.

But if you can tolerate them, they are an excellent exercise. Use a grip about one hand width wider than for your regular bench, and pause at the chest as with regular benches. These are a good exercise for those lifters who are planning on competing raw, but they would be of little use to those benching with a shirt.

3–Second Pause Benches* – As the name implies, pause the bar at the chest for a slow three count ("1,001—1,002—1,003"). Doing this will improve your lift off of the chest, and it will make the wait for the press signal at a contest seem short. This is another good exercise for raw benchers but not shirted benchers.

Cambered Bar Benches* – A cambered bar is bent up and across in the middle (see picture on next page). The idea of using it is by keeping the "bend" at the top, you can lower the weight to below the chest. This will then help you get the weight off of the chest at the bottom position, so these might be a good exercise for raw lifters. However, they can be rather awkward to do. The bent part has a tendency to flip down. Also, they can be dangerous as the bend is so high that one could end up going too far down and pull a muscle.

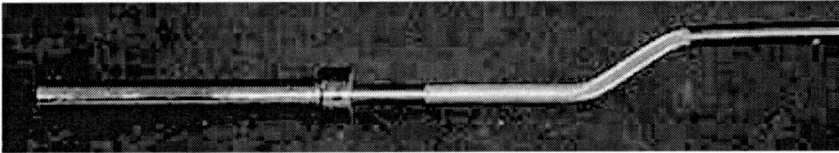

A safer alternative would be to use dumbbells. The advantage of dumbbells is you can lower the weights lower than on barbell benches, just as with a cambered bar. But unlike a cambered bar, if something doesn't "feel right" you can quickly dump the weights and maybe avoid injury.

Flyes/ Peck Dec/ Cable Crossovers – These are very popular chest exercises, but none of them are near as effective for building muscular size or strength as benches and variations thereof. There would also not be near as much carry-over to benches from flyes and the like as from bench variations. But flyes and the like could provide some benefit to raw lifters in helping the push off of the chest, and they might have a place at the end of a chest workout to pump up the pecs. They would be most helpful when rehabbing a pectoral injury.

Helps the Top Part of Benches

A word of warning to shirted benchers, if you concentrate on using the exercises to follow, it is very possible that your raw bench will stagnate or even go down. The reason for this is your drive off of the chest will weaken. But this does not matter. All that matters is that your weights on these exercises and especially on your shirted bench is going up. But this is one reason why it is difficult to go back and forth between raw and shirted benching.

Chain, Band, and Reverse Band Benches* – These three exercises will be dealt with in Chapter Thirteen.

Lockouts/ Rack Benches* – These are partial bench presses. The idea is to start these from just below your "sticking point." To do partial benches, you could just do benches as normal, but only go part way down. But the problem with this is the danger factor. You can handle a lot more weight on partial benches than on regular benches.

As such, I would recommend putting a flat bench in a power rack. Set the safety bars a couple of inches below your sticking point. There are then two possible ways of doing these. For the first, set the hooks in the power rack at the appropriate height to be used as the bench up-rights. Take the bar off of the hooks as normal, but then lower the bar until it taps the safety bars and then press it up.

The second method would be to rest the bar on the safety bars. Slide underneath the bar, press it up from a dead stop, and then lower it and rest it fully on the safety bars. Then again press it up from the dead stop.

Experiment with each method to see which works best for you. Or use one method for one routine, and the other for the next. Given the heavy weights utilized, it might be prudent to wear wrist wraps when doing this exercise. The same would go for the next two exercises.

Board Benches* – This exercise is similar to power rack lockouts. Only here, you place two to four boards (nailed together) on the chest. Lower the bar until it taps the boards and then press the weight.

Ideally, the boards should have a handle extending out of one end (see picture on next page). A spotter can then hold this handle to keep the boards from falling off of the lifter's chest.

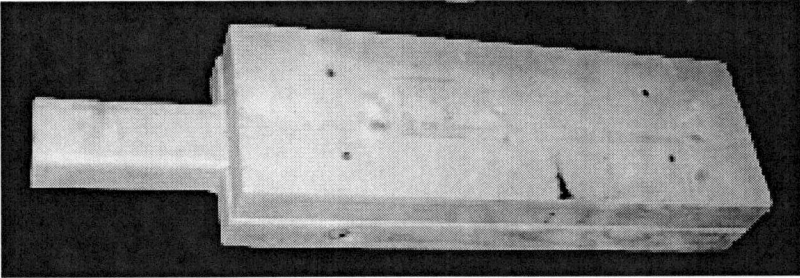

Floor Press* – Yet another way to do partial benches. Simply lie on the floor in a power rack. Use the hooks in the power rack for the uprights. Take the weight off of the racks and lower the bar until the elbows just touch the floor and then press up.

Rack–Speed Benches* – Speed work in general will be addressed in Chapter Thirteen. But this exercise is a specific form of speed work for those whose sticking point is in the middle part of the lift. Put a bench in a power rack and use two sets of safety bars. One set of safety bars is placed so that the bar is about 3–4 inches off of the chest and the other set of bars about 2–3 inches below lockout. Place the bar on the bottom set of safeties.

Slide underneath the bar. Quickly press the bar up and just tap the top set of safety bars and then lower it quickly and just tap the bottom set of bars. Repeat for the required number of reps, then rest the bar on the bottom set of safeties, and slide back out.

Close Grip Bench Presses* – This is a great bench press assistance exercise. It is good for working the anterior (front) deltoids and triceps in a way that will directly benefit the bench press. This exercise especially helps the top third of the lift. The grip should be as close as is comfortable. I grip the bar on the smooth sections of a power bar, in-between the center and outer knurling sections. My hands are thus about 9" apart. The elbows should be kept close to the body.

On the next page are pictures of the three different bench grips. The first was my regular bench grip at the time of this picture. The second is my wide grip bench. The third is close grip benches.

But I should mention, some lifters use a grip more like my wide grip for their regular bench. But that is usually lifters using a shirt. The wider grip causes more stretch in the shirt and thus more push from it. But for me, a strain in my left pec forced me to move my regular grip in about half an inch on each side after this picture was taken. My raw bench has progressed well since doing so.

157

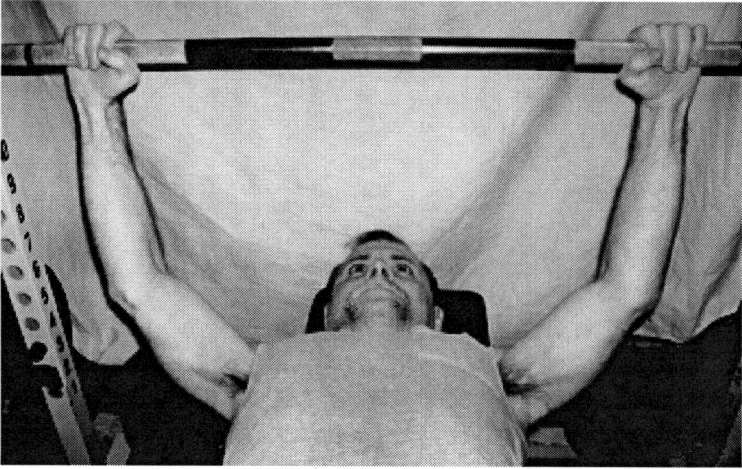

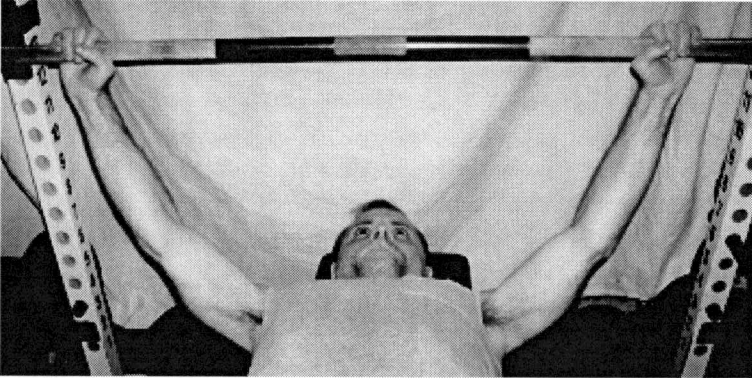

Miscellaneous Exercises

Overhead Presses* – Overhead presses work the upper pecs, anterior (front) deltoids, and triceps like benches, so they provide benefit for the bench press, especially for the middle part of the lift. However, most of the stress when doing presses is on the medial (middle/ top) delts, which are mainly used in a supportive role in benches. As such, the carry-over to benches is not as great as with the previous exercises. But still, presses can have a place in a powerlifter's routine to maintain muscular balance in the shoulder. They are a great size and strength builder as well. They can be done with a barbell or with dumbbells.

Upright Rows – Upright rows are a unique exercise in that they are both a bench press and a deadlift assistance exercise. They are a bench assistance exercise since, as with presses, they work the medial delts. However, they are a deadlift exercise in that they work the traps. They also work the biceps.

The wider your grip the more upright rows work the delts, and the narrower the grip, the more they work the traps. Also the delts do most of the work until the upper arms are about parallel, and then the traps take over. So to focus on the delts, use a wide grip and only come up to until the upper arms are parallel to the floor. To focus on the traps, use a narrow grip and raise the bar to chin level. To work both evenly, use a shoulder width grip and raise the bar to the top of the chest.

However, it is important to mention that some consider upright rows to be a dangerous exercise. They put the shoulder in an unnatural position, which can lead to injury. But if they are done, be careful to use correct form. Stay upright with no forward or backward bending, and be sure to raise and lower the bar in slow, controlled manner.

Laterals (Front and Side) – Front laterals work mainly the anterior delts, so there would be some carry-over to benches. However, the various bench variations would be more effective. Side laterals work mainly the medial delts, so they would be of little benefit to benches. Presses would be a more effective exercise for powerlifters to include than side laterals for shoulder development. But either form of laterals might be useful to pump up the delts after a chest/ shoulder workout.

Note that bent over laterals work the rear (posterior) delts and thus would be more of a deadlift assistance exercise.

Triceps Exercises – Close grip benches, dips, band and chain benches, and the various partial bench movements described previously work the triceps very effectively and in a manner that would have direct carry over to benches. The triceps also get a lot of work from any other pressing movement. For many, this will provide more than adequate triceps work. In fact, including direct triceps work could lead to overtraining the triceps. Also, you have to be careful as such exercises can be taxing to the elbows.

However, many find isolation triceps exercises benefit the lockout on the bench and/ or serve to pump up the triceps at the end of a bench workout. For such purposes, there are many good triceps exercises, but the various forms of triceps presses and cable triceps pushdowns are probably the best.

A very effective way to do pushdowns is to use a Triceps Strap Rope (pulley strap attachment), available from APT (pictured to the right). When doing these, be sure to fan your hands out at the bottom. Doing so really hits the triceps.

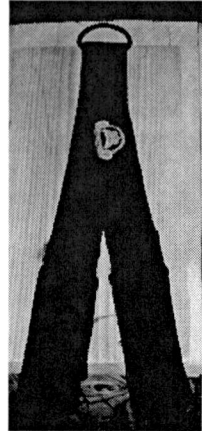

Rotator Cuff Exercises – The rotator cuff is "A set of muscles and tendons that secures the arm to the shoulder joint and permits rotation of the arm" (Dictionary.com). The important point here is the rotator cuff rotates the arm, but it does not get worked when doing pressing or pulling movements. Specific exercises need to be done to strengthen it. This is important as rotator cuff injuries are very common and can easily sideline an athlete, including powerlifters. As such, it is important to do rotator cuff work as "prehab" to prevent injuries.

Rotator cuff exercises are usually done with very light weight plates or dumbbells. They involve rotating the arm towards or away from the body. A full description of such exercises is beyond the scope of this book, but videos of such exercises are available on this writer's fitness Web site. Here it will be said that one of the best ways to effectively work the rotator cuff is with a Shoulder Horn. It is available from Elite Fitness (see Appendix #1). To the left is a picture, with one arm in the start position and the other in the bottom position. These can be done moving the arms together or alternating arms, as seen here.

Chapter Twelve
Deadlift Assistance Exercises

This chapter will discuss assistance exercise for deadlifts (DLs). They are divided by which part of the deadlift they most benefit.

Helps All Aspects of Deadlifts

Stiff Leg Deadlifts* – This is a great deadlift assistance exercise. But careful attention must be paid to form to prevent injury. In fact, some recommend against them due to the risk of injury. There is great stress on the low back and hamstrings. Only advanced lifters should try theses. Most especially, if you lack flexibility, you could pull a hamstring.

Stiff Leg Deadlifts (SLDLs) should be done in a slow, controlled manner, on both the ascent and descent. Some advocate standing on a platform while doing them. This way, you can lower the bar to your ankles and really stretch the lower back and hamstrings. However, others claim this extra stretch is dangerous to the lower back. As such, they advocate the opposite: only lowering the bar to about knee level, stopping in mid-air, and then returning to an upright position.

Personally, I think SLDLs should be done from the floor or standing on a low platform, 3" high at the most. Pause the weight at the floor as should always be done with regular deadlifts. Also as with DLs, keep you head up as much as possible so you don't overly round your back. However, if you experience any undo comfort in the lower back or hamstrings, discontinue them.

Note that the name is *Stiff* Leg DLs, not *Straight* Leg DLs. The point is, there should be a slight bend in the knees, as seen in the picture. This prevents undo stress on the knees and lessens the chance of pulling a hamstring.

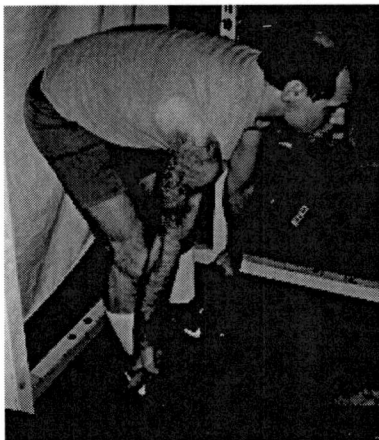

SLDLs are an excellent exercise for strengthening the low back and hamstrings in a way that has direct carry-over to DLs. They are especially important for those who use a sumo (wide) stance for DLs as the sumo stance does not work the low back as much as conventional (close) stance DLs do. However, even sumo stance deadlifters should use a close stance for SLDLs.

Back Pulls* – These are basically SLDLs done on a cable pull machine. Doing them this way gives a "smoother" feel to the lift. But the down-side is, as you progress, cable pulls machines will not have enough weight. So switch to SLDLs once you start pulling the stack.

Good Mornings* – Like SLDLs, Good Mornings (GMs) are a very effective low back and hamstring exercise. However, also like SLDLs, many believe GMs are too dangerous to be worth the risk. They place even greater stress on the low back and especially hamstrings than SLDLs. Making them especially dangerous is it can be difficult to keep correct form, but correct form is vital to preventing injury.

Put the bar on the back in the "low" power squat position, not high on the traps as for high-bar squats. The bottom position of the exercise should be when your upper body is at or just above parallel. As with SLDLs, use a slight bend in the knees. When bending forward, move your butt back so as to keep the center of gravity over your hips. Do them in a slow, controlled manner. If you experience any undo comfort in the lower back or hamstrings, discontinue them.

Good Mornings should be done in a power rack. Set the safety bars so that at the bottom position the bar is just above the safeties. If you miss a rep, you can lean forward a little more and set the bar on the safeties and duck out from under it. If done without the rack, the only way to get out would be to dump the bar over your head, and that could have traumatic results.

The pictures below were taken without weight on the bar so the reader can see the above points demonstrated.

Note that my hamstring injury mentioned earlier in this book occurred while doing GMs. What I think happened is I was having problems keeping my form correct. Specifically, I was trying to keep my legs slightly bent but was having trouble doing so. On the rep that I got injured, maybe my leg had completely straightened, thus putting even more stretch and strain on the hamstring, leading to the injury. Take that as a word of warning.

Hyperextensions – These are another effective low back and hamstring exercise that is similar to good mornings. But with hyperextensions, the machine will hold you in proper form, so they might be a safer alternative to GMs. But again, form is critical. Despite the name, you should *not* "hyper" extend at the top. Stop when the body is straight. Pause, and then slowly lower yourself. Pause, and then start up again. There should be no "swinging" of the body. They should be done in slow, controlled manner. If you experience any undo comfort in the lower back or hamstrings, discontinue them.

To add resistance, weights can be held at the chest. Set the weights on the floor in front of the hyperextension stand and pick them up when in the bottom position. An alternative would be to use a curl bar. Again, set it on the floor and pull it up behind your head and onto the same place you hold the bar for squats. But with either method, there is a limit to how much weight you can add, so adding reps not weight will eventually be the only way to increase resistance.

Note also that these are not as demanding as GMs, possibly because of the machine holding you in place and the lighter weights that are used. They also seem to work mainly the low back while GMs work both the low back and hamstrings. As such, I consider hyperextensions to be a "minor" assistance exercise rather than a "major" one.

Opposite Stance Deadlifts* – If you use a conventional stance, then do sumo stance DLs as an assistance exercise, and vice-a-versa. Conventional stance DLs work the low back and hamstrings more than sumos, while sumos work the hips and quads more than conventional stance DLs, so the two forms complement each other nicely. And you just might find out in time you can actually use more weight on the "opposite stance" and want to switch to it for your competition stance. But whatever the case, it is good to experiment with both stances.

Conventional stance DLs would especially be a good assistance exercise for those who pull sumo. In fact, they would be a safer alternative for low back and hamstring work than the preceding exercises.

Helps the Bottom Part of Deadlifts

Platform Deadlifts* – This exercise is ideal for overcoming difficulties getting the weight off of the floor. There is nothing more embarrassing than to get psyched up for a deadlift at a contest and then to barely budge it! Even if your sticking appoint is later in the lift, Platform Deadlifts (PDLs) will still help as you will be stronger at the bottom and thus have more strength left for later parts of the lift. The same could be said for all of the bottom end exercises in the previous two chapters, but this effect seems to be greater with PDLs.

To do this exercise, you stand on blocks 2-4" high while performing your DLs. If you're doing conventional DLs, you can stand on a couple of 45 or 100 pound plates stacked on top of each other to the desire height, a couple of boards nailed together, or even a couple of stacked rubber mats.

But for sumo DLs, it gets a little trickier. Weight plates will slide if you try to stand on two sets. But a way to avoid this is to set up inside of a power rack. You can wedge the weights against the side of the rack to keep them from slipping. Another option would be to nail together three or four planks, cut to the required length (pictured using four ¾" thick planks). Be sure they're long enough to accommodate your stance but not so wide that you'll hit the planks when you set the weight on the floor.

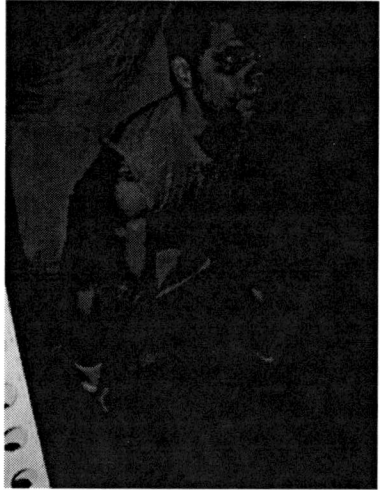

However, even sumo pullers might find it best to do these with a conventional stance, for the reasons mentioned previously.

Helps the Top Part of Deadlifts

Chain, Band, and Reverse Band Deadlifts* – These three exercises will be dealt with in Chapter Thirteen.

Rack Pulls* – As the name implies, these are done in a power rack. Set the pins about 1-2" below the knees or just below wherever your sticking point is. Lift the bar from the pins as if you were completing a DL. The idea here is to overcome a sticking point and to work the top part of the lift. However, be sure to use the same form as you do on regular deadlifts. There is a tendency to alter your form with rack pulls. But if you do, the carry-over will not be as great as expected.

Given the heavy weights utilized, the use of a belt might be prudent when doing this exercise. Most also find they need to wear wrist straps in order to hold onto the bar. These were discussed and pictured in Chapter Two. It should also be noted that rack pulls are a very demanding exercise, so be careful about overtraining. Only do them every other week or even only once a month for this reason.

Upper Back Exercises – The upper back is used greatly in DLs, especially when locking out, so any upper back work would have some carry-over to DLs. But the best types are variations of rows and cable pulls as these most closely approximate the DL movement.

Lat pulldowns and chin-ups/ pull-ups are also very effective lat exercises, but the carry-over to deadlifts would be less than with rows and cable pulls. However, such movements would benefit the bench press as the lats are utilized in a supportive role when benching. As such, a combination of rows/ cable pulls and lat pulldowns/ chin-ups/ pull-ups would probably be best.

Shrugs can also be done to work the traps. When you do shrugs, you're supposed to actually shrug your shoulders! I say this as all too often I've seen guys at gyms pile on hundreds of pounds on the bar, and then barely shrug their shoulders. That would always upset me as that is how bars would get bent at the gym.

Shrugs are another exercise for which wrist straps should be used. But rack pulls and shrugs are the only such exercises. For all other exercises, do not use wrist straps in order to strengthen the grip.

Miscellaneous Exercises

Leg Curls – These are very effective at working the hamstrings. They were invaluable when I was rehabbing my hamstring injury. I intend on doing them at least on occasion from now on in order to prevent such injuries. In fact, after that injury I replaced the FID Bench I had with one that had a leg curl/ extension attachment (pictured).

Side Bends – These are one of best methods there is for working the obliques. Thick obliques are important for providing stability for doing squats and DLs. But since they are basically a "pull" exercise, they are best done on DL days. Do them one side at a time, holding a dumbbell on the side you are bending away from. Do not hold dumbbells in both hands as the weights will offset each other.

It is important to do one or two warm-up sets on each side before doing your work sets. The reason for this is to be sure the obliques are warmed-up so as to prevent injury. Also, as subsequent reps are done you should notice that you can bend a little further, so it would be best to loosen up with warm-up sets so all of your work reps can be done through as full of a range of motion as possible. But be very careful of overtraining your obliques when doing these.

Forearm/ Grip Exercises – Any pulling exercise will work the forearms and improve your gripping strength. However, if you're finding that you're loosing your grip on DLs, then some direct forearm/ gripping work will be needed.

I have always found that reverse curls eliminate any grip problems I might be having. They can be done with a barbell, curl bar, dumbbells, or cable machine.

Wrist curls are another good option. These should be done with both an overhand and an underhand grip. While doing the underhand grip, be sure to "roll" the bar down to your fingertips and roll it back up again before bending your wrists up.

Another good exercise is to use a wrist roller. You can purchase one from APT (pictured) or make it. Get a 2" thick wooden dowel. Drill a hole through the middle, attach a chain to it, and attach a hook of some kind at the other end. You then wrap and hook the chain around a weight. Stand and hold the dowel with the arms bent and elbows at the sides (not arms straight as in the picture). The weight should be on the floor. Roll the weight up and then back down. Do this with both an overhand and an underhand grip.

Biceps Work – The biceps are not really used in DLs or in either of the other two powerlifts. However, there is quite a bit of strain on the biceps when doing DLs. Moreover, with the amount of work the triceps get in training the bench press, it would be prudent to add some bicep work for injury prevention and to maintain muscle balance. The biceps are worked in most upper back exercises, like rows and cable pulls. That will suffice for some, but most will want to add a few "curls for the girls."

A wide variety of curl exercises can be done. But watch your form as many "cheat" so much that the biceps get very little actual work. Using a preacher curl pad when doing curl bar curls will prevent such cheating. My new FID Bench has such an attachment (pictured).

Another great way to do curls is with dumbbells. Let the dumbbells hang at the sides, end facing forward. Then as you curl the weights up, rotate the dumbbells so they are parallel with the torso. This way both functions of the biceps are worked—curling the arm upwards and rotating the forearm.

Similar to this would be Zottman curls. Start with an underhand grip and curl the dumbbells up. At the top rotate your hands so they are now in an overhand position, then curl down. At the bottom, rotate the hands to underhand again, and repeat.

To focus on the rotating forearm function of the biceps and to give the wrist some work, try wrist rotations. For these, weight plates are put on just one side of a dumbbell. Then grasp the dumbbell as far to the other side as possible. Sit on a bench, place the forearm on your thigh, and rotate the wrist.

Chapter Thirteen
Bands and Chains/
Speed Work

The use of bands and chains has been mentioned previously. This chapter will describe their use. Later, speed work will be discussed.

Bands and Chains

The use of bands and chains are especially recommended for those who compete equipped. The bands and chains mimic the effects that the gear gives and provide extra work for the top part of each lift. However, those who compete raw will benefit from their use as well, but such lifters should be sure to balance off band and chain work with exercises that work the bottom part or all aspects of each lift.

Bands

Bands are most popularly used on benches. For this exercise, for someone benching around what I do (220 with a shirt), you need a pair of "mini-bands." Those with bigger benches than I have might need to use two or three sets of bands to give sufficient resistance for the de-sired effect. These bands basically look like fan belts, only a little longer. They are available from APT.

To set-up the bands, loop each end of each band around the bar against the inside collars of the bar so that they will be inside of the weights. Then insert a 70-80 pound dumbbell through the bottom loops. The dumb-bell should then stretch the band so that the dumbbell is resting on the floor. The bands will add about 70 pounds total of resistance at the top of the lift, so just the bands and an empty bar is the equivalent of about 115 pounds at the top.

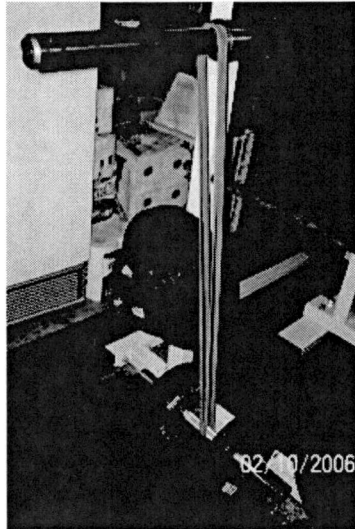

Once the bands are set-up, bench as usual. But what will happen is as the bar is pressed from the chest the bands will stretch and add resistance, so the effect will be that of gradually adding resistance. This is the same effect a bench shirt gives. It helps the most at the bottom of the lift but gradually helps less as the bar is pressed, so, in essence, the weight gets heavier as the bar is pressed. As such, bands are an ideal training method for those who will be competing with a bench shirt.

Along with in mini-band (1/2") size, bands are also available in "light" (1-1/8"), "average" (1-3/4"), and "strong" (2-1/2") sizes. Each larger size gives increasing resistance. These heavier bands are generally used on squats. The light size is for those squatting less than 450 pounds, the average size for those squatting 450-650, and the strong size for those squatting over 650.

When I first tried using light bands on squats, I had a couple of problems setting them up. First, you're supposed to loop the bands over the bar and then "choke" them near the floor around the bottom of the power rack or dumbbells. "Choking" means to wrap the band around the support and then through itself (see picture to the left).

However, the power rack I was using was not bolted down, so I couldn't use it, so I used dumbbells. But the problem was, with as short as I am, the bands are too long. And choking them around the dumbbells didn't do much. So instead, I had to choke them around the bar, wrapping them around a couple of times.

Second, when I initially set them up, I was not able to walk the weight out in the power rack. It jerked me around too much. If I had a monolift to work out with, that would not have been a problem. But eventually, I figured out how to set it up so that I could walk it out. The key was setting things up so you only walk out a very

12/20/20

short distance. It still jerks around some, but not so much as to make it unmanageable (see picture on the preceding page).

Using bands on deadlifts is even trickier. There are two ways to set them up, both of which require the use of a power rack. The first requires a power rack in which the bases on each side are bolted to the floor but are elevated enough that you can get the bands underneath. You choke the bands around each base, wrapping them around three times then pull the other end over the bar, and then deadlift as usual.

However, if your power rack (like mine) does not fit this description, then you will need to use dumbbells. What I do is to put the dumbbells inside of the bases on each side of the power rack. I then choke the bands around the bar, wrapping them three times, and then pull the other end around the dumbbells. But I found this still wasn't short enough, so I had to wrap them twice around the dumbbell bars.

This was easy for me to do since I use changeable dumbbells, so put the bands on first then the weights. But if you're using pre-set dumbbells, then it might be difficult to get the bands wrapped around the dumbbells. But if you can get it set up, the bases will keep the dumbbells from being pulled out underneath the weights. For conventional stance deadlifters, then deadlift as usual. But for sumo stance deadlifters, you have to put your toes in-between the weights on the dumbbells. See picture below for the set-up.

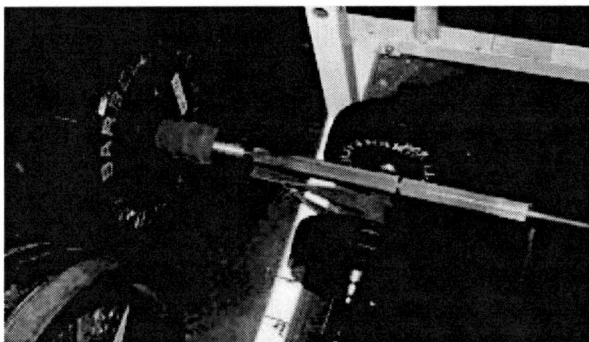

There is also available a jump stretch platform that will make the deadlift set-up easier. The platform is a sheet of metal with metal loops on each side. You wrap the bands around the loops and stand on the sheet metal. Your bodyweight plus the weight of the bar holds the platform down when pulling. There are separate sized platforms for conventional and sumo deadlifts. The latter is rather expensive, which is why I have not bothered with it. But if the reader is interested, it is available from Elite Fitness (see Appendix #1).

Reverse Bands

Another way to use bands is to use light, medium, or heavy bands in a "reverse band" fashion. For this, you choke the bands around the top of a power rack or around safety bars set near the top. You then place the bar through the loops at the bottom and place sufficient weight on the bar to pull it down into place. The bands then give the effect of a suit or shirt in "pulling" the bar up from the bottom, but less so as the bar is raised.

This setup can be used for all three powerlifts. Different placement of the safety bars at the top of the power rack and/ or wrapping the bands around more than one time around the top of the rack when choking them can be used to adjust the height of the bottom of the bands where the bar is placed.

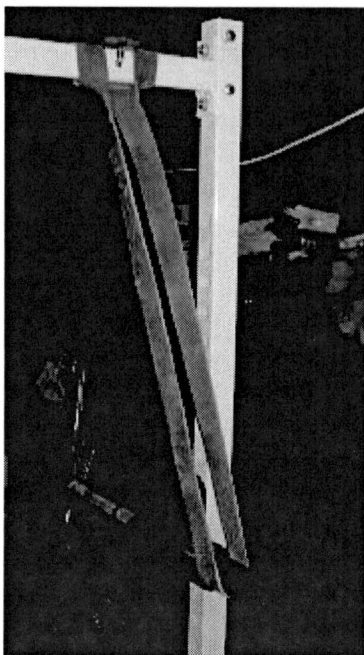

The ideal is to have the band tension setup so that the bands add about what your gear adds. So if your squat gear adds a hundred pounds, then the bands should as well. Pictured is the setup for reverse band squats using average bands.

Chains

Chains are great way to train and are definitely worth the cost. I got my chains from Topper Supply Company (see Appendix #1). They are also available from APT Pro Gear. The idea behind using chains is similar to bands. As you lift the bar, the chains will come off of the floor gradually adding weight to the bar. This will mimic the effect of a bench shirt or squat suit. Ideally, the change in weight from the bottom to the top of the lift should be such that it feels like the effect of your suit or shirt.

Chains are available in 5/8" and ½" sizes. I got the 5/8" size. The full set consists of two each of a main heavy chain, a lighter leader chain, and a metal "triangle" that connects the two. But some chain setups do not use the triangle. The leader chain instead connects directly to the heavy chain. But with the triangle, the total weight is a little over 50 pounds, so just the chains and an empty bar is the equivalent of about 95 pounds at the top of the lift.

As a little tip, the main chains tend to slip off of the "triangle" in the middle of the set-up. So I purchased a couple of pairs of "C-clamps" from a hardware store and use these to hold the chains in place (see the picture to the left). Also from a hardware store, I purchased a couple of clasp-type hooks (the kind used on cable machines in most gyms) to use on the leader chains. These hold better than the hooks that came with the chains.

Initially, I found the change in weight from bottom to top to be sufficient. But later when using better gear, I needed to add another pair of heavy chains to get the right effect. These can be ordered separately. With the two pairs of heavy chains, the total setup weighs about 90 pounds, or about 135 pounds with an empty bar. My multi-ply gear contest bests are 415 – 220 – 410. This will give you some idea of how much chain weight you'll need for each lift.

To set up the chains, the leader chain goes around the bar and then through the triangle, connecting back onto itself. The main chain(s) then hang doubled over the triangle, so that the middle of the chain is over the triangle and each half is hanging down. Loop the leader chains over the bar and hook the clasps onto the leader chains so the length of the main chain is such that at the top position as much chain as possible is off of the floor but is still touching the floor. In the bottom position as much of the main chain as possible should be lying on the floor. Pictured to the right is the setup for chain squats.

Later I got some chain collars from APT. The chains attach to the collars, then the collars slide onto the bar like regular collars.

For squats and benches the leader chains should be placed inside of the weights, against the inside collars of the bar. But for deadlifts, I put the triangles directly on the bar, placed at the ends of the bar to

173

prevent setting the weights down on the chains. They can be kept in place by using two sets of clip-type collars, one on each side of the triangles. I still use the leader chain, hanging it from the triangle with the heavy chains just for the little extra weight.

Also for deadlifts, I like to I lay out the chains away from the bar for each set. This makes the first rep very difficult since the chains have to drag across the floor towards the weights. As such, this setup is beneficial even for raw lifters. After the first rep, the chains bunch up underneath the bar, so there is less resistance at the start. This makes the rest of the reps more then for top end work. See the picture to the left for the setup for the start of deadlifts.

Advantages of Bands and Chains

There are several advantages to using bands and chains over other forms of assistance exercises and even over doing the actual powerlifts with gear.

First, the point of using chains and bands is that the "feel" of the lift is very similar to doing the actual powerlift with gear. There is more tension at the top of the lift than at the bottom. Yet, they are all full range of motion exercises and thus the carryover to the actual powerlifts is greater than when doing partial movements (like board benches).

Second, chains and bands provide variety into the workout. I mention in various places in this book the importance of periodically changing your assistance exercises. This is so that your body does not adapt to a particular exercise. But by training the actual powerlifts every workout, your body will adapt to them, and that could lead to stagnation. One approach to try to keep this adaptation from happening is to cycle from higher to lower reps. Alternating the actual powerlifts with chain and band work is another way of changing the exercise and thus preventing stagnation.

Third, putting on a tight suit or shirt and wrapping your knees for every set is difficult and time-consuming, so workouts with gear tend to be rather long. But setting up the chains and bands is relatively easier and quicker, so the workouts are shorter. Workouts with gear also seem to be more demanding on the body than working with chains and bands. So using the chains and bands instead of gear on the powerlifts for some of the workouts gives a break from the difficulties of using gear but still provides a similar training effect.

Fourth, when doing chain and band work, it is best not to wear any supportive gear, not even a belt. This way, the joints and low back get strengthened. However, since the tension is sub-maximal when the joints are at their least advantageous position (such as the bottom position of a squat), the risk of injury is far less than it would be doing the actual powerlifts raw.

Speed Work

Researchers at the College of New Jersey recently discovered that adding a jump squat to your workout can boost strength by as much as 13 percent in 5 weeks. In the study, men who did jump squats twice a week during the last third of a 15-week program improved their standard barbell squats by an average of 66 pounds. "The jump squat trains your muscles for explosive power, a stimulus for gains that traditional lifting doesn't provide," says lead study author Jay Hoffman, PhD. Try adding the move to your routine (*Men's Health* magazine. May 2006, p.52).

Speed work (a.k.a. explosive work, dynamic work) is not done very often by those who lift weights. In fact, later in the same issue of *Men's Health*, the following factoid is give, "9 – percentage of men who incorporate explosive training into their workouts" (p.166). However, as the above quote indicates, speed work can be very beneficial to strength gains. There are various movements that can be done, which will be described in this chapter.

Performing Jump Squats

Men's Health describes the performance of jump squats:
Stand with your feet slightly more than shoulder-width apart and hold a pair of light dumbbells at your sides. Lower your body until your thighs are parallel to the floor, then bend forward slightly at the hips so your shoulders move in front of your feet. Push off of the floor explosively to jump straight up

as high as possible. Land with your knees soft and immediately sink down into your next squat.

The plan: Do four sets of five repetitions in weeks 1 and 3, and four sets of eight reps in weeks 2 and 4 (May 2006, p.166).

Jump squats can also be done with a light barbell. The only difficulty is trying to hold the bar down to keep it from flying up off of the shoulders. But then, I read on a Web page somewhere that if the bar isn't coming up off of your shoulders, you're not doing them correctly.

However, there is a risk of injury doing jump squats. Most obviously, you could twist an ankle. Second, you could pull a muscle. And third, long-term, they are hard on the knees.

But to lessen the risk of the first, you just need to be careful and really concentrate while doing them. And wear sneakers with a heel. The heel will balance you. On the second potential problem, be sure you are warmed up before doing them. On the third point, again, wear good sneakers, and only do them occasionally, not every week year-round.

On the sets and reps, some recommend a "speed day" separate from your regular workout which involves doing eight sets of three reps. To be clear, the speed work is the primary thing done on that day. The reps are kept low as this more approximates the powerlifter's goal of a 1RM.

But many other powerlifters do their speed work after their regular lifts. And in that case, only 3-4 sets should be done. But with either method, take 30-60 seconds rest between sets. As for reps, I've found that from 3-6 reps works best.

Jump Deadlifts/ Clean-Shrugs

Similar to jump squats is "jump deadlifts." These are done the same way as jump squats but with holding the bar in deadlift position and taking a deadlift stance. But a couple of points need to be noted in doing them.

First, it is best to use an overhand grip with both hands rather than the normal "mixed grip" that most powerlifters use on deadlifts (one hand overhand, one underhand). With a mixed grip, the bicep on the arm in the underhand position gets jerked on the way down and a pulled muscle could easily result. But this shouldn't be problem in the overhand position.

Second, if you use enough weight, you'll only jump a few inches off the ground. This is true for jump squats as well. In fact, most likely, both lifts are safer if you use more weight and jump lower than if you use less weight and jump higher. There's less risk of twisting an ankle or a pulling a muscle with a lower jump.

But how much weight should be used? Not much. For my first workout doing them, I did a warm-up set with just the bar, and then added a pair of 25s for a total of 95 pounds. That seemed about right. After a couple of weeks, I was up to using 115. For comparison, I deadlifted 400 at a preceding contest. This means we're talking about using about one-quarter of your 1RM.

Third, the first time I did jump deadlifts, I was using my toes/ calves too much. But with practice, I learned to push up more from my heels like on regular deadlifts. The idea on each rep is to drop down as much as possible, then explode up, using your entire lower body.

Fourth, even if you wear wrestling or similar shoes without a heel for regular deadlifts, you should wear sneakers with a heel for jump deadlifts. You need the heel to cushion the landing and for balance.

A variant of jump deadlifts is clean-shrugs. The difference with clean-shrugs is your feet do not leave the floor. You raise the bar quickly off of the floor, and then come up on your toes and purposely shrug your shoulders, keeping the arms as straight as possible throughout. Either would work for explosive work.

Explosive Push-ups

For working the upper body and as assistance for bench presses, explosive push-ups are a good speed exercise. The idea here is simple. You do push-ups as normal, except you push up hard enough so that your hands come off of the floor. You then "catch" yourself on the way down. There are two ways to do these to be sure you are exploding up on each rep.

The first is to do "clap" push-ups. When your hands come off the floor, you clap once then quickly put them back in push-up position. In order to have time to do the clap, you have to really push yourself up into the air, so the clap ensures that you explode up on each rep.

Another method would be what I call "Rocky" push-ups. These are seen in the training sequence in the first *Rocky* movie. Rocky did one-arm push-ups, alternating arms in a quick fashion. Specifically, you push-up with one hand while holding the other hand behind your back. Then while you are in the air, quickly alternate arms and do another rep. By putting one arm behind your back, it forces you to push up hard into the air so you have time to switch arms. For a good demonstration of these, watch the movie! If you haven't seen it, it is an excellent movie, one of my all-time favorites.

In any case, done either way, explosive push-ups really pump up the chest and work well for explosive/ speed work.

The Olympic Lifts

Olympic weightlifters perform the snatch and the clean and jerk. Both of these are explosive movements. However, the skill level is very high on both of these exercises, so much so that I won't even attempt to describe them in writing.

Basically, I would say you should only do these movements if you have someone who knows what they are doing coaching you on the proper execution. Otherwise, you could easily end up hurting yourself. But with such a coach, these exercises would be excellent ways to develop explosiveness.

Chain and Band Speed Work

All three powerlifts can be performed in a speed fashion. The idea here is simple; you keep the weights light and just do the lifts as normal but in a very rapid fashion. However, where the problem comes in is at the top of each lift.

On squats, if you squat up fast, you most likely will end up doing jump squats, with your feet coming up off of the floor and the bar off of you back. The only way to avoid this would be to purposely slow down near the top of the lift. But then half of your effort will be spent slowing down rather than exploding. A similar situation would exist with deadlifts. On benches, if you push the bar up in a rapid fashion, it will "jerk" your arms at the end, possibly leading to joint problems. But a way to avoid these problems would be utilize chains and bands.

With the resistance being lower at the bottom of the lift, you can really "explode" out of the bottom. You then try to maintain your speed as much as possible throughout the movement. But with the resistance getting greater as you go up, you'll inevitably slow your ascent. By the time you get to the top, the resistance will have slowed you down so there will be not any "jerking" at the top, and the potential problems described above will be avoided.

Speed squats, benches, and deadlifts can be performed using chains, bands, and reverse bands. You could also do overhead presses, rows, and other exercises with chains and bands. The sets, reps, a rest

178

periods should be similar as for jump squats and deadlifts and explosive push-ups. Keep the reps rather low and the rest periods between sets short.

As for weight, it is generally recommended to use about half of what you can do for your 1RM. So if you can squat 400 pounds, you would use 200 pounds for your speed work. But note, this 200 pounds includes the bar weight plus the weight of the chains or the amount of resistance the bands add. The latter can be hard to gauge, but with a little experience you will get a feel for how much resistance the bands are adding.

It should be noted that using chains and bands for speed work is more suited to equipped lifters than raw lifters. The reason is, with the light weights and deloading of the chain and bands, there is very little tension at the bottom of each lift. So raw lifters will not be getting much work at all in the part of the lift where they need the most work.

Instead, raw lifters might want to try doing the powerlifts in speed fashion without chains or bands. As discussed, this can have drawbacks, but with practice, you can get the hang of it and learn how to do them without the previously mentioned problems.

Short, Very Intense Cardio

The idea of doing short, very intense cardio was mentioned previously in this book. The idea is to do just a few minutes of cardio but at a very intense pace. It was said that this provides the same cardiovascular benefit as two hours of cardio done at a moderate pace. But another benefit of such cardio is that it functions as speed work.

Specifically, it was mentioned that I do step-ups on my squat box on squat days, I hit a heavy bag on bench days, and on deadlift days I jump rope. It was also said that a speed bag would work for use on bench assistance days.

Each of these exercise are by their very nature speed work. In fact, boxers have long utilized a speed bag and jumping rope for their "speed work."

To be even more speed-like, jump-ups onto a box can be done instead of step-ups. But be very careful you don't fall and get injured. Also, to provide some cushioning, I nailed a portion of a rubber floor mat on the top of my wooden squat box.

My Plan

For quite some time I did speed work after my regular workouts using jump squats and deadlifts and explosive push-ups or chains and bands. But I never felt they benefited me that greatly.

However, I also tried doing speed benches on my bench assistance day instead of other kinds of bench assistance, and that worked out well. But I think the reason it did so was not so much because it developed "explosiveness" as is claimed but simply because it was a light workout. More about what to do on bench assistance day will be discussed in the next chapter.

But here, it will be said that now I mainly use the short, very intense cardio at the end of my workouts. That way, I kill two birds with one stone so to speak, getting in both my cardio and my speed work in at just six minutes. But the key is to do them in a truly intense and thus quick fashion.

Jump Rope

My initial jump rope was just a cheap, plain rope. But I now use one that has beads on it. I know that sounds girlish, but the beads are red and black, my favorite color scheme, just like most of my power gear and the cover of this book.

But the important point is the beads serve a purpose; they add centrifugal force to the rope. That keeps the rope circling outward and makes jumping easier. With my old jump rope, I'd mess up and have to re-start about every 20 seconds or so. But with the beaded rope, I am able to jump my planned several minutes without messing up. Jumping straight through is much harder than getting a "break" every time I'd mess up, so the training effect is better.

Section Four

Putting it all Together

Chapter Fourteen
Training Routine Format

It is now time to put together the information from the preceding chapters into possible training routine formats. Four similar but somewhat different formats will be presented.

Workouts Splits

For each routine, lift four days a week, rotating through four basic workouts: Squat/ Bench/ Deadlift/ Bench Assistance. But how the body parts are split up and how many exercises and sets are done vary somewhat between the routines.

Split One:

For quite some time after I started powerlifting again, I used the following split:

The outline is:
Day One: Squat, Upper Back.
Day Two: Bench, Arms, Abs.
Day Three: Deadlift.
Day Four: Bench Assistance, Arms, Abs.

Day One:
Squat
One Major Squat Assistance Exercise
Two Upper Back Exercises

Day Two:
Bench
One Major Bench Assistance Exercise
One Curl Exercise
1-2 Ab Exercises

Day Three:
Deadlift
One Major Deadlift Assistance Exercise
Leg Curls
Calves Raises

Day Four:
Two Major Bench Assistance Exercises
One Reverse Curl Exercise
1-2 Ab Exercises

The main idea here is to follow up each powerlift with one major assistance exercise, then on bench assistance day to do two major bench assistance exercises. The upper back work on Day One offsets the upper back work from deadlifts on Day Four.

With doing the powerlifts each week, this split works well with the first three cycles described in Chapter Eight, namely, the Basic Cycle, the Mini-Cycles, and the Alternate High/ Low Reps plan.

When using this split, I only did two work sets for all exercises. This split worked well over a period of time. However, there were two main problems with it.

First off, Day One was always longer than the other three workouts. The reason for this was two-fold. First, squats tend to take longer than benches or deadlifts, especially when lifting equipped. Second, moving from legs to upper back was a major change and required doing almost the same number of warm-ups for the first upper back exercise as for the first exercise of the day.

The second problem with this split is the workouts in general tended to take too long.

Split Two:

For the preceding reasons, I eventually moved to a different split. It was also here that I started doing the short, intense cardio at the end of my workouts and started including more isolation work. I also became more specific on the type of assistance exercises to do as I had figured out what worked best.

The outline is:
Day One: Squat, Abs, Cardio
Day Two: Bench, Upper Back, Cardio.
Day Three: Deadlift, Abs, Cardio.
Day Four: Bench Assistance, Upper Back, Arms, Rotator Cuff.

Day One:
Squats or Major Squat Assistance Exercise
Leg Extensions and/ or Calves Raises
Lower Abs Exercise
Step-ups

Day Two:
Bench or Major Bench Assistance Exercise
Row-type Upper Back Exercise
Curl or Reverse Curl Exercise
Heavy Bag

Day Three:
Deadlift or Major Deadlift Assistance Exercise
Leg Curls and/ or Hyperextensions
Upper Abs Exercise
Jump Rope

Day Four:
Bench Assistance Exercise
Chest and/ or Shoulder Isolation Exercise
Lat pulldown/ Pull-ups-type Upper Back Exercise
Triceps Exercise
Rotator Cuff

The biggest change from the preceding split is to do only one main exercise on each workout day rather than two, so for instance, either squats or one squat assistance exercise is done. As such, this split works best with last three cycles mentioned in Chapter Eight, namely, the Alternate Weeks routine, the Four Week Rotation, and the Off-season/ In-Season plan.

When using this split, initially I did four work sets on the power-lifts or major assistance work so the total number of work sets would be the same as with the previous split, but I found that to be too much, so I dropped to three work sets. But some might be able to handle four sets. In that case, you might want to skip the following minor assistance exercise. I continued with two sets for all minor assistance work.

With only doing one major exercise, there is time savings not having to move from one major exercise to another.

The other big change was to split up the upper back work from two exercises being done on squat day, to one exercise being done on each bench day. With the upper back also being worked on deadlift day, I was initially concerned this would lead to overtraining the upper back, but I found this was not a problem as long as I only did two work sets on each upper back exercise. With working upper back after benches rather than squats, not as many warm-ups sets are needed.

I also found it best to include one row-type exercise (where the bar is pulled towards the chest from the front), and one exercise where the resistance is upward, as in lat pulldowns and pull-ups.

For the previous split, I worked abs on bench days to even up the length of the workouts. But this did not fit as well as working abs on squat and DL days, so I moved the ab work to those days. That then gave me time to add triceps work on the bench assistance day.

I also only did one main exercise on bench assistance day, but again, for three work sets.

Split Three:

The above split worked well with the Off-season/ In-Season routine, but when I decided to go back to using the Alternate Weeks routine, I wanted something a little different. This split combines elements of the previous two.

The outline is:
Day One: Squat, Abs, Cardio
Day Two: Bench, Upper Back, Cardio.
Day Three: Deadlift, Abs, Cardio.
Day Four: Bench Assistance, Upper Back, Arms, Rotator Cuff.

Week A:

Day One:
Two Major Squat Assistance Exercises
Upper Abs Exercise
Step-ups

Day Two:
Two Major Bench Assistance Exercises
Row-type Upper Back Exercise
Heavy Bag

Day Three:
Two Major Deadlift Assistance Exercises
Lower Abs Exercise
Jump Rope

Day Four:
Two Bench Assistance Exercises
Lat pulldown/ Pull-ups-type Upper Back Exercise
Biceps Exercise
Rotator Cuff

Week B:

Day One:
Squats
Calves Raises
Upper Abs Exercise
Step-ups

Day Two:
Bench
Chest, Shoulder, or Triceps Isolation Exercise
Row-type Upper Back Exercise
Heavy Bag

Day Three:
Deadlift
Leg Curls or Hyperextensions
Lower Abs Exercise
Jump Rope

Day Four:
Two Bench Assistance Exercises
Lat pulldown/ Pull-ups-type Upper Back Exercise
Forearms Exercise
Rotator Cuff Exercise

The basic pattern here is to do two major assistance exercises during Week A and on Bench Assistance day, but only two work sets are done for each exercise. Then the actual powerlifts are performed during Week B for three or four work sets, combined with one minor assistance exercises for two work sets. But again, that following exercise can be skipped if four work sets are done on the powerlift. Two work sets are also performed for the rest of the exercises.

The reason for going back to two major assistance exercises is so that a top end and a bottom end or all aspects exercise can be done for each lift each routine.

Split Four:

This final split works best with the Alternate High/ Low Reps routine. Like Split One, the powerlifts are done each week followed by one major assistance exercise, both for two work sets. The rest of the

187

exercises are the same as for Split Three, so there is no reason to lay-out the format. But some might want to skip the minor assistance exercises to keep the workouts from getting too lengthy.

The main point is, by doing the actual powerlift each week, the reps can be alternated. Then by following the powerlift with one major assistance exercise, both a top-end and a bottom-end or all aspects exercise can be included with each routine by alternating weeks.

Following are pairings for the assistance exercises that will work well for this and the preceding split.

For this split, I would recommend following the completely raw, high reps powerlift with a top-end exercise, and the equipped, low reps powerlift with a bottom-end or all aspects exercise. In that way, all parts of each powerlift are worked each week. For Split Three, raw lifters should do the bottom-end or all aspects exercise first; equipped lifters should do the top-end exercise first.

Squats
Low Squats / Partial Squats
Dead Stop Squats / Reverse Band Squats
Pause Squats / Chain Squats
Manta Ray Squats / Band Squats
Sting Ray Squats / Reverse Band Squats

Bench:
Dumbbell Bench / Lockouts or Board Benches
Pause Bench / Close Grip Bench
Legs up Bench / Chain, Band, or Reverse Band Bench

Deadlifts:
Platform DLs / Rack Pulls
Reverse Band DLs / SLDLs
Chain DLs / GMs and Shrugs
Conventional DLs / Platform DLs (for raw, sumo pullers)

On the second DL pairing, even though SLDLs would be the more important exercise for raw lifters, I found that it was best to do it second so as to be more thoroughly warmed up. Also, my low back was too sore if I did the SLDLs first to effectively work the RB DLs.

Finally, just to note a point, I've presented all of these routines in the order of Squat/ Bench/ Deadlift/ Bench Assistance as that is easiest to remember. But after a contest I generally do the Bench Assistance workout first, as it just seems most natural to start with Bench Assistance day since of course the three powerlifts were done at the contest.

188

Bench Assistance Day

The kind of major assistance exercises done on bench assistance day deserves special mention. But first, there are some powerlifters who only lift three days a week with the following split:

Monday: Squat
Wednesday: Bench
Friday: Deadlift

However, I always found this split to be rather strange. You are in essence working the lower body twice a week but the upper body only once a week. Moreover, most find that only working the bench once a week is not sufficient work. On the other hand, most also find that doing heavy benches twice a week is just too much.

Back in my college lifting days, it was common for lifters to do a "light" bench workout on the second bench day. This would involve doing regular benches but not pushing very hard. That type of program does work well, but it always seemed like a waste of time to always be doing a light workout once a week.

For that reason, many lifters will do only bench assistance work on the second day. In this way, the benching muscles are still being worked but in a somewhat different fashion on each day. That difference enables you to work hard on both days. This makes sense as it is actually the pattern with the squat and deadlift days. Both lifts work the lower body, but in a different manner.

But I found that not just any bench assistance exercise would do. If I did say band benches on bench assistance day, that would still be too much. The problem is the difference between regular benches and band benches is not great enough.

So instead, I found that if I did what I call "non-flat bench assistance" that would work out well. By this, I mean incline or decline benches, overhead presses, and dips. All four exercises work the pressing muscles but from a different angle than benches. This enables full effort to be exerted on both Bench and Bench Assistance day.

Another popular thing to do on Bench Assistance day is speed work. I found this also works very well. With doing speed benches on a separate day, then up to eight sets can be done. But with less than a minute rest between sets, the workout does not take that long.

However, I do not think it works because of anything "special" about speed work. I think it works mainly because doing even eight sets of speed work is still a light workout as only very light weights are used. As such, the separate speed day is really not much different from what powerlifters did back in my college lifting days.

So either non-flat bench assistance exercises or speed benches work well for the main exercise(s) on bench assistance day. The reader will need to experiment to see which works best for you.

Personally, I prefer the non-flat exercises as this enables me to incorporate different exercises into my routine. If I am using Split Two, I alternate weeks, doing an exercise for the lower pecs (e.g., declines or dips) one week and an exercise for the upper pecs and shoulders (e.g., inclines or presses) the next week. If I am using the other splits, Week A I do declines and presses, then Week B I do inclines and dips.

All that said, if you are only able to lift three days a week, then it is possible to do so by using any of the preceding four days a week plans but only lift three days a week. In this way, you would only be doing each basic workout every 9-10 days rather than once a week. Some might even find this extra rest time to be beneficial, but others will find it to be too long of rest between working the same lift. But it is an option if time is short. Another option is presented next.

Two Days a Week Plan

It was mentioned in Chapter Seven that it is possible to lift only twice a week and make progress. But it was also said that a potential problem is that it does not leave much time for variety.

However, a way to at least partially remedy that problem would be to use an Alternate Weeks Routine. In this way, major assistance work can be included in the routine. A basic plan would be as follows.

Week A/ Day One:
Major Squat Assistance Exercise
Major Bench Assistance Exercise
Row-type Upper Back Exercise
Upper Abs Exercise

Week A/ Day Two:
Major Deadlift Assistance Exercise
Bench Assistance Exercise
Biceps Exercise
Lower Abs Exercise

Week B/ Day One:

Squats

Benches

Lat pulldown/ Pull-ups-type Upper Back Exercise

Upper Abs Exercise

Week B/ Day Two:

Deadlift

Bench Assistance Exercise

Forearms Exercise

Lower Abs Exercise

With only one major assistance exercise being done for each lift, it would be best to choose exercises that work all aspects of the lift.

Another option would be to use an Off-Season/ In-season routine. In that case, two different major assistance exercises can be alternated during the off-season, one a top-end exercise and the other a bottom end or all aspects exercise. But then the actual powerlifts should be done each week during the in-season.

With only one exercise being done for each body area each workout, it would probably be best to do three work sets for each exercise.

Assistance Exercises Selection

With any of the preceding workout splits, it is easy to plug in assistance exercises to do. The following list of different possibilities is provided so the reader can easily pick an exercise for one routine, but then find an alternative exercise to switch to for the next routine. When possible, choosing a bottom-end or all aspects assistance exercise plus a top-end exercise each routine is a good plan for all types of lifters. Most of these exercises were discussed in Section Three.

For Top-End Work:

Powerlifts done with bands, reverse bands, or chains.

Partial movements: partial squats, bench squats, board benches, bench rack lockouts, floor benches, rack pulls.

Close grip benches would also be included here.

For Bottom-End Work:

Squats: low squats, dead stop squats, box squats, pause squats.

Benches: wide grip benches, 3-count pause benches, cambered bar benches.

Deadlifts: Platform deadlifts.

For All Aspects Work:

Squats: Manta Ray (high bar; close stance) squats, Sting Ray (front) squats, wide stance squats, lunges, leg presses.

Benches: Dumbbell benches (alternating arms or arms together), feet on bench benches, reverse grip benches.

Non-flat bench assistance: Incline benches, decline benches, overhead presses (barbell or dumbbells for preceding three exercises), dips on dip bars or on gymnastic rings, upright rows.

Deadlifts: stiff leg deadlifts, opposite stance deadlifts, good mornings and shrugs.

Note that since good mornings only work the lower back, it is good to combine them with shrugs to work both the lower and upper back. Those two exercises together would then constitute the one deadlift assistance exercise.

Note also that hyperextensions could be used in the place of GMs. However, I consider them more of a minor assistance exercise, as they are not as demanding as GMs or other deadlift assistance exercises.

Additional Exercises:

Note: Full descriptions of all of these options are beyond the scope of this book. But videos of most of these exercises being performed are available on this writer's fitness Web site (see Appendix #3).

Row-type upper back exercise: Barbell rows (with a wide, medium, or close grip), dumbbells rows (with elbows out, elbows in, or underhand), curl bar rows, cable pulls, various row machines.

Lat Pulldown exercises: Done overhand with a wide, medium, or close grip, with an underhand grip, a mixed grip (one hand overhand, one hand underhand; reverse hands each set), or a "V" grip handle.

Pull-ups exercises: Done with an overhand grip (pull-ups), underhand grip (chin-ups), mixed grip, parallel grip, or using a "V" grip handle placed over the pull-up bar (alternate on each rep which side the head goes to).

Chest isolation exercises: Flyes, Peck Deck, Cable crossovers.

Shoulder isolation exercises: Front or side dumbbell laterals.

Triceps exercises: Triceps extensions/ presses (using a barbell, dumbbells, curl bar, or triceps bar, and done standing, sitting or lying, a.k.a. "skull crushers"), triceps pushdowns (using a straight bar, curved bar, or pulley strap), various arm machines.

Biceps exercises: Barbell curls, dumbbell curls, curl bar curls, preacher's curls, Zottman curls, hammer curls, cable curls, various arm machines, wrist rotations.

Forearms exercises: Reverse barbell curls, reverse dumbbell curls, reverse curl bar curls, reverse preacher's curls, wrist curls (palms up and palms down), wrist roller.

Rotator Cuff exercises: Lying, up/ lying, down/ lying, out/ lying, in/ sitting, front/ sitting, side/ lying on side/ Shoulder Horn (arms together or alternating arms).

Leg curls and leg extensions exercises: Legs together or alternating legs, done on a variety of machines or using ankle weights.

Calves exercises: Standing (barbell or dumbbell), sitting (barbell or dumbbell, various calves machines.

Upper abs exercises: Crunches, decline crunches, sit-ups, decline sit-ups, crunch-side-bend combo/ Twisting versions of: crunches, decline crunches, sit-ups, decline sit-ups.

Lower abs exercises: Reverse crunches, dip bar (or hanging) reverse crunches, leg raises, dip bar (or hanging) leg raises/ one-leg dip bar (or hanging) leg raises, Twisting versions of reverse crunches, dip bar reverse crunches, leg raises, dip bar leg raises.

Upper and lower abs: Bicycle abs, crunch-reverse crunch combo, various abs machines. Note: For any given routine, be sure to include at least one twisting exercise or side bends to work the obliques.

Yearly Training Program

It's now time to put all of the preceding information together into a yearly training program. First to be looked at is post-contest plans.

I usually work out on Sunday, Monday, Wednesday, and Thursday. If the contest had been on a Saturday, I will usually wait until Thursday or Friday of the following week for my first workout, which will be a bench assistance workout. That way, I have a full 4-5 days rest. My next workout will then be squats on Sunday, over a week after the contest, benches Monday, and deadlifts on Wednesday, and bench assistance again on Thursday, and so on.

If I am going to be using an Alternating Weeks routine, this will give me two different sets of workouts. It will thus take me two full weeks to put in each of my eight workouts. For each of these first workouts I might follow the suggestion of doing sets of six reps until I do one relatively heavy set for each main exercise for each workout.

After the second week, it will be time to start working harder. I will do my warm-ups as described previously, and then start with a little more weight than for the top set of six I used in my previous workout. I will then increase the weights for the second set for the drop reps approach, doing four reps. I'll then be going 2 x 5-6, 3-4.

If I am doing three work sets on the powerlifts, I will increase the weights for each set so as try to do 6, 5, 4 reps. I'll stick with that for a couple to a few weeks.

For example, below is how my weights and reps progressed on squats in my most recent routine, using an Alternating Weeks routine. This routine started after a four week break, so I used two weeks of doing sets of six rather than just one. This gave me time to get back in lifting shape and my weights back up before tackling heavy workouts. Warm-ups are in brackets. All lifts were done completely raw.

Week 2:   [45/15, 95/8, 135/6, 185/6] 205/6
Week 4:   [45/15, 115/8, 155/5, 195/3] 215/6, 225/6, 235/6
Week 6:   [45/15, 115/8, 170/5, 225/3] 245/6, 255/5, 265/3
Week 8:   [45/15, 115/8, 170/5, 225/3] 245/6, 257/5, 270/4
Week 10: [45/15, 125/8, 190/5, 230/3] 255/6, 267/5, 280/4

At this point, it will time to get into heavier lifting. So I might simply add twice as much weight between sets and thus use the 5-6, 3-4, 1-2 plan. Or I might switch to the "drop reps with back-ff set" scheme.

If I am going to be using the Alternate High/ Low Reps routine, then the first week (lifting completely raw), I will work up to one somewhat hard set of eight reps, maybe followed by a somewhat hard set of six. The second week (using gear), I will work up to one somewhat hard set of four reps and maybe of two reps. I will then increase the weights the next two weeks and go into the regular pattern of 2 x 7-8, 5-6 odd numbered weeks and 2 x 3-4, 1-2 even-numbered weeks.

Another option will be to follow the same sets and reps scheme as my previous routine, but to drop all of the weights by about 10 percent. For instance, if I am using the "drop reps with back-off set" scheme and my last squat workout before a contest went 300/3, 325/1, 250/7, then my first workout after the contest I might go 270/4, 295/2, 225/8. I will then gradually work back up from there.

The most important point of all of this is that at the start of each new routine, and especially right after a contest, you need to "deload" by cutting back on the volume, intensity, and/ or poundage and gradually work back up. It is a good idea to "deload" on cardio work as well. To do so, at the start of a new routine, cut back on the time and intensity of your cardio and then gradually work back up.

That said, my last heavy workout before a contest will be about a week before, depending on how my workout rotation goes. Ideally, I want to have at least a week of rest after my last workout for each lift but less than two weeks.

Then the last week before a contest will be mainly rest or maybe a light workout or two. If my last heavy workout for a lift is close to two weeks before the contest, then I will probably put in a light workout for that lift about a week before. That workout will consist of my planned warm-up sets and opener for the contest. The next chapter will discuss picking contest attempts.

After a contest, again, I will take several days off and then start all over again. When I do, I will start a new routine with different assistance exercises from my previous routine. If there is an extended time between contests, then I will probably use two or three 8-12 week routines between contests or use the Off-Season/ In-Season routine.

As for how many contests to enter a year, in college, I entered as many as 4-5 contests a year. But after my 21 year break from competing, the first year I started competing again I entered three contests. Since then, I have entered only one or two a year.

But entering only one contest a year is not really enough. I have done so on occasion because health or other problems forced me to forgo entering a second planned contest. However, only one contest a year is simply too much time between contests. It also puts too much "pressure" on having to perform well at that one contest with not having competed for twelve months.

However, entering more than three contests a year is just too much. Most likely, at best, you will just keep totaling the same amount contest to contest. You might even find your lifts dropping contest to contest. There is always a drop in strength after a contest, and with entering more than three contests a year, there simply will not be enough time to recover and get your lifts back up for the next contest.

As such, I would say the ideal would be to plan on entering 2-3 contests a year.

Ideally, I like to have my contests for the next year planned out at the beginning of the year. This can be done by checking *Powerlifting USA* and the Web sites for various federations. This is not always possible, but at the least it helps to know when your next contest will be several months in advance.

Also, given that I live in Pittsburgh, I try to avoid contests in the winter. I am just too fearful that I will be prepared for a contest when a major snowstorm will hit and prevent travel to the contest. So my "contest season" lasts from early spring to late autumn. I would guess many lifters have a similar schedule.

What this means is, the ideal time to take an extended break would be after the last contest in the fall or maybe over the Christmas holiday season. You should then have plenty of time to get prepared for a contest in the spring.

It was only this past year that I first took an extended break in December 2008/ January 2009. I actually had planned on entering a contest in January for the first time as there was to be a contest near my home. But I was forced to forgo the contest and take a break when I felt my body was breaking down. As it turned out, there was a snowstorm that day, and I later found out only a dozen lifters showed up.

In any case, it was with having to take that break that I realized what had been missing in my training, an extended break. Since I had started lifting six and half years before, I had not taken more than a week off at a time. That may sound like dedication, but in fact, the lack of a longer break probably hurt my long term progress. So take the tip, and take a longer break once a year.

The next chapter will present detailed training logs so the reader can see how all of the points presented in this chapter and in this book work out in actual practice.

Chapter Fifteen
Sample Workout Logs

This chapter will reprint a sampling of my workout logs from the last couple of years. The first two sets of workouts were my workouts leading up to contests. For both of these, I was competing in the 114 pound weight class and in the Open and Masters II (45-49) divisions.

In these logs, warm-ups are in brackets. All weights are in pounds. Workout times include set-up, warm-up, lifting, cardio (if done), stretching (if done), and clean up.

When I post my logs on my Web site, I often include comments about the workouts. Those are omitted here unless they are needed to understand the logs. The logs are also modified somewhat for use here.

For the first of these logs I was using spin-lock collars that weighed five pounds each. I usually leave the collars on the bar after my workouts and thus for my first warm-up set the next workout. As such, for some workouts, my first warm-up set was 55/15, and my second set with a pair of 45s added was 145/8. But later, I got a pair of metal Quicklee collars, which weigh just one pound each. I ignore that weight, so just the bar is 45 pounds and with a pair of 45s, 135 pounds. Always be sure to account for differing collar weights.

Alternate High/ Low Reps Routine

The first sets of workouts were leading up to IPA Pennsylvania State Championships, Saturday September 22, 2007, for which I wore multi-ply gear. I used the Alternate High/ Low Reps routine from Chapter 8 and something similar to Split Three from Chapter 14, except Week A I did the powerlifts completely raw followed by the powerlifts done with chains or bands, both for two work sets. For Week B, I used a 3 x 3, 2, 1 rep scheme on the equipped powerlifts. I was only working out three times a week at this time.

Week 7 of 8

Bench Assistance
Wednesday – 8/29/07

Speed Band Bench (mini-bands): [45/15, 95/10, add bands: 45/6, 60/3]
70/3 x 5 (weight/reps x sets)
Standing Barbell Press: [45/10, 60/6, 75/3] 85/6, 95/4

Curl Bar Rows: [65/6, 90/3] 105/5, 105/5
Reverse Curl Bar Curls: [40/10] 52/10, 52/10
Rotator Cuff (two exercises): [10/10] 13/12, 13/12
Stretching: ~10 minutes
Workout Time: 1:30 (hour: minutes)

Squats
Friday – 8/31/07

Completely Raw Squats: [55/15, 145/10, 195/6, 235/3] 255/6, 265/5
Reverse Band Squat (average bands): [255/6, 315/3] 350/3, 350/3
Twisting Leg Raises (reps to each side): 17, 11
Stretching: ~10 minutes
Workout Time: 1:37

Benches
Labor Day – 9/3/07

Completely Raw Bench: [45/15, 95/10, 115/6, 130/3] 145/6, 155/6
Chain Bench (set-up weighs about 90 pounds):
[55/6, 90/5] 110/3, 110/3
Lat. Pulldown (medium grip): [55/8, 80/4] 97/10, 97/9
Hammer Curls: [20s/10] 26s/10, 26s/9
Stretching: ~10 minutes
Workout Time: 1:19

Deadlifts
Wednesday – 9/5/07

Deadlifts:
Completely Raw Deadlifts: [55/15, 145/10, 225/6, 285/3] 315/6, 325/4
Reverse Band DLs (light bands looped around the safety bars in the top hole of my power rack): [255/6, 315/3] 360/4, 375/3
Sit-ups: [--/10] 12/12, 12/12
Stretching: ~ 10 minutes
Workout Time: 1:25

Bench Assistance
Friday – 9/7/07

Speed Reverse Band Bench (light, #3 bands):
[45/15, add bands: 115/10, 135/6]: 150/3 x 5
Dumbbell Press: [10s/10, 22s/6, 30s/3] 35s/6, 37s/4
Dumbbell Rows (elbows in): [37/6, 47/3] 57/6, 60/5
Reverse Dumbbell Curls: [20s/10] 26s/10, 26s/9
Rotator Cuff: [10/10] 13/12, 13/10
Stretching: ~10 minutes
Workout Time: 1:20

Final Squats Pre-contest
Monday – 9/10/07

Equipped Squats
(Gear: Crain squat shoes, power belt; Titan single-ply briefs; Ginny canvas suit; APT 2.5m Black Mamba knee wraps, APT wrist bands)
[55/15, 145/10, add briefs: 245/6, add suit: 335/3] add belt and wraps: 375/3, 395/2, 415/1
Jump Squats: 75/6, 75/5, 75/5
Twisting crunches (reps to each side): [--/12] 2.5/10, 2.5/8
Stretching: ~10 minutes
Workout Time: 1:35

Final Benches Pre-contest
Wednesday – 9/12/07

Equipped Benches:
(Gear: Crain Double Xtreme Bench Shirt; APT 24" Black Mamba wrist wraps): [45/15, 95/10, 115/6, add shirt and wraps, 155/3, 180/1] 200/3, 215/2, 230/1
Lat Pulldowns (underhand grip): [50/8, 80/4] 105/8, 105/8
Dumbbell Wrist Rotations: [10/12] 14/12, 14/12
Stretching: ~10 minutes
Workout Time: 1:18

Final Deadlifts Pre-contest
Friday – 9/14/07

Equipped Deadlifts:
(Gear: Crain power belt; Frantz double-ply poly deadlift suit; APT knee sleeves and wrist bands; Nike wrestling shoes)
[55/15, 145/10, 205/6, suit: 270/3, belt and wraps: 330/1] 370/3, 390/2
Dumbbell Calves: [15/10] 20/15
Leg Raises: 25
Stretching: ~ 10 minutes
Workout Time: 1:20

I skipped the final set of each exercise as this workout was rather close to the contest. Ditto the next workout.

Bench Assistance/ Final workout pre-contest
Monday – 9/17/07

Speed Band Bench (mini-bands): [45/15, 95/10, add bands: 45/6, 65/3] 75/3 x 3
Standing Barbell Press: [45/10, 65/6, 80/3] 90/6
Curl Bar Rows: [65/6, 90/3] 105/6
Reverse Curl Bar Curls: [40/10] 55/10
Rotator Cuff (two exercises): [10/10] 14/12
Sit-ups: [--/10] 15/12
Stretching: ~10 minutes
Workout Time: 1:09

Contest Results

My attempts at the contest were:
Squat: 380, 400, 415 (missed third attempt)
Bench: 200, 210, 220
Deadlift: 370, 390, 405 (missed third attempt)
Total: 1010

I went 7/9, which is rather good. I missed the third squat attempt on depth. Benches went as planned, getting all three attempts. The third deadlift I missed mainly because I was "out of gas" due to the heat and not having been able to fully rehydrated after weigh-ins, as will discussed in Chapter 21.

Off-Season/ In-Season Routine

These next sets of workouts were leading up to NASA Northeast State Championships, Saturday, June 7, 2008. At this contest, I competed unequipped, wearing a belt, wrist wraps, and knee sleeves.

I used the Off-season/ In-season routine and Split Two. Following are my workout logs for the final two weeks of the off-season and the final three weeks of the in-season. In the off-season, I alternated two different sets of exercises. During this time I had stopped stretching after my workouts, but I had started doing cardio. Now, I do both.

Off-season/ Week 9 of 10

Squats
Thursday – 3/6/08

Reverse Band Squats (average #4 bands choked around the top of my power rack, set so there is virtually not tension at the top of the lift): [55/15, add bands: 195/10, 245/6, 295/3] 325/6, 335/5, 345/5
Bicycle Abs (reps to each side): 25, 25
Step ups: 6:00 (minutes: seconds)
Workout time: 1:05 (hour: minutes)

Benches
Sunday – 3/9/08

Dumbbell Benches: [20s/15, 30s/10, 40s/6, 50s/3] 57s/7, 60s/6, 62s/4
Curl Bar Rows: [60/8, 85/4] 97/7, 102/6, 107/5
Rotator Cuff (Lying on side): 10/12, 10/12
Heavy Bag: 6:00
Workout time: 1:09

Deadlifts
Monday – 3/10/08

Good Mornings: [45/15, 75/10, 105/6, 130/3] 145/7, 152/6, 160/6
Barbell Shrugs: [145/8, 185/4] 205/8, 215/8, 225/7
Crunches: 50/20, 50/20
Jump Rope: 5:00
Workout time: 1:02

Bench Assistance
Wednesday – 3/12/08
Overhead Presses: [Dumbbells: 10s/15, Barbell: 45/10, 60/6, 75/3]
87/7, 92/5, 97/4
Lat Pulldowns (wide grip): [60/8, 90/4] 100/8, 105/5, 105/5
Reverse Curl Bar Curls [45/10] 57/8, 57/8
Rotator Cuff (lying, down): 12/12, 12/12
Workout time: 0:59

Off-season/ Week 10 of 10

Squats
Thursday – 3/13/08

Manta Ray Squats: [55/15, 125/10, 175/6, 220/3] 245/7, 255/6, 265/5
Standing Barbell Calves: [125/12] 145/13, 145/13
Dip Bar Reverse Crunches: 20, 16
Step ups: 6:00
Workout time: 1:10

_____

Benches
Sunday – 3/16/08

Reverse Band Benches (light #3 bands choked around the top of my
power rack, set so there is very little tension at the top of the lift):
[45/15, add bands: 115/10, 145/6, 170/3] 190/6, 197/5, 210/3
Dumbbell Rows (elbows out): [40/8, 50/4] 57/7, 60/6, 60/6
Rotator Cuff (sitting, side): 13/12, 13/12
Heavy Bag: 6:00
Workout time: 1:10

_____

St. Patrick's Day Deadlifts
Monday – 3/17/08

Chain Deadlifts (chain set-up weighs about 90 pounds):
[55/15, 145/10, add chains: 145/6, 225/3] 250/6, 265/5, 280/4
Sitting DB Calves: [50/10] 70/12, 70/12
Twisting sit-ups (reps to each side): 12, 9
Jump Rope: 5:15
Workout time: 1:13

_____

Bench Assistance/ Last Workout of Off-Season
Wednesday – 3/19/08

Dips: [bwt./10, 25/6, 40/5, 55/3] 70/7, 75/6, 80/5
Lat Pulldowns (medium grip): [60/8, 90/4] 105/8, 110/6, 110/5
Dumbbell Wrist Curls [17/10] 20/12, 20/10
Rotator Cuff (lying, in): 15/12, 15/12
Workout time: 1:04

In-season/ Week 8 of 10

Mother's Day Squats
Sunday – 5/11/08

Unequipped Squats:
Gear: Crain: squat shoes, power belt; APT: heavy knee sleeves.
[55/15, 145/8, 185/6, add belt and knee sleeves: 225/3, 265/1]
295/4, 325/1, Completely Raw: 255/8
Leg Raises: 25, 20
Step ups: 6:00
Workout time: 1:06

Benches
Monday – 5/12/08

Unequipped Benches:
Gear: APT: bench belt, 24" Black Mamba wrist wraps.
[45/15, 95/10, 115/6, 135/3, add belt and wraps: 155/1]
172/4, 185/1, Completely Raw: 155/7
Barbell Rows (medium grip): [55/8, 85/4] 97/7, 102/6, 107/5
Rotator Cuff (lying, side): 11/12, 11/12
Heavy Bag: 6:00
Workout time: 1:14

Deadlifts
Wednesday – 5/14/08

Unequipped Deadlifts:
Gear: Crain: power belt; APT: knee sleeves; Nike wrestling shoes.
[55/15, 145/10, 210/6, add belt and knee sleeves: 270/3, 330/1]
365/4, 395/2, Completely Raw: 305/8

Standing Barbell Calves: [145/10] 165/12, 165/12
Twisting Sit-up (reps to each side): 12, 10
Jump Rope: 5:00
Workout time: 1:19

Bench Assistance
Thursday – 5/15/08

Presses: [DBs: 10s/15; BB: 45/10, 60/6, 75/3] 85/6, 90/5, 95/4
Lat. Pulldowns: [55/8, 90/4]; Pull-ups: 5/8, 7.5/6, 10/4
Dumbbell Curls [25s/8] 29s/8, 30s/7, 31s/6
Rotator Cuff (lying, out): skipped
Workout time: 1:05

My shoulders were feeling overtrained, so I skipped the rotator cuff work here and for the duration of this routine. I was also feeling a little overtrained in general, so I skipped my workout on Sunday, moving it to Monday. With doing so, I felt fine for that workout.

In-season/ Week 9 of 10

Squats
Monday – 5/19/08

Unequipped Squats:
Gear: Crain: squat shoes, power belt; APT: heavy knee sleeves.
[55/15, 145/8, 195/6, add belt and knee sleeves: 235/3, 275/1]
305/3, 330/1, Completely Raw: 265/6
Leg Raises: 25, 25
Step ups: 6:00
Workout time: 1:14

Benches
Wednesday – 5/21/08
Unequipped Benches:
Gear: APT: bench belt, 24" Black Mamba wrist wraps.
[45/15, 95/10, 120/6, 140/3, add belt and wraps: 160/1]
177/3, 190/1, Completely Raw: 155/7
Barbell Rows (medium grip): [55/8, 85/4] 100/7, 105/5, 110/4
Heavy Bag: 6:00
Workout time: 1:00

204

Deadlifts
Thursday – 5/22/08

Unequipped Deadlifts:
Gear: Crain: power belt; APT: knee sleeves; Nike wrestling shoes.
[55/15, 145/10, 210/6, add belt and knee sleeves: 275/3, 335/1]
375/3, 405/1, Completely Raw: 325/6
Standing BB Calves: 1[45/10] 170/12, 170/12
Twisting Sit-up (reps to each side): 12, 12
Jump Rope: 5:00
Workout time: 1:12

Final Bench Assistance
Sunday – 5/25/08

DB Decline Bench: [20s/15, 35s/10, 47s/6, 57s/3] 65s/6, 67s/5, 70s/4
Lat. Pulldowns: [55/8, 90/4]; Chin-ups: 7.5/7, 10/7, 15/5
Reverse Curls: [DBs: 10s/8, BB: 45/4] 57/8, 60/7, 62/5
Workout time: 1:10

In-season/ Week 10 of 10

Final heavy squats pre-contest
Monday – 5/26/08

Unequipped Squats:
Gear: Crain: squat shoes, power belt; APT: heavy knee sleeves.
[55/15, 145/8, 195/6, add belt and knee sleeves: 240/3, 280/1]
310/3, 335/1, Raw: 270/6
Leg Raises: 25, 20
Step ups: 6:00
Workout time: 1:14

Infected finger

I had planned on putting in final heavy bench and heavy deadlift workouts similar to the preceding squat workout. However, the morning before that squat workout, I woke up with pain and swelling in my left index finger. I didn't think much of it at the time, but within a couple of days, it had really swollen. I went to the doctor, and he told me it was infected. He put me on antibiotics and told me I shouldn't lift for a few days. Mind you, this was less than two weeks before the contest, so I had to miss my planned final two heavy workouts.

By Sunday before the contest, the swelling had not gone down and I had developed pus in the finger. Monday, I needed to go to the doctor again to get it drained. But I knew I needed to do something. I couldn't go two full weeks before the contest without working out at all, so I put in a couple of light workouts. By "light" I mean my planned warm-ups and openers for the contest.

Note also, the contest was to be in kilos, both the weights in the warm-up room and on the platform, hence, the odd weights here. I was using my 1¼ pound plates to approximate the kilo equivalents.

Light Workouts

Light Squats and Deadlifts (warm-ups and openers)
Sunday – 6/1/08

Unequipped Squats:
Gear: Crain: squat shoes, power belt; APT: heavy knee sleeves.
[55/15, 145/8, 197/6, add belt and knee sleeves: 242/3] 282/1

Unequipped Deadlifts:
Gear: Crain: power belt; APT: knee sleeves; Nike wrestling shoes.
[145/8, 210/6, add belt and knee sleeves: 277/3] 342/1

Workout time: ~1:10

Light Benches (warm-ups and opener)/ Final workout pre-contest
Monday – 6/2/08

Unequipped Benches:
Gear: APT: bench belt, 24" Black Mamba wrist wraps.
[45/15, 95/8, 122/6, add belt and wraps: 142/3] 160/1
Workout time: 0:26

The next chapter will discuss how the contest went. But here, I will say my finger was still swollen come contest time. But I managed to hold onto all of my deadlifts without using that finger. And the contest went very well, despite all the problems.

Alternate Weeks Routine

The next workout logs to be included in this chapter are the final two weeks of my most recent completed routine. This ten week routine was begun January 7, 2009, after I took a four week break.

In addition, in December at the time of my last workouts, I was just recovering from the hamstring injury that occurred on October 22, 2008, so it had been over 12 weeks since I had worked out heavy on steady basis. Plus, I had lost several pounds during that time off.

However, by the end of this routine my lifts for reps were almost back up to where they were before the injury and extended break. Just goes to show that the workout program in this book is very effective.

For this routine I was using the Alternate Weeks routine and Split Three. I started this routine doing sets of six for all main exercises the first four weeks. I then did 2 x 5-6, 3-4 for major assistance work the next four weeks. For Week 9 shown here, I dropped down to 2 x 4-5, 2-3. For the powerlifts, I did 3 x 6-3 for all these weeks.

At this time, I had tentative plans to enter an ADAU Raw Power contest in the late spring or early summer.

Week 9 of 10

Squats
Thursday – 3/5/09

Low Squats: [45/15, 115/8, 150/5, 185/3] 210/5, 225/3
Partial Squats: [225/6, 275/5, 315/3] 350/5, 375/4
Sit-ups: [7.5/10] 15/10, 15/8
Step ups: 6:00
Stretching: ~10 minutes
Workout time: 1:21

Benches
Sunday – 3/8/09

DB Benches: [20s/15, 38s/8, 45s/5, 55s/3] 62s/5, 65s/4
Rack Lockouts: [115/6, 135/5, 155/3] 170/5, 180/3
DB Rows (underhand grip): [30s/8, 45s/5] 52s/7, 55s/5
Heavy Bag: 6:00
Stretching: ~10 minutes
Workout time: 1:20

Deadlifts
Monday – 3/9/09

Reverse Band Deadlifts: [45/15, add bands: 185/8, 275/5, 355/3] 385/5, 410/3
SLDLs (on 3" high platform): [135/8, 185/5, 230/3] 255/5, 270/3
Twisting Leg Raises (reps to each side): 17, 17
Jump Rope: 3:30
Stretching: ~ 10 minutes
Workout time: 1:11

Bench Assistance
Wednesday – 3/11/09

Decline Bench: [45/15, 95/8, 125/5, 150/3] 170/5, 180/3
DB Presses: [17s/8, 27s/5] 35s/6, 35s/5
Lat. Pulldowns (wide grip): [55/8, 80/5] 100/10, 105/6
Preacher Curls: [35/10] 42/10, 45/10
DB Flyes: [10s/10] 12s/13, 12s/13
Stretching: ~10 minutes
Workout time: 1:10

I usually do rotator cuff work at the end of this workout, but I thought it more important to do DB flyes to work on a tender left pec. I'll probably continue to do flyes on bench assistance day for a while.

I had been feeling a little overtrained going into this workout. But the next day (Thursday) was my planned monthly day off. By Sunday, after three days of rest, I felt much better.

Week 10 of 10

Squats
Sunday – 3/15/09

Completely Raw Squats: [45/15, 125/8, 190/5, 230/3] 255/6, 267/5, 280/4
DB Calves: [25/10] 35/12, 40/9
Crunch-Reverse Crunch Combo (with 3# ankle weights):
[20/10] 30/16, 35/15
Step ups: 6:00
Stretching: ~10 minutes
Workout time: 1:20

My knees had been bothering me some the previous couple of weeks. They felt okay during this workout, but they were sore afterwards. It was nothing serious, but enough to make me leery about going any heavier without knee support. As a result, I decided not to enter an ADAU contest like I had thought of doing, since they do not allow knee support. Instead, I decided to enter a RAWU contest as RAWU allows knee sleeves in its raw division.

Benches
Monday – 3/16/09

Completely Raw Benches: [45/15, 95/8, 115/5, 135/3] 152/6, 160/5, 167/3
BB Rows (medium grip): [55/8, 80/5] 90/7, 95/5
Triceps Pushdowns: 45/12, 45/12
Heavy Bag: 6:00
Stretching: ~10 minutes
Workout time: 1:04

My pec felt fine, even on the heavy triple. That was a relief, as my pec problem could have derailed my plans to compete unequipped. But after this workout, I doubt it will be a problem.

Deadlifts
Wednesday – 3/18/09

Completely Raw Deadlifts (sumo): [45/15, 135/8, 215/5, 295/3] 330/6, 345/4, 360/skipped
Leg Curls (legs together): [20/10] 30/10, 30/10
Dip Bar Reverse Crunches (with 3# ankle weights): 22, 20
Jump Rope: 3:00
Stretching: ~10 minutes
Workout time: 1:10

My right hamstring cramped up on me during this workout. I managed to put in most of the workout, but I had to skip the top set of DLs. It bothered me some afterwards. Fortunately, with starting a new routine, I had already planned on "deloading" the next couple of weeks.

Bench Assistance
Thursday – 3/19/09

Incline Bench: [45/15, 75/8, 97/5, 117/6] 132/5, 140/3
Dips: [25/8, 45/5, 65/3] 80/5, 90/3
Lat. Pulldowns (V Grip): [55/10, 85/6] 100/9, 100/7
Reverse Curl Bar Curls: [40/8] 52/9, 52/9
DB Flyes: [10s/10] 12s/14, 12s/14
Stretching: ~10 minutes
Workout time: 1:20

Alternate High/ Low Reps Routine

The final workout logs to be included in this chapter are my six most recent weeks of workouts prior to publishing this book. These workouts were my first weeks for the new routine I started after the preceding one. As such, the first two weeks are "deload" workouts.

For this routine, I am using an Alternative High/ Low Reps routine and Split Four. This routine will take me to my next planned contest, RAWU Northeast Regional and Pennsylvania State Championships, June 13-14, 2009 in Greencastle, PA. I will enter their "Raw" division, wearing a belt, wrist wraps, and knee sleeves.

Week 1 of 11

Squats
Sunday – 3/22/09

Completely Raw Squats: [45/15, 95/8, 135/5, 175/8] 200/8, 225/8
Chain Squats (chains set-up weights about 90 pounds):
[95/6, 115/6] 135/6, 155/6
Crunches: [25/12] 35/15, 40/15
Step ups: 3:00
Stretching: ~10 minutes
Workout time: 1:28

Since this is a deload week, my plans were to work up to one somewhat heavy set of eight on the powerlifts and one somewhat heavy set of six on major assistance work. I'll then do 2 x 8, 6 and 2 x 6, 4 respectively for my next workouts. I also cut back on the time and intensity of my cardio, but then I will gradually work back up.

Benches
Monday – 3/23/09

Completely Raw Benches: [45/15, 95/8, 115/8] 125/8, 135/8
Reverse Band Benches (#3, light bands): [135/8, 155/8] 175/8, 185/8
Curl Bar Rows: [55/8, 65/8] 75/8, 85/8
Heavy Bag: 3:00
Stretching: ~10 minutes
Workout time: 1:14

Deadlifts
Wednesday – 3/25/09

Completely Raw Deadlifts: [45/15, 135/8, 185/8, 225/8] 265/8, 285/8
Platform Deadlifts (sumo, on 3" platform): [135/8, 185/6] 225/6, 245/6
One-Leg Dip Bar Leg Raises (reps to each side): 15, 15
Jump Rope: 1:30
Stretching: ~10 minutes
Workout time: 1:14

Bench Assistance
Thursday – 3/26/09

DB Decline Bench: [20s/15, 30s/6, 40s/6, 50s/6] 55s/6, 60s/6
BB Presses: [45/8, 55/6, 65/6] 75/6, 80/6
Pull-ups: bwt/6, bwt/6
DB Curls: [10s/10] 15s/10, 20s/10
DB Flyes: [10s/10] 12s/15, 12s/15
Stretching: ~10 minutes
Workout time: 1:22

Week 2 of 11

Squats
Sunday – 3/29/09

Unequipped Squats
Gear: Crain: squat shoes, power belt; APT: Convict knee sleeves:
[45/15, 115/8, 165/4, add gear: 215/4, 255/4] 275/4, 295/2
Pause Squats: [95/8, 135/6] 155/6, 175/6
Bicycle Abs (reps to each side): 15, 15

Step ups: 3:30
Stretching: ~10 minutes
Workout time: 1:31

I had only planned on doing sets of four, working up to one somewhat heavy set. But instead, I decided to go a little lighter on that set than I had planned, but then to do a somewhat heavy double as I need to get used to low reps again. I will do the same for benches and deadlifts for my next workouts and then gradually increase from there.

I tried APT's Convict knee sleeves for the first time for this workout. They are very supportive but also more difficult to get on and off than I prefer, so I will go back to using APT's heavy knee sleeves.

Benches
Monday – 3/30/09

Unequipped Benches
Gear: APT: bench belt, 24" Black Mamba wrist wraps:
[45/15, 95/8, 115/5, add gear: 135/3] 150/4, 160/2
Feet on Bench Benches: [95/8, 115/6] 135/6
DB Rows (elbows out): [30/8, 40/8] 50/8
Heavy Bag: 3:30
Stretching: ~10 minutes
Workout time: 1:12

Deadlifts
Wednesday – 4/1/09

Unequipped Deadlifts (sumo)
Gear: Crain: power belt; APT: knee sleeves; Nike wrestling shoes:
[45/15, 135/8, 185/4, add gear: 235/4, 285/4] 335/4, 355/2
Good Mornings: [45/8, 75/8] 95/8, 105/8
Shrugs [135/8] 185/8, 195/8
Leg Raises: 20, 15
Jump Rope: 1:45
Stretching: ~10 minutes
Workout time: 1:23

Bench Assistance
Thursday – 4/2/09

DB Incline Bench: [10s/15, 20s/8, 30s/8] 35s/8, 40s/8
BB Decline Bench: [95/8, 115/6 135/6] 145/6
Chin-ups: bwt./ 8, bwt./8
Reverse BB Curls: 45/10, 45/10
DB Flyes: [10s/10] 14/10, 14/10
Stretching: ~10 minutes
Workout time: 1:07

This workout ended my deload period. After my normal two day rest, Sunday I started back into harder workouts.

Week 3 of 11

Squats
Sunday – 4/5/09

Completely Raw Squats: [45/15, 115/8, 165/5, 210/3] 235/8, 255/6
Chain Squats (chains set-up weights about 90 pounds):
[95/6, 140/3] 165/6, 185/4
Crunches: [30/10] 45/11, 50/10
Step ups: 4:00
Stretching: ~10 minutes
Workout time: 1:24

Benches
Monday – 4/6/09

Completely Raw Benches: [45/15, 95/8, 110/5, 125/3] 140/8, 150/6
Reverse Band Benches (#3, light bands): [145/6, 175/3] 195/6, 205/4
Curl Bar Rows: [55/8, 75/4] 90/8, 100/6
Heavy Bag: 4:00
Stretching: ~10 minutes
Workout time: 1:18

Deadlifts
Wednesday – 4/8/09

Completely Raw Deadlifts: [45/15, 135/8, 200/5, 265/3] 295/8, 315/6
Platform Deadlifts (conv. stance, 2-1/4" platform): [135/8, 185/5, 225/3] 255/6, 275/4

One-Leg Dip Bar Leg Raises (with 3# ankle weights; reps to each side): 12, 12
Jump Rope: 2:00
Stretching: ~10 minutes
Workout time: 1:13

Last time I did PDLs, I used my competitive, sumo stance, but I changed to a conventional stance here to give the low back and hamstrings more work than they get with sumos. I also switched to a slightly lower platform (three ¾" thick planks rather than four).

Bench Assistance
Thursday – 4/9/09

DB Decline Bench: [20s/15, 35s/8, 45s/5, 55s/3] 62s/6, 67s/4
BB Presses: [45/8, 60/5, 75/3] 85/6, 90/4
Pull-ups: bwt/8, bwt/8
DB Curls: [15s/10] 22s/10, 25s/8
DB Flyes: [10s/10] 14s/12, 14s/12
Stretching: ~10 minutes
Workout time: 1:18

I was very tired by the end of this workout. But it just happened to work out that my planned monthly day off was on Easter Sunday, so I didn't work out again until Monday. By then, I felt fine.

Week 4 of 11

Squats
Monday – 4/13/09

Unequipped Squats
Gear: Crain: squat shoes, power belt; APT: heavy knee sleeves:
[45/15, 125/8, 175/5, add gear: 215/3, 255/1] 285/4, 305/2
Pause Squats: [135/5, 165/3] 185/6, 200/4
Bicycle Abs (reps to each side): 20, 20
Step ups: 4:30
Stretching: ~10 minutes
Workout time: 1:23

The APT heavy knee sleeves worked great. They are very easy to pull up and down but provided plenty of support. My knees felt fine.

Benches
Wednesday – 4/15/09

Unequipped Benches
Gear: APT: bench belt, 24" Black Mamba wrist wraps:
[45/15, 95/8, 115/5, 130/3, add gear: 145/1] 160/4, 170/2
Feet on Bench Benches: [95/8, 115/5, 130/3] 145/6, 155/4
DB Rows (elbows out): [35/8, 45/4] 52/8, 57/5
Heavy Bag: 4:30
Stretching: ~10 minutes
Workout time: 1:16

Deadlifts
Thursday – 4/16/09

Unequipped Deadlifts (sumo)
Gear: Crain: power belt; APT: knee sleeves; Nike wrestling shoes:
[45/15, 135/8, 195/5, add gear: 255/3, 315/1] 345/4, 365/2
Good Mornings: [45/8, 70/5, 95/3] 115/6, 125/4
Shrugs [135/8, 185/4] 205/8, 220/5
Leg Raises: 20, 20
Jump Rope: 2:15
Stretching: ~10 minutes
Workout time: 1:27

My jump in weight from my first to my second set on the power-lifts in Week 4 was not quite as large as usual. But that is because I was just getting back into lower rep training. I will probably increase the jump slightly for the next workouts.

Bench Assistance
4/19/09

DB Incline Bench: [10s/15, 20s/8, 30s/5, 37s/3] 45s/8, 50s/6
BB Decline Bench: [95/8, 120/5 140/3] 155/6, 165/4
Chin-ups: [bwt./ 8] 2.5/6, 2.5/6
Reverse BB Curls: [45/8] 50/8, 50/8
DB Flyes: [10s/10] 14/15, 14/12
Stretching: ~10 minutes
Workout time: 1:21

Squats
Monday – 4/20/09

Completely Raw Squats: [45/15, 115/8, 170/5, 220/3] 245/8, 265/6
Chain Squats (chains set-up weights about 90 pounds):
[105/5, 150/3] 175/6, 195/4
Crunches: [30/10] 45/12, 45/12
Step ups: 5:00
Stretching: ~10 minutes
Workout time: 1:22

Benches
Wednesday – 4/22/09

Completely Raw Benches: [45/15, 95/8, 115/5, 130/3] 145/8, 155/6
Reverse Band Benches (#3, light bands): [145/5, 180/3] 200/5, 210/3
Curl Bar Rows: [65/8, 80/4] 95/8, 105/5
Heavy Bag: 5:00
Stretching: ~10 minutes
Workout time: 1:11

Deadlifts
Thursday – 4/23/09

Completely Raw Deadlifts: [45/15, 135/8, 205/5, 275/3] 305/8, 330/6
Platform Deadlifts (conv. stance, on 2.25" high platform): [135/8, 185/5, 235/3] 265/6, 285/4
One-Leg Dip Bar Leg Raises (reps to each side): [--/10] 5s/10, 5s/10
Jump Rope: 2:30
Stretching: ~10 minutes
Workout time: 1:26

Bench Assistance
Sunday – 4/26/09

DB Decline Bench: [20s/15, 35s/8, 47s/5, 57s/3] 65s/6, 70s/4
BB Presses: [45/8, 65/5, 80/3] 90/6, 95/4
Pull-ups: [bwt/8] 2.5/6, 2.5/6

DB Curls: [17s/10] 25s/10, 27s/8
DB Flyes: [10s/10] 14s/15, 14s/15
Stretching: ~10 minutes
Workout time: 1:19

Week 6 of 11

Squats
Monday – 4/27/09

Unequipped Squats
Gear: Crain: power belt, squat shoes; APT: heavy knee sleeves:
[45/15, 125/8, 170/5, add gear: 215/3, 260/1] 290/4, 315/2
Pause Squats: [135/5, 175/3] 195/6, 215/4
Bicycle Abs (reps to each side): 25, 20
Step ups: 5:30
Stretching: ~10 minutes
Workout time: 1:26

    This was the first time since my hamstring injury last October that I had three 45s on each side of the bar for squats, and it felt good!

Benches
Wednesday – 4/29/09

Unequipped Benches
Gear: APT: bench belt, 24" Black Mamba wrist wraps:
[45/15, 95/8, 115/5, 135/3, add gear: 147/1] 162/4, 175/2
Feet on Bench Benches: [115/5, 135/3] 150/6, 160/4
DB Rows (elbows out): [35/8, 47/4] 55/8, 60/5
Heavy Bag: 5:30
Stretching: ~10 minutes
Workout time: 1:28

    I was having a hard time focusing for this workout, so it took longer than usual. But my work sets went well. In fact, this was the best benches have felt all year. The double was with strength to spare.

Deadlifts
Thursday – 4/30/09

Unequipped Deadlifts (sumo)
Gear: Crain: power belt; APT: heavy knee sleeves; Nike wrestling shoes: [45/15, 135/8, 195/5, add gear: 255/3, 315/1] 350/4, 375/2
Good Mornings: [45/8, 80/5, 110/3] 125/6, 135/4
Shrugs [135/8, 190/4] 210/6, 210/6
Leg Raises: 25, 20
Jump Rope: 2:45
Stretching: ~10 minutes
Workout time: 1:27

Another very good workout. The double was again with strength to spare, so my lifts are all coming along nicely.

Bench Assistance
Sunday – 5/3/09

DB Incline Bench: [10s/15, 20s/8, 30s/5, 40s/3] 47s/8, 52s/6
BB Decline Bench: [95/8, 120/5 145/3] 160/6, 170/4
Chin-ups: [bwt./ 8] 2.5/8, 5/5
Reverse BB Curls: [45/8] 50/10, 52/8
DB Flyes: [12s/10] 15s/8, 15s/8
Stretching: ~10 minutes
Workout time: 1:25

More Workout Logs

Posted on my fitness Web site are my workout logs going back to when I first started lifting weights again in the spring of 2002. Each week, I post my workout logs for the preceding week on that site, on my MySpace blog, and in the Weight Trainer's United forum (see Appendix #3). I also post on these sites details before and reports afterwards for any contest I might enter.

These posts will include details for the remaining weeks for the last routine presented here, along with what happens at the RAWU contest I have plans to enter. My plan at this writing is to use the Alternate High/ Low Reps plan through Week 8. I then might switch to the "drop reps with back-off set" scheme for the last three weeks. That way, I will do the powerlifts for low reps each of those last weeks.

Hopefully, I will be able to gradually increase my top weight set for the powerlifts each workout. If things go as planned, I should be in a position to set some unequipped PRs at the RAWU contest.

Chapter Sixteen
Contest Attempts

It is now time to discuss the all-important issue of your contest attempts. This is of course what powerlifting is all about—your three attempts on each lift at a contest. But first, it would be good to present a few suggestions about packing for a contest.

Packing for a Contest

Chapter Two described all of the different gear you might need for a contest. You can use that chapter as a checklist when packing. Check and double-check to be sure you have everything before leaving for the contest.

I like to pack each piece of gear in a small garbage bag or "zip" bag. That way, the gear doesn't get tangled up. It is also good to keep pairs of items like knee wraps in the same bag.

It was also mentioned in Chapter Two that you will need one or two large gym bags to carry all of your gear with you. But I also usually take a small gym bag. After I change into my gear, I will put into that small bag whatever I will need for the lift at hand. That way, you will not be fishing around in your large bag for needed items.

The items in the small bag will include a clipboard with my warm-up weights and planned attempts and a kilogram conversion chart if necessary, a pencil or pen, a calculator, a hand towel, and chalk, along with whatever wraps I will need for the lift at hand, plus baby powder for deadlifts.

Preparing for Your Attempts

An important part of a powerlifting contest is the social aspects of the sport. You can meet a lot of interesting people at a powerlifting contest, and it is good to socialize and make some new friends.

However, the time for socializing is before you start warming up. That is one reason to arrive plenty early to a contest. But once you start warming up, it is time to start focusing on why you are there, to do your best on your contest attempts, and it takes time to get into the right mental focus to do so.

Your warm-ups are also when you need to be familiarizing yourself with the equipment for the contest. Hopefully, there will be similar equipment in the warm-up room as on the contest platform. You should check out what's on the platform before the contest begins and see how it compares with the warm-up room equipment.

Most especially, if there is monolift on the platform and one in the warm-up room, be sure to practice with it if you are not familiar with it. Also, don't forget to determine your rack height and give that to the scorer's table.

Also, be sure to check the contest bar that will be used for each lift. The markings on the bar might be different from what you are used to, so be sure you know before your attempts where you will need to grip the bar. You might want to measure your training bar and take a measuring tape to the contest just to be sure.

Chapter One mentioned about keeping an eye on what is happening on the platform so as to properly time your warm-ups. Be sure you are done warming up in plenty of time.

Once you are warmed up, make your way to the contest area. Find a chair to sit on and place your small gym bag beside it, and then stay put there. Make that your "space" where you will get zoned into your contest mind.

It is at this point that I will basically isolate myself, cutting off any talking. I don't mean to be unfriendly, but it takes a lot of concentration to be truly prepared for a heavy lift.

You also need to be paying attention to the announcer so as to know when to start getting prepared, both mentally and in regards to your gear, and especially on squats if you are using knee wraps.

You do not want to wrap too early as waiting too long after wrapping will cut off circulation to your lower legs. But it is even worse to start wrapping too late and have to rush the job. Poorly wrapped knees can easily lead to a missed attempt.

I get my wraps in hand when I am announced as being "in the hole" and begin wrapping as soon as I am announced as being "on deck." You will have plenty of time while they load the bar for that lifter and the lift is performed. Before your name is called as being "up" you should be done wrapping. If not, then start earlier on your next attempt.

After wrapping your knees, tighten your wrist wraps if you're using them, get up (or have someone pull you up), and have your straps pulled up if you're wearing a suit, and then tighten your belt.

When your name is called you will probably still have a little time before your one minute starts to begin your lift while they change the weight on the bar, unless you are using the same weight as the previous lifter. Once the bar is loaded, it will be announced and your one minute time will begin.

It is vital that all of your gear is already in place when the bar is announced as loaded. You need to use some of that one minute getting yourself psyched up for your lift. Some lifters like myself scream, some slap themselves in the head (again, like me), some have someone else slap them, some sniff an ammonia capsule (yuk!), while others are perfectly quiet, instead focusing their energies inward.

Whatever works for you is perfectly acceptable. Just be sure all of the antics do not take too long and use up your time limit. Also be sure all of the antics occur off-platform. In some federations, you can be red-lighted for head-slapping and the like on the platform. Also be sure all of your gear is properly adjusted before getting on the platform as again, you can be red-lighted for adjusting gear on the platform.

Once you are psyched up and focused, step onto the platform and get positioned. Take a breath and concentrate on the job at hand. The most important point is to have absolute confidence that you will get the lift. Any doubts and you could psych yourself out and miss the lift.

The rest of the world should be oblivious to you at this point. It's just you and the bar. But keep just enough outside focus to pay attention to the head judge's commands. Let out one more scream if you must and start your lift.

Be sure to follow all of the judge's commands as described in Chapter One. When you are finished with your lift, check the lights board to see if your lift passed and then clear off of the platform as quickly as possible.

Wait until after you are off of the platform to start to undo your gear. You then need to decide on what weight you will use for your next attempt. Give that to the scorer's table and then sit back down. Roll up your wraps and then rest for a few minutes. It will then be time to do it all over again for your second and third attempts.

After squats, you should have plenty of time to get out of your gear and get your gear ready for benches. You should also plan on eating and/ or drinking something. What to eat and drink during a contest will be discussed in the next section. You should also have some time for more socializing in-between lifts. But again, once you start to warm-up for benches, you needed to re-focus.

Timing your warm-ups for benches was discussed in Chapter One. Here, it will just be said to be sure you get into your bench shirt in plenty of time. If you are using wrist wraps, replace the knee wraps in your small gym bag with those.

The same pattern again repeats for deadlifts. Only now, be sure to put your bottle of baby powder into the small gym bag.

Picking Contest Attempts

Picking your weights for your attempts involves deciding how much to open up with and how much to jump in weight from your first to the second attempts and from your second to your third attempts. What weights you pick for your contest attempts will be based on how your final workouts before the contest have gone, specifically what the weights were that you used for a given number of reps.

Many recommend opening with the weight you used for a triple in training. The second attempted is about what you used for a single or double in training. And the third attempt is then for a personal record (PR), which is to say, more weight than you lifted in the gym or ever before at a contest.

However, this attempts scheme is based on a couple of premises. The first is the jumps between attempts should not be that large. The amount of weight you can use for a triple is only about 5% less than a double. Then a similar jump would be used from your second to third attempts. This means, your opener would be just 10% less than your final attempt.

With this plan, the idea is you want to lift as much as possible on your first attempt just in case you miss your next two. If you do, you will still have gotten in reasonably high attempt.

But one problem with this philosophy is that your opener is so close to your max that a bomb out is very likely. And even if you get in your opener, going 1/3 on a lift is not very satisfying either.

The other problem with this philosophy it is based on the idea that you will be so psyched up at a contest that your will be able to lift more than you ever have in training. Some will even refer to people who lift less in a contest than in training as "weenies."

However, I have never found that I am able to lift more in a contest than I have done in training. Call that what you will, but the previous discussion about not lifting under ideal conditions at a contest must be remembered. Also, I am able to get myself rather psyched up in training, so there is not much of a difference come contest time.

Moreover, I usually cut weight for a contest, and that loss of weight can cause a loss of strength. At the least, losing weight will offset any advantage one might get from extra "psych" at a contest.

In fact, the loss of strength from cutting weight is a common reason for bomb outs at contests. Most lifters find that benches are most affected by cutting weight, squats the second most affected, and deadlifts the least affected. You need to take that into account when picking your attempts.

But this does not mean you can expect a big day on deadlifts despite cutting weight. Remember also that a powerlifting contest can last several hours. It is a long, grueling day. All of that waiting around at a contest for your time to lift can drag you out. Also remember, that you will be doing all three lifts on the same day, so come deadlifts, you could very well already be exhausted.

Another issue to consider is that many, myself included, often have a hard time sleeping the night before a contest. You might also be tired out from a long travel the day before or the morning of the contest, packing and unpacking for a hotel stay, and other reasons.

And finally, you have to be prepared for the judging being stricter than you might think. In Chapter One it was mentioned that on squats, it is a good idea to sink you first squat extra low so there is no doubt it will pass. On benches, you need to be prepared for an extra long wait for the "Press" command.

In both cases, it would be good for your opener to be extra light to be sure it passes. After your openers, you will have a better idea what the judging will be like and can adjust your attempts accordingly.

Given all of these factors, I think a good idea would be to go into a contest "assuming" you will go at least 2/3 on each lift. In other words, you should not be looking at your opener as a weight that you will be finishing with. Your opener has only one purpose—to keep you in the contest. That's it. As such, it should be a weight that you know you can get no matter how terrible you feel and no matter what goes wrong and how strict the judging is.

This all takes us back to the rep range you used for your last workouts before the contest. If you're using the 5-6, 3-4, 1-2 rep range, then the weights you used for your last workout for those three sets would be your contest attempts. This will give you about a 10% increase attempt to attempt, or 20% from your opener to third attempt.

It might sound light to open with a weight you did for 5-6 reps, but again, it is not what you start with that matters, but what you end with. With this scheme, you are very likely to go 3/3 on all three lifts.

The reason for this is you will be handling the same weights with the same weight jumps that you used previously in a workout, so the "feel" of the weights should be very familiar. But since you are only doing one rep rather than 5-6 and 3-4 on the first two sets, you should still be "fresh" for your final attempt. Those first two attempts will not be hard enough to significantly tire you out.

The downside to starting lighter and taking bigger jumps between attempts is if you miss your final attempt you will "lose" more on your total than if you had smaller jumps but still went 2/3. But again, you're more likely to go 3/3 if you take larger jumps and start lighter.

If you're using the 3-4, 1-2, 7-8 rep plan, then the same principles apply. Only now your weights from your first two sets in your last workout will be your second and third attempts. Your opener will actually be your final warm-ups set from your last workout. I know that sounds really light, to open with a warm-up set. But if you think about it, that is what your opener is, a warm-up for the rest of your attempts.

Of course, the weights can be adjusted somewhat based on how hard your sets felt in training and exactly how many reps you got. If you got six reps on your first set with the first rep range, then you might want to open with a little heavier weight than you used for that set than if you had only gotten five reps.

Your final attempt should be what you got for a single not a double. But that should be planned for in your last workout. In other words, for your last workout before a contest you should be using a weight for your 1-2 rep set that you figure will be a near max single.

The preceding conservative approach is the type of plan I would recommend for the beginner powerlifter. But the intermediate to advanced lifter might get away with ignoring some of this advice and going a little heavier on your opener and taking somewhat smaller jumps between attempts. Such a lifter might also be able to handle a slightly greater training load.

In that case, I'd recommend adding a set to the "drops reps with back-off set" scheme and thus going 4 x 3-4, 2-3, 1-2, 7-8 for at least your last couple of workouts pre-contest. These four sets should be the bulk of your workout as much more could lead to overtraining.

As before, the last set should be done completely raw. But the first three sets should be done with contest gear, and the weights for those three sets would be your contest attempts. However, I would recommend opening with what you did for four (not three) reps.

That said, your planned attempts might need to change in the course of a contest. If you miss your first attempt, repeat the same weight for your second attempt; do not increase the weight! This is where many bomb out of a contest. They try to stick with their original plan for their second attempts. The only time it might be necessary to increase the weight is if you missed your opening bench attempt due to not being able to touch the bar to your chest due to your shirt. But that is a problem you should have had worked out before the contest.

If your opener is harder than expected, then you might have to swallow your pride and reduce your planned second attempt. Again, do not stick with your original plan if things did not go as planned with your opener. Similarly, if your second attempt is harder than expected, you might have to reduce your third attempt. It is far better to drop your attempts a few pounds and get them than to stick with your original plan and miss attempts.

However, I strongly warm against increasing any attempt beyond what you had previously planned. In the excitement of a contest, you might feel like Superman and that you can lift anything. But most likely, reality will hit home and your unplanned increase will lead to a missed lift or even worse, an injury. Again, if is far better to finish up feeling you could have done a little bit more than to really push it and miss your final attempts.

The one exception to this "rule" would be on deadlifts if the contest is on the line. If you need to pull a few pounds more than you had planned on your third attempt for the victory, then it might be worth going for it. But note, that is a few pounds more, not 50! No matter how psyched up you are, you will not all of the sudden be able to pull significantly more that you ever have before.

The bottom line is a big total will come about by going 9/9, even if all of your third attempts were a little less than full max lifts. If you try to push beyond your limits and only go 6/9, missing all of your third attempts, your final total will be far less.

These comments are not an excuse to not push yourself at all on your third attempts. Ideally, they should be full max or at least very close to full max lifts. It's just that an "extra" five or ten pounds is not going to make that much of a difference on your total but could very well lead to a missed attempt and a greater reduction on your total.

Adding in Gear

At what point in your warm-up sets should you add in gear? This question applies to both workouts and contests, but it will be addressed here in the context of a contest. But the same plan will apply to workouts. The answer to this question will depend on what kind and how much gear you are using.

It was stated previously, that the recommended warm-up reps are 15, 8, 5, 3, 1. The first two sets should be done completely raw regardless of how much gear you are going to be using. Those sets will be very light, so there is no reason to use gear. You want to be sure the body parts that will be supported by gear get warmed up.

But with the set of five you will want to start adding gear if you are lifting equipped. However, many will find that a strong bench shirt or even squat suit will not allow you to get anywhere near down with what will still be a light weight, so it would be a better idea to just add a belt and wraps at that point.

Then on the triple, add in your suit or shirt. You might still not be able to get down, but you need to start getting used to the gear.

However, some might want to switch the above suggestions and add the suit first, then the wraps. The reason I sometimes used this pattern is I would wear my sneakers for the first two sets, but then put on my squat shoes after my suit. In that way, I didn't need to take the squats shoes on and off so much as they are harder to get on and off than low top sneakers. Also, if you are wearing briefs, then you might want to add them first, then your suit on the next set.

Now it was mentioned in regards to the warm-ups sets to space them about evenly apart. However, gear changes this somewhat. When you add in knee wraps for squats, the amount of extra weight they enable you to handle needs to be figured in. So you will probably want to jump by that much more than for the previous set. Then the same goes even more so when you add in your suit or shirt. You will most likely need a bigger jump then than between your previous two sets. If you are lifting unequipped, wait until the triple to add your belt and wraps.

Examples

The best way to demonstrate the preceding points is to present my contest attempts from two recent contests. For perspective, it will help to include my final heavy workouts for each lift. The first of these contests was before using the rep ranges and attempts plans previously discussed, but this will give you an idea of the different options.

2006 APF PA States

First to be looked at is 2006 APF Pennsylvania States, for which I used multi-ply gear. At this time, I was using a 4 x 4-1 rep plan.

Squats:
Final Workout:
Gear: Crain: squat shoes, power belt, double-ply Genesis squat suit, wrist wraps; Titan: 2.5 meter THP wraps.
[55/15, 145/10, add squat shoes and suit: 235/6, add belt and wraps: 325/3] 360/4, 385/3, 405/1, 420/1

Contest:
Warm-ups: free/15, 45/12, 135/8, add shoes and briefs: 225/3, add suit: 295/3, add belt and wraps: 350/1
Attempts: 375, 400, 415 (all attempts passed)

Benches:
Final Workout:
Gear: Crain: power belt, Double Xtreme shirt; Inzer: wrist wraps.
[55/15, 95/10, 125/6, add shirt: 155/3, add belt and wraps: 170/1] 195/4, 205/3, 215/2, 225/1

Contest:
Warm-ups: 45/15, 95/10, 125/6, add shirt: 160/3 (couldn't touch), add belt and wraps: 180/1 (couldn't touch)
Attempts: 200, 215, 220 (missed third attempt)

Deadlifts:
Final Workout:
Gear: Crain: power belt, Frantz: double-ply poly deadlift suit; APT knee sleeves and wrist bands, Nike wrestling shoes.
[55/15, 145/10, add suit and wrestling shoes: 235/6, add belt and wraps: 325/3] 355/4, 375/2, 400/1, 420/1

Contest:
Warm-ups: 135/10, add briefs: 225/4, add suit and shoes: 295/1, add belt and wraps: 350/1
Attempts: 375, 400, 410 (missed third attempt)

Note that in training at this time I was using five pound spin-lock collars, so my "base weight" with a pair of 45s on the bar was 145. But at the contest were wire-type collars, which have a meaningless weight, so the base weight is only 135. Also note that at some contests a specialty squat bar will be used, which weighs 55 pounds rather than the 45 pounds of a normal power bar or Olympic bar. Be sure to account for this difference between different types of collars and bars when loading the bar for your warm-ups.

That said, as can be seen, on squats I opened with ten pounds less than I had tripled in training, and I finished with five pounds less than I had singled in training, going 3/3.

On benches, I opened with five pounds less than I had tripled in training. My second attempt was what I had doubled in training. But then I missed my third attempt, which was five pounds less than I had singled in training. That miss was probably because I had cut significant weight for this contest.

On deadlifts, my final workout did not go as planned, but I still attempted what I had originally hoped to do. This was obviously a mistake given that I missed on my third attempt with ten pounds less than I had done in training. That miss could very well have been due to going too heavy on my first two attempts.

Note also that on deadlifts I skipped the initial 15 rep warm-up set as I was plenty warmed up at that point, so it was not necessary.

Overall, I went 7/9, which is not bad. But still, I was not very satisfied with this performance. I really thought I should have gotten my final bench and deadlift attempts. But winning Best Lifter made it a very good day nevertheless.

2008 NASA NE States

Next to be looked at is 2008 NASA Northeast States. At this contest, I competed unequipped, wearing a belt, wrist wraps, and knee sleeves. I was using a 3-4, 1-2, 6-8 rep range in training.

Note that I use pounds in training, but the weights at the contest in both the warm-up room and on the platform contest were in kilograms. That accounts for the "odd" weights indicated.

Squats:
Final workout:
Gear: Crain: power belt, squat shoes; APT: heavy knee sleeves.
[55/15, 145/8, 195/6, add belt and knee sleeves: 240/3, 280/1]
310/3, 335/1, Raw: 270/6

Contest:
Warm-ups: bar/15, 143/8, 198/5, add belt and knee sleeves: 243/3
Attempts: 281, 309, 331 (all attempts passed)

Benches:
Final workout:
Gear: APT: bench belt, 24" Black Mamba wrist wraps.
[45/15, 95/10, 120/6, 140/3, add belt and wraps: 160/1]
177/3, 190/1, Raw: 155/7

Contest:
Warm-ups: bar/10, 94/8, 121/5, add belt and wraps: 143/3
Attempts: 160, 176, 187 (all attempts passed)

Deadlifts:
Final workout:
Gear: Crain: power belt; APT: knee sleeves; Nike wrestling shoes.
[55/15, 145/10, 210/6, add belt and knee sleeves: 275/3, 335/1]
375/3, 405/1, Raw: 325/6

Contest:
Warm-ups: 143/8, 209/5, add belt and knee sleeves: 276/3
Attempts: 342, 375, 402 (all attempts passed)

My basic plan for my openers was to round up from what I had done for my final warm-up set in training to the closest weight that could be used due to the kilograms. Then I rounded down from what I had used for my first two work sets in training for the second and third attempts at the contest.

For squats, my final warm-up in training was 280, so took 281 for my opener. My two work sets were 310, 335, so I called for 309, 331 at the contest. A similar plan was used for benches and deadlifts.

This plan worked out very well as I went 9/9. Not only that, but my third attempts on all three lifts were full max efforts; I could not have done any more on that day, so I picked my attempts perfectly.

Contest Anecdotes

This chapter will conclude with a couple of contest anecdotes that illustrate a couple of previously mentioned points.

The first concerns a point mentioned in Chapter Nine. It was said there that a thumbless grip on benches is very dangerous. I say this due to an incident that happened at a contest I entered in college.

One of the heavier weight lifters was attempting something like 500 pounds. Using a thumbless grip, he got the bar almost to lockout, but it then slipped out of his hands and crashed onto his chest. The bar came out too quickly for the spotters to catch the weight.

The lifter lay on the bench in extreme pain and barely able to breathe. An ambulance had to be called, and the lifter was taken out on a stretcher. Needless to say, this put a damper on the normal excitement of a contest and caused a long break in the action.

When the contest was finally ready to resume, the meet director gave a short speech about how dangerous a thumbless grip is and strongly warned against it. I can remember him saying, "I know some lifters think it can add five pounds or so to their bench, but it is not worth it." But then the first lifter up when the contest resumed used a thumbless grip. The meet director looked dumbfounded, and I found it hard to believe as well.

I later learned that the lifter who had been injured had shattered his sternum and fractured a couple of ribs. He never competed again.

At a more recent contest, a similar incident happened. But this time, the lifter using a thumbless grip was wearing a very tight, double-denim shirt. The shirt was so thick and tight that when the bar slipped, it bounced up off of his chest, and the spotters caught it on the rebound. The lifter jumped up off of the bench and motioned that he was okay, kind of like the Pepsi Max 2009 Super Bowl commercial where men get hit in various ways but declare, "I'm good."

I guess this is another way gear can protect the lifter that could be added to what was said in Chapter Five. But much better would be to use your thumbs when benching and thus not to lose your grip.

On a less serious note, at another contest in college, one of the lifters came up with a "bright" idea. He would psych himself up for his final deadlift attempt by going outside of the high school gymnasium the contest was being held at and down the street a block or so. He would then come running down the street screaming, fly into the gym, up to the bar, and rip it up off the floor.

But what happened was as he was running down the street screaming a police officer stopped him. By the time he explained what he was doing, his minute had expired and he missed the attempt. A good illustration of what was said in this chapter to not let your psyching up antics take too long so as to use up your minute to start your lift.

A point not yet mentioned in this book is that if two lifters in the same weight class total the same amount, or if two lifters lift the same weight at a single lift contest, then the lifter with the lighter weigh-in bodyweight wins. This became important to me at the second of the two bench press contests I entered in the summer of 1985, mentioned about in the "About the Author" chapter.

I competed at 123s. I got my opener with 200, but then missed my second attempt with 225. Another lifter in my weight class benched 225 on his third attempt. But I had weighed in lighter, so all I had to do was to get that 225 on my third attempt and I would be the winner.

It was a very hard fought lift, moving as slowly as could be, but I got! I looked up from the bench at the lights board. When three white lights came up, I was so excited I jumped up off of the bench and into the air so high that when I came down, both feet were planted firmly on the end of the bench. I have no idea how I managed to jump that high and to not fall off of the bench. But the way I planted my feet would have been a perfect "gymnast's landing."

Incidentally, if two lifters total the same or lift the same weight and had weighed in at the same bodyweight, then after the contest, they are both re-weighed, and the lighter lifter at that time is the winner. If they both weigh the same after the contest, then a tie is declared. But frankly, I have never heard of that happening.

Section Five

Injuries and Back Pain

Chapter Seventeen
Dealing with Injuries

Mention has been made several times in this book about a hamstring injury I sustained on October 22, 2008. Needless to say, I was very discouraged by that injury. But I recovered rather quickly from it. But it would have been much better to have avoided the injury in the first place.

Following the many training suggestions in this book will go a long ways towards helping the reader in avoiding injury. In fact, it was because I didn't follow some of my own advice that I probably ended up with that injury.

This chapter will look in detail at the possible causes of powerlifting injuries and ways to avoid them. It will then look at rehabilitation in case an injury does occur.

To introduce these ideas, I will first reproduce a message I posted about that injury the day afterwards on my fitness Web site, on my MySpace blog, and in the Weight Trainer's United forum (see Appendix #3).

Hamstring Injury

For quite some time, I had it written into my workout plan to skip a workout about once every four weeks. That pattern worked well. But after one such skipped workout a few weeks ago when I felt like I didn't need the break, I decided it wasn't really necessary to skip a workout once a month. Shortly after that I had some setbacks healthwise and had to take a week off. When I started lifting again, I started a new routine. I then lifted for the next five weeks without a break.

This past week was the fifth week, and over the past week my health problems had been flaring up again, and I had lost a quite a bit of sleep as a result. I thought of taking a day off at the beginning of this week but stubbornly stuck to my new plan of not skipping workouts. The night before my workout yesterday (Wednesday, 10/22/08), I barely slept a wink, so I felt terrible. But despite the problems, I went ahead and worked out anyway.

On my fourth rep of my second work set of the day, I felt a "pop" in my left hamstring that really hurt. I stupidly tried one more rep, which caused even more pain. But at least I had sense enough to end the workout at that point. I iced my hamstring throughout the evening and more today. But it still feels terrible. This is the worst injury I have sustained since I started lifting weights again over six years ago. The worse part about it is I should not even have been lifting yesterday!

In my defense of trying that one more rep, very often over the last six years I will experience pain that feels like a pulled muscle, not just while lifting but even when doing everyday activities. This is due to my fibromyalgia. But every time, I will simply ignore the pain and continue, and the pain will eventually go away. If I stopped lifting every time I felt pain I would never work out.

However, what I have been afraid of is that one of these days I would sustain a real injury, ignore it, and make things worse, and that is what just happened. But I should have known things were different this time as the "pop" feeling was different from what I usually feel.

Similarly, given my health problems, I very often have problems sleeping, so again, if I didn't lift every time I had a bad night, I'd never lift. But again, this time was different given that I had lifted for five weeks straight. I knew I needed a break but didn't take it, so I'm really kicking myself right now.

At this point, I know I will need to take a few days off, so I won't lift again until next week. But I'm not sure when I will start back. I will have to see how my hamstring feels and play it by ear. I'm also not sure what I will do training-wise. But I know this ends my current workout plan. I will probably write up a special "rehab" plan.

As I posted previously, I had planned on entering an ADAU bench/ deadlift contest in January. I was mainly planning on entering it for deadlifts. But, of course, it will be deadlifts that will be most affected by this injury. So very likely, that contest in January will no longer be a possibility.

Needless to say, this means I will go back to planning on taking an "extra" day off once a month. But this injury also has me rethinking two other aspects of my workouts.

The first is the exercise I injured myself on was Good Mornings (GMs). Many believe GMs are too dangerous of an exercise to be worth the risk. But I have found GMs to be very beneficial for both my squat and deadlift. I used a combination of GMs and shrugs for my off-season before my last contest, and I really felt that helped me have a very good day on deadlifts at the contest. But now, I'm not so sure if they are worth the risk.

I mention on my Web site that GMs are definitely an "advanced" exercise and should only be done by experienced lifters. I also state that you have to be very careful with your form. But the latter might have been the problem. I felt like I was having problems keeping my form correct. Specifically, I was trying to keep my legs slightly bent but was having trouble doing so. On the rep that I got injured, maybe my leg had completely straightened, thus putting even more stretch and strain on the hamstring.

A similar exercise is stiff-leg deadlifts (SLDLs). Those also many consider to be too dangerous. But I again have found them beneficial and don't seem to have the same problem keeping my form on them. So maybe I will stick with SLDLs from now on for my main off-season DL exercise.

Another plan might be to do conventional stance DLs during my off-season, then switch to my competitive sumo stance during the in-season. Like GMs and SLDLs, conventional DLs also put more emphasis on the low back and hamstrings than sumo DLs, but they are probably a lot safer than GMs and SLDLs.

The second thing I am rethinking is stretching. Long before I had started lifting again, I had been stretching on a regular basis, and continued to do so when I started lifting again, usually stretching for 10-15 minutes after each workout. However, due to my fibromyalgia, that extra 10-15 minutes was proving too tiring on top of an hour or so of lifting. So I dropped off stretching last year, and I have not done any stretching since. It could be that without stretching, my hamstring had tightened up, thus contributing to the injury. So I will have to go back to stretching, even if it is very difficult for me to do so.

In any case, only time will tell how serious this injury is and if or when I will be able to get back into hard training and think about another contest. I say "if" as there have now been several times in the past few years when I had planned on entering a contest but had to cancel my plans due to one problem or another. In fact, until the unplanned week off mentioned previously, I had planned on entering a contest in a couple of weeks.

Needless to say, I am getting frustrated and am thinking maybe it is time I accept that my problem-ridden body simply cannot handle powerlifting anymore. But I do enjoy it and would like to continue, so we shall see what happens.

Preventing Injuries

The preceding message brings out several points worth detailing that very often lead to injuries.

1. Overtraining

Probably the most common reason for getting injured is being overtrained. If you are not fully recovering workout to workout, your body will slowly break down. Eventually, it will reach the "breaking point" and something will give. When that happens, you will be forced to take a break and back off on intensity for a while. But again, it would be far better to take the break before getting injured.

This requires knowing your body and when it needs a break. Planning on taking a break every month or so is one way to ensure you're recovering adequately.

Another aspect of overtraining that needs to be looked at after an injury is your workout volume. Maybe you were doing too many exercises, too many sets of each exercise, working out too many times a week, or pushing too hard on each exercise each and every workout without deloading at any point. All of these points need to be considered when evaluating what led to an injury and anytime you feel overtrained.

2. Exercise Form

The second major cause of injuries is poor form on your lifts. The reason lifters (especially male lifters) very often use poor form is they are trying to lift more weight than they can do with proper form, so they begin "cheating" to hoist up weights that are really beyond their limitations.

This is pure ego, and stupid ego at that. Your lifts done with bad form will never pass at a contest, so it makes no sense to lift that way in the gym. It especially makes no sense to cheat on assistance work in the gym as what you handle on assistance exercises is meaningless. All that matters is that you are working hard enough with proper form to aid your competition lifts.

3. Trying to lift too much weight

Related to the above point is an injury can occur when a lifter tries to lift much more than he or she is actually capable of lifting. This again is pure ego and often occurs when a lifter is "showing off" in the gym. It is also pure stupidity. You are not all of the sudden going to be able to lift a significant amount more than you have before. Slow, gradual increases are the best way to improve your lifts over the long term, not trying to make gigantic gains in a single workout.

Powerlifters have also gotten injured when trying to lift far over their capacity at a contest. That issue was addressed in the previous chapter.

4. Exercise Selection

Some exercises are simply more dangerous than others. This book has detailed some you need to especially be cautious with. For each of these exercise alternatives are available and might be safer choices. Newer lifters should definitely avoid more advanced exercises. But if you do such exercises, be sure you are thoroughly warmed up and that you use proper form

5. Flexibility

This point is actually controversial as there are some who believe that stretching does not help to prevent injuries. But it only stands to reason that with an exercise like Good Mornings where a body part is being stretched that if that body part is flexible it is less likely to be injured that if it is tight.

However, the detractors are correct on one point—stretching before a workout is not wise. Doing so can actually weaken the muscle, leading to injury. Also, stretching "cold" can also be dangerous and lead to injury. Stretching should always be done after a workout.

Immediate Steps to Take

If an injury does occur, there are several steps that should be taken immediately.

1. STOP!

The most important immediate thing to do when an injury occurs is to stop doing what you are doing! That sounds rather basic, but it very difficult for many to do.

You are psyched up for a workout, when something happens. It is so hard to stop and end the workout right there, but that is what must be done. If you do so much as one more rep as I did, you can make things much worst. I probably would have recovered even faster than I did if it were not for that one additional rep. Under no circumstances should you try to complete the workout.

Even more difficult is if the injury occurs at a contest. You will need to decide if trying to finish the contest is worth potentially being laid up for weeks afterwards. It is also possible that pushing through an injury to try to complete a contest could end your lifting career altogether. As such, most likely, it is not worth pushing through the pain, and you are best just accepting that your day is done. As the saying goes, "Live to fight another day."

But making all of this most difficult is deciding if you really did injure yourself. This is especially difficult for someone like me who regularly experiences non-injury related pain.

But a better approach than doing another rep to deciding what has happened is to stop and rest a couple of minutes. Then try doing the movement you were doing with no weight. If that causes any pain, then you know it is best not to try doing it with weight.

If it doesn't cause pain to use your bodyweight, then try a rep with very light weight, and take it from there. But again, you are best off not risking it.

2. R.I.C.E.

This acronym stands for: Rest, Ice, Compression, Elevation. The rest part has already been mentioned. Stop what you are doing.

The next three points relate to blood flow. Blood flow to the area must be slowed down to prevent swelling and further tissue damage.

If you are in a gym or at a contest, most likely you will not have access to an ice pack, but most powerlifters will have knee wraps with them. That will do nicely for the "compression" part of the acronym by wrapping the injured area. If you are a raw lifter and thus do not carry wraps, you might want to keep an "Ace" bandage or a knee wrap in your gym bag just for this purpose. However, be sure the blood is not restricted too much causing the area to turn blue.

Once you get home, apply ice as soon as possible. It is a good idea to keep a frozen ice pack in the freezer at all times, just in case. The blue, soft gel ice packs found in pharmacies and other stores are excellent for this purpose. They remain flexible even when frozen, so they can be wrapped around an injured body-part.

But for my hamstring injury, what worked best was a small, hard ice block that is made for use in a food cooler. I would lie down and place the hard ice pack under my hamstring.

Also if possible, elevate the area to further reduce blood flow.

The ice and wrap should be removed after 15-20 minutes and the body part lowered. The ice should be re-applied every hour for the next 48-72 hours.

You should also continue to rest for the next three days. That means no workouts. It would be best to not even try to "work around" the injury as you could still aggravate it even if not working that body part directly.

Rehabilitation Program

After three days, the rehabilitation program should begin. Exactly what you should do will depend on how serious the injury is.

1. When to see a doctor:

If the injured area is still hurting greatly after three days, you should probably see a doctor. If there is any swelling or discoloration, you should definitely see a doctor. That could indicate the muscle has pulled away from the tendon. In that case, surgery might be needed. At the very least, you should be under the care of a trained physical therapist.

What follows is assuming it is a minor muscle "pull" or strain that can be rehabilitated on your own.

2. Strengthening the injured area:

The first step is to work on is gradually re-strengthening the inured area. What exercises should be done in this regard will of course depend on what body part is injured. For my hamstring injury, I did deadlifts and leg curls. Of course, squats also utilize the hamstrings, but not as directly, so the focus here will be on deadlifts, but I followed the same principles on squats.

For my first deadlift workout, I started as always with a set with the bar. I then used the previously mentioned idea of doing sets of six until a hard set was reached. But in this case, I started even lighter and made smaller jumps in weight between sets. And I wasn't working up to a hard set but only until I felt any pain. It was then that I stopped.

I used that approach for the next several workouts. But I gradually increased the weight and the number of "heavy" sets. I put "heavy" in quotes as the weights I used initially for what would be my work sets were nothing but very light warm-up sets.

This is a very important point that you need to accept. It will be weeks before you are handling anything near what you had used before the injury. Just accept it.

The important point here is it is better to come back from an injury slower than you have to rather than trying to come back too fast and re-injuring it. A re-injury will take much longer to heal.

3. Stretching the injured area:

After the lifting portion of the rehab program, you need to stretch the area to regain range of motion. But be very careful when doing so. Most likely, the injured area will be very tight. Only use a very easy stretch. Do not even come close to causing any pain, but each workout try to stretch it a little bit farther. Eventually, but slowly, your flexibility will return.

4. Working around the injury:

You need to keep working out with the non-injured body areas. However, you might have to back off on the intensity. For instance, after my hamstring injury, even for upper body workouts, I was still leery about pushing too hard and aggravating my hamstring. On benches, I didn't want to work hard enough that I needed to use "leg drive," so all I did for my first bench workout was basically warm-ups.

You might also need to change some of your exercises so as not to aggravate the injury. For instance, I had been doing decline benches, but I was afraid the way you "hang" from your legs when doing them would be problematic, so I did dips instead.

I was also afraid doing rows with a barbell would aggravate my hamstring, so I did them with a dumbbell instead, one arm at a time, with one knee on a bench and the other foot on the floor with the knee slightly bent. That prevented any strain on my hamstring.

For curl bar curls, I set the bar down on my squat box so I wouldn't have to bend down to pick it up.

Even when hitting the heavy bag, I didn't move around like I usually do; instead, I kept my feet in one place and again, I didn't work that hard.

It was all such a drag, having to worry about every little thing. But I was hoping if I was just cautious for a couple of weeks my hamstring would be okay, and I was right in that regard. Altogether, it took about five weeks for my hamstring to be fully healed.

5. Heat and Ice:

Many recommend that after 48-72 hours, you should switch from using ice to using heat on the injured site. However, I have never found heat to be helpful, with one exception. It is beneficial to use heat on the area for 10-15 minutes immediately pre-workout. That way, the area will be warm and looser for the workout. But then afterwards, it is helpful to use ice to quench any inflammation from the workout. The pattern of heat before and ice afterwards seems to be very beneficial.

Rehab Progression

To give some specifics on what to expect, below are my workout logs for deadlift day throughout my rehab program.

Week One

Tuesday – 10/28/08

Deadlifts (sumo):
[45/15, 135/6, 185/6] 225/6
Leg Curls: --/ 12, 3/10
Reverse Crunches (on floor): 12, 12
Jump Rope: skipped
Stretching: 10-15 minutes
Workout time: 0:52

I debated on whether I should use a conventional or sumo stance for DLs. Sumo is my competition stance. They of course do not work the hamstrings as much, so I probably will be able to handle heavier weights sooner without aggravating my hamstring, but conventional DLs would probably rehab the hamstring better. As a compromise, I decided to go with the sumo stance but to also do leg curls to isolate the hamstring.

My hamstring felt reasonable good for this workout. It only started hurting with the set with 225, so I stopped there. But that was all I had hoped to pull as it would give me a good place to increase from.

I don't have a leg curl machine, so I am doing the leg curls to re-hab my hamstring by standing and bending my leg up. I have a pair of three pound and of five pound ankle weights, so I'll be able to utilize them as I am able. I will do the leg curls on both squat and deadlift days, so I'll be doing them twice a week.

Week Two

Monday – 11/3/08

Deadlifts (sumo):
[45/15, 135/8, 185/6] 225/6, 245/6
Leg Curls: [--/10] 3/12, 3/12
Reverse Crunches: 15, 13
Jump Rope: skipped
Stretching: 10-15 minutes
Workout time: 0:59

My hamstring felt reasonably good, and I probably could have pulled more, but I didn't want to push it. Also, last week I did one "heavy" set of DLs, so this week I did two, and next week I hope to do my normal three sets.

The only time I felt anything in my hamstring was on my second set of reverse crunches. I felt a "twinge" on my 13th rep, so I stopped there. I was going to try some jumping rope, but with the twinge, I thought it best to skip it.

Week Three

Monday – 11/10/08

Deadlifts (sumo):
[45/15, 135/8, 185/5, 220/3] 245/6, 260/6, 275/6
Leg Curls (alternating legs): [--/10] 5/10, 7.5/10
Reverse Crunches (on floor): 20, 15
Jump Rope: 1:00
Stretching: 10-15 minutes
Workout time: 1:09

Prior to this workout I got a new FID [flat, incline, decline] Bench with a leg curl attachment. It worked very well for doing the leg curls to rehab my hamstring.

The only time my hamstring bothered me was jumping rope, but I figured I need to get back into at least some light cardio before I lose my aerobic conditioning. I just jumped for one minute at a very slow pace. Hopefully, I can gradually increase the pace and time.

Week Four

Monday – 11/17/08

Deadlifts (sumo):
[45/15, 135/8, 190/5, 245/3] 275/6, 290/6, 305/6
Leg Curls: [2.5/10] 7.5/10, 10/10
Reverse Crunches: 25, 25
Jump Rope: 1:30
Stretching: 10-15 minutes
Workout time: 1:17

My hamstring and deadlift are coming along rather nicely.

Week Five

Monday – 11/24/08

Deadlifts (sumo):
[45/15, 135/8, 205/5, 275/3] 305/6, 320/6, 335/6
Leg Curls (alternating legs): [5/10] 10/10, 12/10
Dip Bar Reverse Crunches: 15, 15
Jump Rope: 1:45
Stretching: 10-15 minutes
Workout time: 1:16

This was the first workout since my hamstring injury that I felt confident working hard on DLs, and work hard I did. The final rep of the last set was a full effort. And with that, my DL is back to where it was before the injury.

My hamstring did not bother me at all during this workout, but it hurt slightly afterwards. But after I iced it, it felt fine. So I'll probably continue my pattern of heat before my workouts and ice afterwards for some time. With doing so, I think I will be fine.

Final Notes:
Shortly after this workout, I ran into some problems health-wise and had to take the four week break from lifting mentioned previously in this book. If it had not been for that, I probably would have been able to enter the contest in January I had been planning on. But as it was, I refocused on a contest later in the year. But at least my hamstring was fully recovered when I started lifting again.

Also, a few months after my hamstring injury, I decided to do Good Mornings again. This can be seen in last set of workout logs in Chapter 15. I did so as I believe GMs really help both my squat and DL. Also, I had been doing leg curls since that injury but still had a problem with my other hamstring. My thought is GMs are a good way to strengthen hamstrings in a manner that has more carryover to DLs.

However, I am careful to watch my form. Also, when I injured my hamstring, I was doing GMs as my first exercise of the day. But now, I am doing them after DLs, so my hamstrings will be more warmed up. Proper form and being thoroughly warmed up are important when doing any exercise, but especially so for an exercise like GMs.

Muscular Imbalances

It was mentioned in the "About the Author" chapter that I injured my right shoulder in a bicycle accident. Specifically, I fractured the clavicle and scapula and cracked the shoulder socket. That accident occurred on July 28, 1999, or as of this writing, almost a decade ago. But my right shoulder is still weaker than the left.

At the time of the accident, I was working out with Nautilus equipment, so I did not notice the problem. This relates back to the point in Chapter Seven about machines not being as effective as free weights. In this case, the machines kept me from coming up uneven. But as soon as I started using free weights, I had a hard time coming up even when using a barbell on benches, overhead presses, and rows.

To work on this muscular imbalance I have incorporated a lot of dumbbell work. With dumbbells, the stronger side is not able to "pull" the weaker side along as with a barbell. Specifically, I have been doing dumbbell benches, presses, laterals, rows, and rotator cuff work.

When doing the dumbbell work, when working one arm at a time like with dumbbell rows or when alternating arms on benches and presses, I always start with my weaker side. And I do the same number of reps with both arms, even if I would be able to do more with the stronger side as doing so would exaggerate the muscular imbalance.

This dumbbell work has helped considerably. I no longer have trouble coming up even on benches. However, it has not totally corrected the problem. I especially notice this on dumbbell presses. I have a difficult time locking out my right arm. This is probably because the bones did not heal properly; there is a "bump" on the top of my right shoulder, but still, it is a big improvement. So take my experience as a tip. If you have any such muscular imbalances or problems coming up even on benches, then incorporate dumbbells into your training.

Chapter Eighteen
Overcoming Back Pain

Low back pain is a very common problem for powerlifters. In fact, it was back pain that forced me to stop powerlifting back in college. Later it completely crippled me for six years. But eventually I completely overcame the pain.

Available on my fitness Web site is a paperback booklet and eBooklet titled *Overcoming Back Pain: A Mind-Body Solution* (see Appendix #2). This chapter will present a condensed version of that booklet.

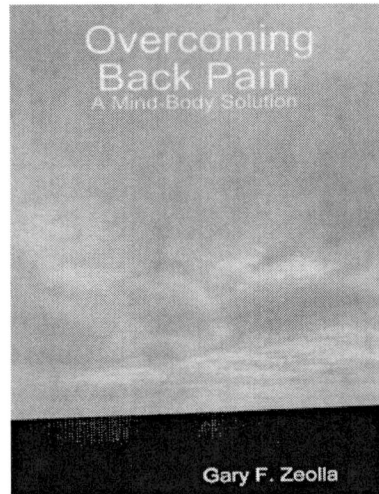

Introduction

In college I was on the Penn State Powerlifting Team. I won two Pennsylvania Collegiate titles, one National Collegiate title, and I broke several collegiate records. My best lifts in the 123 pound weight class were (in pounds): squat: 425; bench press: 240; deadlift: 435.

However, in November of 1982, during my senior year, while warming up for a squat workout I felt a jabbing pain in my lower back. Since I was just warming up I couldn't see how I could have hurt myself, but I took a week off of lifting just to be sure.

But then, at the end of that week, I was in a car accident. It was not a serious accident and everyone seemed okay at the time. But the next day, I woke up with excruciating low back pain. From then on I was unable to do much of anything at the gym. During the rest of my senior year, every time I tried to lift a weight of any significance, the jabbing back pains would come back.

Over the next several years the pain worsened to the point where I was unable to lift anything over 20 pounds. I also had to avoid any strenuous activity, especially anything that would require "twisting" in one direction or another. The only thing I did to stay in shape during this time was casual walking. The fear of pain kept me from engaging in anything more strenuous.

245

Crippling Back Pain

I maintained this fearful lifestyle for several more years. As long as I was careful I was able to at least function normally. But then on June 4, 1994 I lifted a heavy object. Immediately, I knew something was terribly wrong. The pain gradually worsened over the next few weeks until it became unbearable, so I went to the emergency room.

The ER doctor took X-rays and gave me some pain pills. He told me to go home, lie down in bed, and move as little as possible for the next two weeks. I can remember clearly the doctor saying, "I can't emphasize this enough. Rest, Rest, Rest!"

Now I was really frightened. With such a prescription, I thought my back must be in terrible shape if so much as moving could cause damage. Not wanting to hurt myself any further, I followed the doctor's advice. But over the next two weeks, my back did not improve. As long as I lay in bed I was okay, but as soon as I got up, the pain would come back. What this experience did was to engrain it in my mind that the only way I could relieve the pain was by lying down.

After the two weeks, I could barely get around. I could be "up" (sit, stand, walk) for only a few minutes before I had to lie down again due to developing pain. At this point, my doctor sent me to physical therapy. There, they had me do stretching and strengthening exercises.

Over the next several weeks I improved somewhat, but not much. I was now able be up for all of 30-60 minutes before I had to lie down. Needless to say, this pattern left me with no life to speak of. In addition, I would now experience pain if I lifted anything over two pounds. Yes, you read that correctly: two pounds! Here I was a former National Collegiate Powerlifting Champion, and now I couldn't even lift a half-gallon of milk.

Traditional and Alternative Treatments

Over the next few years I made the round of traditional doctors. An MRI showed I had a compressed lower spine and a "bulge" on one of my disks. I went to see a couple of surgeons, but both said surgery would not help. Then I tried spinal taps, traction, and a T.E.N.S. device, but none of these provided any relief. As a result, I took lots of acetaminophen to deal with the pain.

Next I began to investigate alternative treatments. I tried chiropractic, acupuncture, massage, and trigger point therapy treatments. The only one of these that helped at all was the trigger point therapy, but it didn't help that much. With traditional and alternative treatments providing little relief, I began to see what I could do on my own.

Throughout this time I continued to do stretching and strengthening exercises and kept walking as best as I could. This exercise seemed to help some, so I decided to get serious about exercise. I began doing strength training at a Nautilus Center, and I gradually increased the distance and speed I was walking. I even started bicycling and swimming for the first time in years. I also really started to watch what I ate.

I tried various supplements like MSM, SAMe, glucosamine, and various vitamins and minerals. The only thing that seemed to help at all were calcium and magnesium capsules. I also tried various creams, ointments, and sprays, but with no lasting effect.

But one thing that did seem to help was lying on an ice pack. And somewhat contradictory, heat would also help, especially wet heat. Engaging in relaxation techniques like mediation and prayer also seemed to help some. After a few months of trying these different treatments on my own, I was doing a little better, but still not much.

Putting the above together, the only treatments that seemed to provide any relief were: physical therapy and exercise, trigger point therapy, a healthy eating plan, calcium/ magnesium capsules, ice, heat, and relaxation techniques. But it made me wonder what the connection was between these seemingly diverse treatments.

The Mind-Body Connection

In the summer of 1999, I read Dr. John Sarno's book *Healing Back Pain: The Mind-Body Connection.* Dr. Sarno's theory is that the vast majority of cases of back pain are caused by extreme emotions, especially suppressed anger. Physical findings like herniated, bulging, and compressed disks are meaningless. Such supposed abnormalities are simply the normal result of aging as many people without back pain have them.

Sarno's idea is that suppressed anger or other strong feelings cause the muscles in the back to become perpetually tense or tight. This tightness in turn reduces blood flow and thus oxygen to the muscles. It is this reduced flow of blood and oxygen that causes the pain. The mind causes the

JOHN E. SARNO, M.D.

HEALING BACK PAIN

The Mind-Body Connection

WITHOUT DRUGS • WITHOUT SURGERY
WITHOUT EXERCISE
BACK PAIN CAN BE STOPPED FOREVER

pain to distract the person from noticing and thus having to deal with the suppressed anger.

To be clear, Sarno is *not* saying that the pain is "All in your head." There is a very real pain caused by a real physical manifestation, the tense muscles, which Sarno calls Tension Myositis Syndrome (TMS). The mind comes in as the cause of the tight muscles.

Now this idea tied together all of the diverse treatments that I had found helped somewhat. Each of these treatments, in one way or another, either increases blood flow directly or relaxes the muscles, which in turn increases the blood flow.

Another thing that Sarno dwells on is the cycle of pain and ever increasing restrictions that one gets into with chronic pain, and how the mind can convince a person they need to do a certain activity or avoid another to stay out of pain. My perceived need to lie down every 30-60 minutes and fear of lifting anything over two pounds were perfect examples of these phenomena.

It took me a while to accept Sarno's ideas. But by the spring of 2000, I knew Sarno was describing my situation perfectly, so I began to follow Sarno's suggestions as outlined in his book. First I began using Sarno's mind techniques. These entail talking to your brain. Now this does sound silly, but it works. What I would do is repeatedly tell my mind, "There is nothing wrong with my back." Or if I would experience pain I would simply tell my brain to "Get lost!"

If I did get angry about something and start to feel pain, I would tell my brain, "Yes I'm angry, but that's no reason to cause me pain." The idea is to recondition your mind so it no longer uses pain as a distraction from anger.

Next I had to deal with the anger. What Sarno recommends and what I did was to start writing down a list of everything I could possibly be angry about, upset, stressed out, or have any other strong negative feelings about. I went all the way back to college when I first experienced pain. I ended up with a very long list, and I kept adding to it over time as I kept remembering more things. I would read and pray over the list daily, asking God to forgive me for harboring anger over people I should have long since forgiven or over events that were out of my control.

Then I started to deal directly with the problems the pain had been causing me. Sarno recommends going about things gradually as it takes time to recondition the mind, so that's what I did. I gradually started staying "up" for longer periods every day until I was able to stay up the entire day without pain. Then I gradually began lifting heavier and heavier weights, first at home and then at the gym. I also began engaging in activities that required twisting quickly.

Over a period of about two months I overcame my fears of being up, lifting, and twisting. By the end of the summer of 2000, I felt like I had completely overcome my back pain. Sarno's theories on the mind-body connection proved to be an answer to prayer for me.

Powerlifting Again

In the spring of 2001, I started using free weights again for the first time in almost 20 years. Later that year I developed health problems unrelated to back pain and had to stop lifting for a while, but I began again in the summer of 2002.

By the winter of 2002-2003, I began handling some pretty decent weights, so much so that I started thinking about competing again. To date, I have competed in nine contests. I now hold a total of 39 powerlifting records and have been the #1 or #2 ranked master powerlifter in the USA in my weight class for each year I have been lifting again. So after taking a 21-year break from powerlifting, I am once again competing with a high degree of success.

My best lifts from these contests are as follows:
Squat: 415
Bench: 220
Deadlift: 410

I have never experienced any back pain while competing at these contests. So after six years of not being able to lift more than two pounds without experiencing pain, I was able to once again squat and deadlift over 400 pounds!

Moreover, some of these contests required a three to four hour drive from my home near Pittsburgh, PA to get to the contest site. And I experienced no pain whatsoever while sitting for that time period. In fact, I now sit for hours on end with no back pain whatsoever.

So nine years after I overcame my back pain, I am living my life back pain free. And I would say that my story should prove beyond any doubt that Sarno's methods in dealing with back pain work. After what I had been through, it really is nothing short of miraculous that not only am I able to live my life back pain free, but that I am able to powerlift at a high competitive level again.

I will close this story by saying I am very thankful for my recovery. And I hope and pray that my story will be an encouragement to the reader.

Books on Back Pain

Healing Back Pain was only one of three books by Sarno that I read. I also read a book by Fred Amir that was based on Sarno's book. Sarno also now has a newer book out that I have not read, but I am sure is very good as well.

Amir, Fred. *Rapid Recovery from Back and Neck Pain*. Santa Clara, CA: Health Advisory Group, 1999.

Sarno, John. *Divided Mind, The: The Epidemic of Mindbody Disorders*. Harper Paperbacks, 2007.

Healing Back Pain: The Mind-Body Connection. New York: Warner Books, 1991.

Mind Over Back Pain. New York: Berkley Books, 1982.

Mindbody Prescription, The: Healing the Body, Healing the Pain. New York: Warner Books, 1998.

Finally, for much greater details on my experiences, see my booklet *Overcoming Back Pain: A Mind-Body Solution* (see Appendix #2).

Section Six

Nutrition
and Supplements

Chapter Nineteen
Eating Plan Basics

Another book I have written is titled *God-given Foods Eating Plan*. The subtitle is *For Lifelong Health, Optimization of Hormones, Improved Athletic Performance* (see Appendix #2).

As the title indicates, this book looks at what God intended for human beings to eat, as based on what the Bible teaches. In the book, the foods that God intended for us to eat are called "God-given foods" while highly refined and processed foods that bear little resemble to the original God-given foods are called "non-God-given foods." The basic thesis is a healthy eating plan is composed of a variety of healthy God-given foods and avoids unhealthy, non-God-given foods.

Along with the Biblical information, the book includes many scientific studies showing that the proposed eating plan is also supported by much scientific research.

That research includes looking at what foods and food groups increase or decrease the risk of degenerative diseases like cancer, heart disease, and dementia. That is the "lifelong health" part of subtitle. This point is important for powerlifters to consider but is often neglected. Too many powerlifters have died young or been sidelined due to heart attacks and other very preventable health problems.

The "optimization of hormones" part of the subtitle refers to what type of eating plan best optimizes hormones like growth hormone, testosterone, and insulin. These hormones are extremely important to the powerlifter. Optimizing their levels will have a dramatic effect on a lifter's progress, ability to recover from workouts, and even ability to get psyched up for a workout or contest. They also play an important role in decreasing body fat and increasing muscle mass.

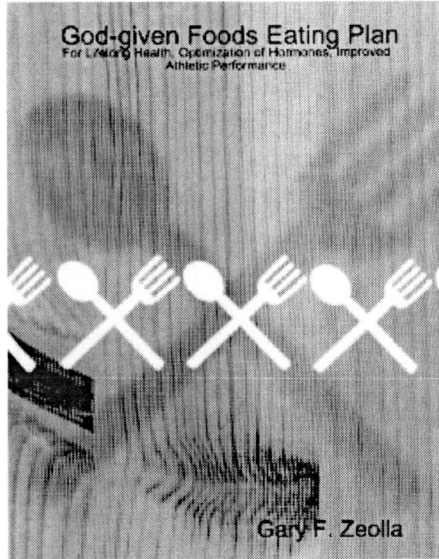

The "improved athletic performance" part of the subtitle refers to suggestions on how to eat optimally to recover from workouts and for adding muscular bodyweight, while reducing body fat.

Needless to say, it is not possible to repeat all of the information from that 260 page book in this book. But this chapter will summarize the chapters that look at different foods and food groups and give the basics on designing an eating plan. For much greater details on all these and other such important issues, see the full *God-given Foods Eating Plan* book.

Note that the following number of servings recommendations are based on a 2,500 calorie eating plan. These numbers need to be adjusted for other caloric levels.

Fruits and Fruit Juices

There are a wide variety of fruits available, such as: apples, apricots, bananas, berries, cantaloupe, cherries, dates, figs, honeydew, granadilla (passion fruit), grapes, grapefruit, guava, jackfruit, lemons, limes, kiwi, kumquats, mangos, nectarines, oranges, papayas, peaches, pears, plums, pineapple, pomegranates, tangerines, and watermelon.

All of these are healthy fruits. But dark or brightly colored fruits with a high water and high fiber content, lower caloric levels, and a low glycemic rating would be best. "Glycemic rating" refers to how much a food elevates blood sugar levels. A low level is best.

Fruits that fit all of these criteria are: apricots, berries (all colors and types), cherries, grapes (especially dark colored grapes), kiwis, and plums. These would be the best fruits. Next best would be various citrus fruits and the more "exotic" fruits like guava and papaya.

Dried fruit, due to its concentrated sugar content, is not as beneficial as fresh fruit. Similarly, the sugar in fruit juices is concentrated to an unhealthy level, and fruit juices are usually highly processed leading to a loss of nutrients and fiber.

Recommended amounts of fruit consumption would be 2-3 servings a day, with a serving being one medium-sized piece of whole fruit, like a medium-sized apple, or ½ to ¾ of a cup of berries. That amount will provide the benefits of fruit without an excessive consumption of fructose ("fruit sugar").

Limiting fructose consumption is important as fructose is not effective for muscle glycogen replenishment. Glycogen is the body's stored form of carbohydrate and is utilized during workouts. It is vital for it to be replenished afterwards so there will be fuel for the next workout. This point is addressed in detail in my *Eating Plan* book.

Vegetables

Vegetables can be classified according to their caloric content. Generally speaking, the lower the caloric content, the greater the nutrient density and the lower the glycemic rating. Also, as with fruits, the brighter the color, the greater is the antioxidant content.

Antioxidants neutralize free radical damage that occurs during a workout and in response to stressors like pollution. Antioxidants also play a vital role in reducing the risk of degenerative disease like heart disease and cancer.

Low calorie veggies include: artichokes, asparagus, beans (green, French, and yellow), bok choy (Chinese cabbage), broccoli, butterbur (fuki), cabbage (all types), cardoon, cauliflower, celery, chard, collard greens, cucumber, eggplant, garlic, kale, lettuce (all types), mustard greens, okra, onions, peppers (all colors and types), purslane, radicchio, radishes (all types), seaweeds (including dulse, spirulina, and kelp), spinach, sprouts (all kinds), rutabagas, turnip greens, water chestnuts, watercress, and zucchini. The glycemic index of these veggies is essentially zero.

Moderate calorie veggies include: carrots, gourds (all types), parsnips, pumpkin, squash (most types), and tomatoes. The glycemic index of these veggies is low to moderate.

High calorie veggies include: yams, sweet potatoes, root vegetables, plantains, corn, white potatoes, and beets. These are listed in order from lowest to highest glycemic. It is best to consume mostly the lower glycemic options.

Low calorie veggies can be eaten freely. The intake of moderate and high calorie vegetables needs to be kept moderate to keep overall carb consumption moderate. However, these veggies are excellent for muscle-glycogen replenishment.

It is best to aim for 8-9 servings of fruits and vegetables a day. With consuming 2-3 servings of fruit, this would mean 5-7 servings of vegetables should be consumed. A serving would be ½ cup of cooked vegetables or one cup of raw vegetables.

Nuts, Seeds, and Peanuts

Nuts include: almonds, Brazil nuts, cashews, chestnuts, hazelnuts, macadamia nuts, pecans, pistachios, and walnuts.

All of these, except chestnuts and walnuts, are especially high in healthy monounsaturated fatty acids (MUFAs). Walnuts are high in alpha linoleic acid (ALA), which can be converted into essential omega-3 fatty acids in the body. Chestnuts are the odd man out, being high in carbs rather than fats.

Seeds include: flax seeds, pumpkin seeds, sesame seeds, and sunflower seeds. All of these are higher in polyunsaturated fatty acids (PUFAs) than MUFAs, except pumpkins seeds, which contain about equal levels of each. Flax and pumpkin seeds are also high in ALA.

Peanuts are actually a legume. But they are similar to most nuts in that they are high in MUFAs.

MUFAs are more beneficial than PUFAs. MUFAs reduce heart disease risk greater than PUFAs do, and MUFAs elevate testosterone levels while PUFAs do not, so emphasis should be on the nuts and peanuts that contain high levels of MUFAs.

The benefits of nuts, seeds, and peanuts can be attained with consuming 1-2 ounces (about 1-2 small handfuls) a day.

Whole Grains and Refined Grains

Whole grains include amaranth, buckwheat, barley, brown rice, corn, kamut, millet, oats, quinoa, rye, spelt, triticale, and wheat.

Oats are probably the "best" whole grain as they have the strongest evidence of their benefits. But much evidence supports the value of the other whole grains as well.

But whatever type of grain is used, it is best to consume grains in their least processed form. Generally speaking, the less a grain is processed, the lower its glycemic rating. The manner in which a grain is milled also has an effect, with stone ground grains being lower glycemic than steel-milled grains.

More specifically, low glycemic whole grains include: stone ground whole wheat bread, sprouted grain bread, rye bread, pumpernickel bread, whole wheat Pita bread, oatmeal, brown rice, bulgur, quinoa, whole grain pancakes and waffles, whole wheat pizza shells, and whole wheat pastas and noodles. These should constitute the majority of grains consumed.

Moderate and high glycemic whole grain products include: whole grain breads other than the ones listed above, whole grain crackers, and whole grain cold breakfast cereals. These can be eaten, but in lesser amounts than the above, and the cereals should be low in sugar. You might need to go to a health food store to get some of these whole grain products.

All whole grains are excellent sources of complex carbs, which are ideal for muscle glycogen replenishment.

However, refined grains are not healthy. The refining process removes most of the original God-given nutrients and fiber. Moreover, without the fiber, the glycemic rating is increased. This makes refined grains less valuable for glycogen replenishment as the carbs are processed too quickly to be effectively converted into glycogen, and refined carbs are more likely to be stored as body fat.

It would be best to consume at least three servings of whole grains a day to attain the benefits these foods have to offer. A serving would be a slice of bread, 1/2 cup cooked rice, 3/4 cup corn, 2/3 cup cooked spaghetti, or ½ cup cooked oatmeal.

Legumes

All legumes (dried beans) are healthy foods, like adzuki beans, broad beans, great northern beans, kidney beans, lima beans, navy beans, and pinto beans, along with chickpeas (a.k.a., garbanzo beans), lentils, and peas. All these legumes are excellent sources of fiber, vitamins, minerals, protein, and low glycemic carbs.

If using canned beans, try to get ones lower in salt, and be sure to rinse them well. Baked beans and other processed beans are not particularly healthy if they have added sugar or artificial ingredients.

Studies show the benefits of legumes can be attained by consuming 2-6 (½ cup) servings a week. Since the carb levels are similar, a serving of legumes should substitute for a serving of whole grains or high calorie vegetables.

Soybeans are a legume that deserves special mentioned. Many claims have been made for soy's benefits, but more recent studies do not support these contentions. Moreover, the quality of soy protein is inferior to protein in animal foods. Also, soy's phytochemicals makes it a controversial food. Some claim soy lowers breast and prostate cancer risk while other claim it elevates the risk. Some studies also show soy lowers testosterone levels. Given these issues, much thought should be taken before consuming soy.

Vegetable Oils

Olive oil is the only truly Biblical oil, so not surprisingly there is much evidence of its health benefits. It is best to get cold-pressed, extra-virgin olive oil.

Unrefined nut and seed oils are also beneficial. What olive oil and unrefined nut oils have in common is they are high in MUFAs and antioxidants. Their consumption is associated with increased testosterone and HDL levels and lowered LDL levels. Unrefined tropical oils (extra-virgin coconut and red palm oils) are also natural oils with purported health benefits.

Refined nut and seed oils can have a limited place for high heat cooking purposes only. But oils derived from low-fat foods like corn and non-foods like canola are highly processed and are excessively high in omega 6s and PUFAs.

Especially problematic is hydrogenated oils and the resultant *trans* fats. Such fats are unnatural and extremely unhealthy. *Trans fats* are also found in fried foods. So any food that contains hydrogenated oil or that is fried would not be a healthy food.

To attain the benefits of olive and other healthy oils, it would be good to consume at least a tablespoon a day.

Olives and avocadoes are unique among fruits in that they are high in fat, namely MUFAs. So a serving of one of these could substitute for a serving of oil.

Coconut and palm oils are also high in fat, but in this case it is saturated fatty acids (SFAs). However, these SFAs are different from those found in animal foods in that they are medium chain triglycerides (MCTs), not long chain triglyceride (LCTs) like most SFAs.

I discuss the many controversies surrounding MCTs in my *Eating Plan* book. But the important points here are MCTs are not as easily stored as body fat as LCTs are, and MCTs are metabolized more like carbs than fats, thus they are a good energy source for workouts.

Red Meat and Poultry

It is shown conclusively in my *Eating Plan* book that the Bible does not support vegetarianism. God gave us meat for food, and meat-eating is assumed throughout Scripture with no negative connotations associated with it. However, certain restrictions are placed on the eating of meat.

Meat can only come from "clean" animals (explained in the book), the cover fat must be removed, and the blood drained. It is also best if the meat comes from animals that have not received hormones or antibiotics and are free-range fed. The meat should also be unprocessed, without added artificial ingredients.

With these restrictions, God-given meats are very nutritious and healthy foods. Lean meat's protein, vitamins, minerals, creatine, and testosterone-elevating properties make it the ideal muscle-building food. Beef, lamb, bison, venison, chicken, and turkey are important examples of clean meats.

However, the corollary to the above is that fatty meats, meats from animals that are not clean, and processed meats are not God-given. It is only with the consumption of such meats that health problems arise. The most important examples of unclean meats are pig products (pork, ham, bacon, sausage).

A modest consumption of meat and fowl for the average person would be a couple of servings a day, with those servings being 3-4 ounces of cooked meat. But powerlifters and those looking to gain muscular bodyweight will want to consume more than that.

Fish

Fish has been shown to have overwhelming health benefits. What makes fish so special is its omega-3 content. All clean fish are beneficial, but especially beneficial are fatty fish like halibut, herring, mackerel, salmon, sardines, trout, and tuna.

Mercury content of fish is a concern. But if only clean fish is consumed, then mercury intake will be kept to a minimum. And the benefits of fish far outweigh any possible detriments.

Important examples of clean fish include the above fatty fish, along with bass, cod, flounder, haddock, and whitefish.

Unclean fish would include catfish, shark, sturgeon, and swordfish. Also unclean are all shellfish and aquatic mammals.

Fish should be consumed at least once a week, up to once a day. These would be 3-4 ounce servings. A serving of fish would replace one of the servings of meat or fowl recommended previously.

Milk

Milk is an excellent source of protein, calcium, and other nutrients. However, the evidence for milk's benefits is split, and there are some potential problems with milk due to its fat and sugar content. So milk consumption should be limited to 1-2 cups per day.

Other Dairy Foods

Cheese is a good source of protein and calcium. The fat content is a concern, but some studies show it is not really problematic. But still, it is best to limit cheese consumption to no more than an ounce a day.

Included cheeses would be cheddar, Colby, Monterey Jack, mozzarella, provolone, and Swiss. However, cheese foods, cheese spreads, and other processed cheeses contain less protein and calcium than real cheese, and they contain many artificial ingredients, so they are best avoided.

Cottage cheese is an excellent source of slow-digesting protein, providing more protein with less fat than hard cheeses. It is also widely available in low-fat versions. But due to its salt content, consumption should be limited to a cup a day.

Butter and cream are both almost pure fat, with very little nutritional content. And the evidence is that the fat is problematic. So butter and cream should only be used in very limited amounts, if at all.

Ice cream is too high in saturated fat and sugar and often artificial ingredients to be a healthy food.

However, yogurt is an especially healthy form of milk due to its beneficial bacteria. It is also higher in calcium and protein than milk. Many do not like the taste of yogurt, but ways to make it more palatable are discussed in my *Eating Plan* book. Due to similar carb content, a serving of yogurt should substitute for a serving of milk.

Protein powders are a processed food. But the processing is to concentrate one main nutrient in milk, the protein content. Other nutrients like calcium are also retained, so protein powders are a good alternate to milk for fat-free, sugar-free protein.

Cheese, cottage cheese, yogurt, and protein powders are all good sources of high quality protein. A total of a couple of servings a day of these foods would be good to consume for this reason. Powerlifters will want to consume even more.

Eggs

Eggs contain the most bioavailable form of protein of any unprocessed food. Eggs are also an excellent source of a variety of nutrients. But due to their cholesterol content, eggs have received a "bad rap." However, studies show eggs can be eaten at an average of one per day without ill-effects on blood cholesterol levels.

Beverages

Water is by far the best beverage. But a moderate consumption of alcohol, especially wine, has reported health benefits. However, the over consumption of wine and other alcoholic beverages can lead to various health and other problems, so much caution should be taken when consuming alcoholic beverages.

Similarly, tea and coffee, if consumed in moderation, can have some benefits due to their antioxidant content, but they can be detrimental if consumed in excess.

Green tea is most famous for its antioxidant content, but black, white, and oolong tea all also contain different types of antioxidants, so it is good to utilized all these types of tea. But note that only freshly brewed tea contains antioxidants. Freeze dried iced tea mix does not.

However, carbonated and non-carbonated soft drinks are chemical connotations, made with refined sugars and artificial ingredients. So such beverages would not be healthy in any sense.

Honey and Other Sugars

Honey is the only Biblical sweetener, and there is evidence of its benefits. But still, it is pure sugar, and the Bible itself says it should only be used in limited amounts.

Other unrefined sugars include molasses and maple syrup. These have some nutrient content, but the amounts are not that great, and they are still pure sugar. In addition, about half of the sugar content in honey, molasses, and maple syrup cannot be used for muscle-glycogen replenishment. So even such unrefined sugars should only be used in limited amounts, no more than one tablespoon total a day.

Brown rice syrup is unique among sugars in that all of the carbs are effective for muscle-glycogen replenishment. Its mixture of carbs is digested over an extended period of time. This makes it good for pre- and post-workout nutrition. It can be found in health food stores.

However, refined sugars, by whatever name they are called, are not healthy. Refined sugars have no nutrient value except for carbs. And those carbs are not effective for muscle glycogen replenishment. In addition, refined sugars are very likely to be stored as body fat.

Besides "sugar" other names for refined sugar that might be seen on an ingredients label are: high fructose corn syrup, corn syrup, corn syrup solids, cane juice, cane syrup, clarified fruit juice, glucose, dextrose, sucrose, fructose, monosaccharides, and disaccharides. All of these should be avoided.

Condiments

Salt (sodium) is a necessary nutrient, but in excessive amounts it can have adverse health effects. So it is best to avoid high-salt processed foods and to use a salt shaker sparingly.

Various spices have different claimed beneficial health effects, but the evidence is lacking in most cases. Also, for some people, too much of some spices can be problematic, so use caution when trying a new spice. But in moderation, spices are a good way to naturally flavor food.

The various processed condiments, like ketchup and mayonnaise, tend to contain excessive amounts of salt, along with sugars, and sometimes unhealthy fats. So if they are used at all, they should be used sparingly. Healthier alternatives can sometimes be found, with salsa being a very good option.

Non-caloric Sweeteners and Other Artificial Ingredients

Stevia is the only natural, non-caloric sweetener. It is preferable to artificial sweeteners, like aspartame and saccharine. Such artificial sweeteners are to be avoided as their safety is questionable. But if you have to choose one, sucralose is probably the safest option.

Also to be avoided are artificial flavorings, colorings, preservatives, and any other artificial chemicals food manufactures add to food. All such ingredients are unnatural with questionable safety.

Desert and Snacks Foods

Most desert and snack foods are composed of unhealthy ingredients, like white flour, refined sugars, hydrogenated oils, lard, and artificial ingredients. Such foods are nutritional worthless, detrimental to health and exercise performance, and very likely to be stored as body fat.

Moreover, commercial desert and snack foods are produced in such a way as to encourage overeating them. Eating things like cake, pies, and candy is the surefire way to an unhealthy and overweight body and poor exercise performance.

Chocolate

Pure chocolate has been shown of late to have various health benefits. However, often the chocolate is mixed with large amounts of unhealthy foods, most notably refined sugar, so such candies should be avoided.

But dark chocolate with at least a 70% cocoa content or unsweetened cocoa powder are ways to attain the benefits of chocolate without an excessive amount of sugar or artificial ingredients. But it only takes a little chocolate to provide the potential benefits, a half to one ounce of dark chocolate or a teaspoon or two of cocoa powder.

Designing an Eating Plan

The first step in designing a performance and health enhancing eating plan is to focus on eating only the foods God intended you to eat. Replacing unhealthy foods with a variety of healthy foods will make a dramatic difference in your health and powerlifting progress.

The second step is deciding on the food choices for each meal and the best proportion of the three macronutrients: protein, carbs, and fat. In my *Eating Plan* book, I recommend the following proportions.

Fat: 30-50%
Protein: 20-35%
Carbs: 30-50%

The book provides much detail on why these are the ideal proportions. But here, if will just be said, you do not need to do a lot of calculations to attain these proportions. Just design each meal as follows. Each main meal should contain a low-glycemic carb source, a high quality protein source, a source of testosterone elevating fat, and a source of antioxidants.

What this translates into for a basic dinner is a potato, sweet potato, or serving of rice, a serving of some sort of meat, a serving or two of vegetables, and a salad with olive oil or flax seed oil for the dressing. Many more examples are given in the book.

The third step is the daily meal schedule. It is best to eat every 2-4 hours, or about 5-7 times a day. Doing so will elevate the metabolism and enable more food to be consumed without a gain of body fat.

This is an important point as the more food you consume the better you will be able to recover from workouts. Or to put it another way, the more you eat, the greater workload you will be able to handle without overtraining. In fact, I have heard it said, "There is no such thing as overtraining, just under-eating."

This is probably an overstatement, but it holds a lot of truth. You simply will not recover from hard workouts if you do not eat sufficient food. But how do you eat a lot of food without gaining body fat? The answer is by putting together all of the points in this chapter and in my *Eating Plan* book.

First off, another statement to remember is, "Not all calories are created equal." By this is meant that some types of calories are much more likely to be stored as body fat than others.

Sugars of all types, high glycemic carbs, saturated fats, and *trans* fats are the most likely to be stored as body fat, while protein, low gly-cemic-complex carbs, and MCTs are the least likely. As such, eating ample amounts of the latter while avoiding the former would be the way to add muscular body weight while avoiding body fat gain.

Second, eating several times a day will fire up the metabolism, causing the excess calories to be burned off as body heat.

Third, hard training, including cardio, will burn off the calories.

Finally, don't try to increase your food intake all at once. That will lead to fat gain and could just make you sick. Instead, gradually in-creasing your food intake over a period of time will train your body to utilize large amounts of calories with laying down body fat.

I am 5'1", weigh 120-something pounds, and am in my late 40s, but I probably eat more than many men larger and younger than I am. I don't eat a whole lot at any given meal, but I eat six times a day. With doing so, the calories add up, but I am anything but fat. A week's worth of my eating plan is presented in the final chapter of my *Eating Plan* book.

Body Fat Percent

A standard scale only tells you if you are gaining or losing body-weight. But it would be good to have an objective way of gauging whether that weight is in the form of muscle or fat. To do so requires measuring your body fat percentage. The following chart presents typical body fat percentages for different body types.

Body Type	Female	Male
Athlete	<17%	<10%
Lean	17-22%	10-15%
Normal	22-25%	15-18%
Above Average	25-29%	18-20%
Overfat	29-35%	20-25%
Obese	35+%	25+% (am-i-fat.com)

A simple but accurate method to measure body fat percent is with skin-fold calipers. These measure the amount of "pinchable" flab on various parts of the body. The measurements are then compared to a chart that gives the fat percent. Such calipers are available from Parrillo Performance and some sporting goods stores. But they require having another person take the body measurements for you.

A way to determine your body fat by yourself is with a body fat scale, like the ones manufactured by Tanita. It is not quite as accurate but is very easy to use (see Appendix #1).

Cheating

Before closing this chapter, it would be good to address a question many ask, is it okay to cheat on occasion and consume unhealthy foods? The answer here really depends on what kind of cheating you have in mind and what is best for you personally.

Some advocate setting aside a "cheat day" in which anything goes all day long. That frankly is nuts. You can consume a lot of very unhealthy food if you eat junk all day long. Moreover, putting that much unhealthy food into your body at once will basically undo any benefits you might receive from eating healthy the other six days. As a result, in the long run, you won't notice much improvement from a healthy eating plan.

But it would be possible to have a "cheat meal" once or twice a week, as long as you don't make it a "pig-out" meal. In other words, a reasonable amount of unhealthy foods for one meal will not cause problems. Such a meal could be timed to coincide with a special event, such as a holiday meal. It would also be okay to have a "cheat food" once in while, such as having an unhealthy desert or snack. For instance, if you really love ice cream, you could plan on having a dish say every Sunday, or even every Wednesday and Sunday.

However, where a problem might come in for some is consuming an occasional cheat meal or food will keep your cravings for unhealthy foods alive. In other words, you might find that if you eat that dish of ice cream on Sunday, you're craving ice cream or other sweets the rest of the week. So for some, it might be best to avoid such foods altogether. By doing so, you will eventually lose any such cravings.

It just depends on the person. Some might find that eating a dish of ice cream once or twice a week will satisfy their cravings so they won't crave ice cream or other junk foods otherwise. But others will find that a dish of ice cream incites their cravings for more and more. It's all a matter of what works best for you.

Another thing to consider is some may find it difficult to stop with a reasonable amount of a given junk food. You might decide to eat a small dish of ice cream but end up eating the whole quart.

One way to avoid this would be to scoop out a reasonable amount into a dish, put the carton back in the freezer, and then go to another room and sit down and eat the dish of ice cream. That way, you'll be less tempted to go back for seconds. The same approach can be used for any kind of junk food or even healthy foods you tend to overeat.

But if that doesn't work, then it would be best to avoid junk food altogether, at least until you get your cravings under control.

Sleep and Stress

In addition to your eating habits, your sleeping habits can have a dramatic effect on your training progress. A lack of sleep will lower growth hormone and testosterone levels, increase the levels of the "bad" hormone cortisol, and upset the balance of the hormones leptin and ghrelin, which can lead to weight (fat) gain. It will also lessen your ability to recover from your workouts. All these points together will sabotage your powerlifting training.

I know how very damaging a lack of sleep can be as I rarely get a good night's sleep due to one or another health problem keeping me awake. There is no doubt this is the prime reason I have not made the progress I feel like I could have made in my training.

But you the reader have no such excuse. If you are serious about being successful in powerlifting, eight hours of sleep a night is absolutely essential. The old adage for gaining muscular bodyweight still hold true today, "Lift big, eat big, sleep big."

Also very damaging is stress. Emotional stress also increases cortisol levels. Stress can also upset the appetite, causing some to eat too little and others to eat too much. In addition, it can increase the risk of various diseases, like heart disease, stroke, immune disorders, colds and flu, gastrointestinal problems, and even cancer. However, relaxation techniques can lower stress and thus reduce cortisol levels.

What this all means is sleep and relaxation are vital for a successful powerlifting career and for good health in general; while a lack of sleep and relaxation can seriously impair your progress, disrupt hormone production, and be damaging to your health.

Chapter Twenty
Pre- and Post-workout Nutrition

What you consume before and after a workout can have a dramatic affect on the quality of the workout and on how well you recover afterwards. But what kind of foods and when to consume them will be determined by your training schedule.

Schedules

I've used two basic schedules for my workouts. At one time, I would work out in the early afternoon, but now I work out in the late afternoon.

When I worked out in the early afternoon, my schedule was to finish eating lunch by 12:30 pm, then to start my workout around 2:00 pm. I found that I needed about an hour and a half or so for my whole foods lunch to digest before a workout. I would then consume a post-workout drink immediately after my workout. Then one to two hours later, I would eat dinner. I found that the liquid post-workout drink would digest within that time, so it did not "spoil" my dinner.

Now, I usually work out after 4:00 pm. That is too long after lunch to not consume something before the workout. So now I will consume a pre-workout drink about 45 minutes before my workout. Again, with being a liquid meal, that is sufficient time for it to digest.

Immediately post-workout I mix 3-4 grams of glutamine in a glass of water and drink that. Glutamine will be discussed in Chapter 22. I then shower and eat dinner. I thus eat dinner about half an hour after the end of my workout.

The main point is, it is best to consume some kind of meal before a workout to provide energy for the workout, but how long before depends on if it is a whole foods or a liquid meal. A whole foods meal will take about twice as long to digest as a liquid meal.

It is then vital to consume nutrients post-workout. If you will be eating a meal within an hour after your workout, that will provide the needed nutrients. But if it is going to be longer than an hour, then it is important to consume a post-workout drink so your body has nutrients to begin repairing muscle tissue and to replenish muscle glycogen.

Whatever your workout schedule, these basic principles will apply. You need food before and after a workout. But the kind of food will greatly affect your workout and recovery ability. Different possibilities will be addressed next.

Pre-Workout Meal

The most important macronutrient to consume pre-workout is carbohydrates (carbs) to provide energy for the workout. But careful attention must be paid to the glycemic response of the carbs.

Low glycemic carbs will cause a minor rise in blood sugar, but the blood sugar then stays elevated for an extended period of time, so low glycemic carbs will provide energy throughout the workout. However, I have found that if the carbs are too low glycemic I do not feel energized enough for the workout, especially at the start of it.

High glycemic carbs, on the other hand, will cause a large spike in blood sugar, but this will in turn cause the body to over-release insulin, and the blood sugar and thus energy levels will plummet. If this happens in the middle of a workout, you'll drag through the rest of it.

What this means is the ideal would be to have a moderate glycemic response from your pre-workout meal.

When I was eating lunch an hour and a half or so before a workout, I found the best carb source was oatmeal. Yes, I ate oatmeal for lunch as it is an ideal low glycemic carb source. I would use about a half a cup of dry oatmeal.

Another option I often used was to make a sandwich using sprouted grain bread (available in the freezer section of health food stores). Such bread is also low glycemic. Either of these meals will provide sustainable energy for the workout.

But I found it helped if I added a teaspoon of honey or a small handful of raisins to the oatmeal. Honey and raisins are natural ways to sweeten the oatmeal and are high in antioxidants. They are both moderate to high glycemic, so they would cause enough of a blood sugar spike to get me started for the workout, but not so much that my blood sugar would drop excessively during the workout. Ketchup or salsa would do the same for the sandwich.

The second most important macronutrient pre-workout is protein. During heavy exercise, along with carbs, the body will utilize amino acids for energy. If there are amino acids in the bloodstream from a recent meal containing protein, the body will utilize those amino acids. But if not, the body will break down muscle tissue for energy. But consuming protein pre-workout will prevent this muscle breakdown. Protein also helps modulate the blood sugar response from the carbs.

When eating oatmeal, I would make the oatmeal using a cup of reconstituted protein powder or drink a cup of protein powder with the oatmeal. When eating a sandwich, I would always use some kind of meat, usually roast beef.

268

The final macronutrient is fat. Some recommend not consuming fat pre-workout as it is hard to digest. But it is for just that reason that I make sure to consume a small amount of fat. Fat provides satiety, so it prevents hunger during a workout.

Just as important, fat increases testosterone levels. But not just any fat does so, only saturated fatty acids (SFAs) and monounsaturated fatty acids (MUFAs) do, polyunsaturated fatty acids (PUFAs) do not.

When eating oatmeal, I added a small handful of nuts or peanuts to the oatmeal, which are high in MUFAs. But I'd be careful not to add too much, or the food would feel like it was "sitting" in my stomach.

For the sandwich, roast beef is high in MUFAs and SFAs, so it would provide both the protein and fat. Despite popular conceptions, red meat actually contains slightly more MUFAs than SFAs. If I used a low fat meat like chicken breast, then I would eat a small handful of nuts with the sandwich.

With the oatmeal, I usually drank a glass of homemade vegetable juice, and with the sandwich, I would eat a side of some kind of vegetables. These would provide vitamins, minerals, and antioxidants.

There are many other options besides oatmeal or a sandwich. The previous chapter gave examples of different low glycemic carb sources, along with many other options for the protein and fat sources.

Pre-Workout Drink

When I was eating a meal 1½ hours pre-workout, I would drink a glass of tea a half an hour before my workout. This would provide caffeine to help get me psyched up and energized for the workout, along with antioxidants to reduce workout-induced free radical damage.

When I changed my schedule and began consuming a pre-workout drink before workouts, I simply used my tea rather than water for mixing the dry ingredients into. I usually make a cup of hot tea the evening before my workouts and mix the dry ingredients into it at that time, then keep it in the refrigerator until workout time. Ice can be added if you need to keep it chilled until workout time. Or you can put the dry ingredients into a shaker bottle and add water when needed. In this case, you would have to use iced tea mix rather than brewed tea.

At the same time I changed my schedule, I was diagnosed with reactive hypoglycemia (low blood sugar). What this means is, when I consume carbs, especially high glycemic carbs, my blood sugar will raise more than for most people about half an hour after eating, but then it will crash down too low an hour after that. With the diagnosis, I attained a home blood sugar monitor, so I now had a very objective way of testing how different carb sources affect my blood sugar levels.

With this condition, one concern I had was keeping my blood sugar from dropping too low by the end of my workouts. As such, I really needed to experiment to find an appropriate carb source for my pre-workout drink.

Many advocate using powdered dextrose. Dextrose is the name for glucose when used in food production. Glucose is the sugar found in the blood and in glycogen, so you would think dextrose would be the ideal pre- and post-workout carb. However, I already knew that dextrose is the worse possible option for a pre- (or post-) workout drink. I had found this out when I first started powerlifting again.

At that time, I began using a creatine complex post-workout that contained dextrose. During that time, I gained weight. I also noticed that I simply could not eat as much as usual as I was always feeling "stuffed," so I was eating less but still gaining weight. With the way my clothes were fitting, it was obvious that the weight gain was due to fat, not muscle or glycogen. It just seemed like my metabolism had slowed down. Meanwhile, I began dragging through my workouts.

I now know what was happening. Dextrose is very high glycemic, so it really spikes then crashes blood sugar. It is also metabolized so quickly that the body is not able to utilize it for energy or for glycogen replenishment, so it is simply deposited as body fat. Also, such a blood sugar spike post-workout neutralizes the growth hormone spike that normally occurs post-workout. All of these factors lead to a slowed metabolism and an increase in body fat.

I am not the only person who has experienced such problems with dextrose, as many people have emailed me who have experienced the exact same problem. So do yourself a favor and avoid dextrose.

The next possible option is maltodextrin. It is metabolized slower than dextrose, so it does not have the problem of causing an increase in body fat. However, maltodextrin is every bit as high glycemic as dextrose. When I tried it pre-workout, my blood sugar had dropped well below normal by the end of my workout.

I also tried two products from Protein Factory (see Appendix #1), *Rice Oligodextrin* and *Oat Muscle*. I recommend both of these items in my *God-given Foods Eating Plan* book as they are advertised as being low glycemic. However, once I tested them using my blood glucose monitor, I found that they both spiked and crashed my blood sugar as much as maltodextrin, so I no longer recommend them.

Another carb source I recommend in that book and mention in the previous chapter is brown rice syrup. Using two tablespoons of it in my pre-workout drink caused a moderate spike in blood sugar, and I

felt energized throughout my workouts. This makes sense given what I mention in the previous chapter about its carbs being digested over a period of time. It would also work well in a post-workout drink since all of the carbs are effective for muscle glycogen replenishment.

However, my blood glucose was a little too low after my workouts. But for those without blood sugar problems this probably would not be an issue. But what might be a problem is brown rice syrup does not dissolve well in cold water. It dissolves just fine if I mix it into my tea while it is still hot, but it would be necessary for some to use a carb source that does not require mixing in hot water. This is also necessary if a similar drink is used at a contest, as will be discussed in the next chapter.

After some more investigation, I came across Ultimate Nutrition's *Pure Muscle Carbs*. It is actually maltodextrin, with a small amount of fructose added to it. I'm not sure if it is due to the presence of the fructose, which is very low glycemic, or if it contains a different type of maltodextrin than the maltodextrin I had used before, but it produced a moderate blood glucose response, and I felt energized for my workouts. Moreover, my blood sugar did not drop too low afterwards, and I have not noticed any fat gaining effects from it. It should also be noted that the amount of fructose is minimal, so this product would also be good for a post-workout drink.

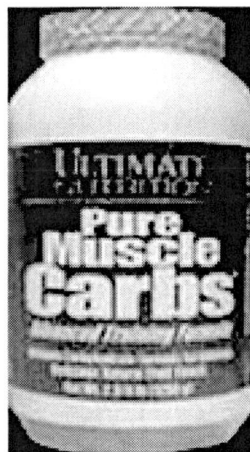

One last product I tried is Optimum Nutrition's *100% Natural Oats & Whey*. This product interested me for several reasons. First, as the name indicates, it is all natural. Second, it would provide both the carbs and protein in one product, so it would be easier to use. Third, the oats are whole grain, with added oat bran, so it is a healthier source of carbs than the refined carbs in *Pure Muscle Carbs*.

Finally, and most important for this discussion, it is low glycemic, producing even less of a blood glucose spike than any of the previous items, and my blood sugar was within the nor-

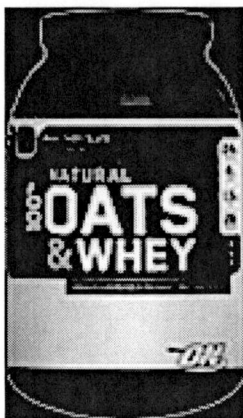

mal range afterwards. However, it is too low glycemic. It does not provide that bit of blood sugar spike I've found I need to feel energized for a workout. But I found if I added a tablespoon of brown rice syrup to a serving of the *Oats & Whey* that worked out well.

However, when you read the fine print of the ingredients list you'll see that the name is somewhat of a misnomer. There is actually more honey and pure cane juice than oats in the product. As a result, it is rather high in sugar. This means this product would not be effective for muscle glycogen replenishment and thus not good post-workout.

All of this is to say that brown rice syrup, UN's *Pure Muscle Carbs* or ON's *Oats & Whey* would all work well for a pre-workout drink. The first two would also be good post-workout.

The protein source for a pre-workout drink is obvious, protein powder. I prefer to use a blended protein, using whey, egg white, and casein, customized at Protein Factory. But many other brands and types of protein powder would work as well.

Now for the most controversial item, the fat source. Again, many say fat should not be used as it takes too long to digest. But again, without any fat, I get hungry before the end of my workout. Fat also further prevents blood sugar spikes and crashes.

The obvious source for the fat is some kind of vegetable oil. But, as already stated, MUFAs elevate testosterone levels while PUFAs do not. This means high PUFA oils like corn or soybean would not be ideal. Much better would be olive oil or high oleic peanut or sunflower oil, all of which are mostly MUFAs.

Another possibility is MCT oil. MCTs were mentioned in the previous chapter. But important here is they are metabolized more like carbs than fats, so using MCT oil in a pre-workout drink is ideal. You get the satiety and testosterone-raising effects of fat, along with another energy source for your workout. So I now often use MCT oil in my pre-workout drink, Ultimate Nutrition's *Premium MCT Gold* to be exact.

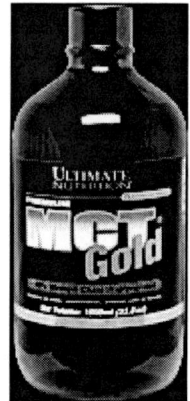

Putting this all together, my basic pre-workout drink is as follows:

Brewed, iced tea – 2 tea bags, 10 ounces of water
Brown rice syrup (2 tbs.) or *Pure Muscle Carbs* (1 – 70 cc scoop)
Blended protein powder – 1 scoop
(or 2 scoops *Oats & Whey* and 1 tbs. brown rice syrup instead of the previous two)
Olive or MCT oil – 1 teaspoon
Creatine – 3-4 grams (to be discussed in Chapter 22)

This drink provides the following nutrient values (when using brown rice syrup and olive oil):

Calories: 298
Carbs: 37g (50% of calories)
Protein: 25g (33%)
Fat: 5.5g (17%)

Another way to look it is the caloric proportion of carbs to protein to fat is approximately 3:2:1 or about 150 calories from carbs, 100 from protein, and 50 from fat. With consuming a total of 300 calories, I have found this ratio provides sufficient carbs for energy but also sufficient protein and fat to modulate the blood sugar response.

But these amounts need to be adjusted based on the reader's body size and personal needs. It would be best to experiment with the different mentioned products and differing amounts and ratios of each ingredient and to see what works best for you.

It should be noted that the overall glycemic response of a meal depends on the type of carbs, the amount of carbs, and the ratio of carbs to protein and fat. So you need to experiment with all three of these factors. But the preceding recipe is a good place to start.

Post-workout Drink

If I were to consume a drink immediately a post-workout as I used to, I would use the exact same formula as above, except for the iced tea. I would add cocoa powder instead for the antioxidant content.

The brown rice syrup and *Pure Muscle Carbs* are ideal for muscle glycogen replenishment. The protein powder will provide amino acids for the body to begin to repair the muscle damage caused by a hard workout. The oil will help to prevent the drop in testosterone that can occur post-workout.

Post-workout Meal

As mentioned, after I shower, I eat a regular dinner. However, even if you consume a post-workout drink, it is still good to eat a regular meal one to two hours afterwards. This will provide sufficient time for the drink to digest, and your body will again be craving nutrients to continue recovery from the workout.

A post-workout meal should be similar to a pre-workout meal in that a low-glycemic carb source should be eaten for muscle glycogen replenishment, a high quality protein source for amino acids for muscle repair, a source of testosterone elevating fat, and a source of antioxidants for neutralizing free radicals. An example would be the meal outlined in the previous chapter, as that is what I consider to be a basic meal pattern, good anytime, post-workout and otherwise.

Adjusted Nutrient Values

There is a problem with the label information for the *Pure Muscle Carbs*. The label states that a "serving" is two (70 cc) scoops, which is said to weigh 55g and provide 208 calories and 52 grams of carbs.

However, when I weighed the contents of just one scoop, it was 45 grams. I can only assume there is much settling and compacting of the contents during storage and shipping. So the product as I now have it is denser than when Ultimate Nutrition did its calculations. The adjusted values for one 45 gram scoop are 166 calories and 43 g carbs.

Meanwhile, according to the label of the Lundberg Farms *Organic Brown Rice Syrup* I use, two tablespoons provide 150 calories and 36 grams of carbs. As such, one scoop of the *Pure Muscle Carbs* provides slightly more calories and carbs than two tablespoons of brown rice syrup. This would slightly change the given values for the drink.

But there would be a greater difference when using the *Oats & Whey*. The scoop that comes with it is an 80 cc scoop, and the serving size is one heaping scoop providing 200 calories, 24 grams of protein, and 22 grams of carbs (vanilla flavor). But doing some weighing, two level 70 cc scoops weigh the same as one heaping 80 cc scoop. I measure it using two 70 cc scoops as it is hard to gauge what a "heaping" scoop is supposed to be.

The blended protein powder I use contains about 25 grams protein, a gram each of carbs and of fat, and about 110 calories per scoop. With the brown rice syrup and oil, this gives the indicated values of the drink containing a 3:2:1 ratio of carbs to protein to fat and about 300 calories.

However, when making a drink using a serving (2 – 70 cc scoops) of *Oats & Whey*, the protein to carb ratio would only be about 1:1, and it would provide only about 240 calories. This could also be why I did not feel sufficiently energized when using just this product. But by adding the tablespoon of brown rice syrup, that brings the carbs up to 39 grams, or again (with teaspoon of oil) about a 3:2:1 ratio of carbs to protein to fat and the calories to over 300.

Another option besides a drink for pre- or post-workout nutrition will be discussed in Chapter 22.

Chapter Twenty-one
Cutting Weight/
Post-Weigh-in Nutrition

In this chapter, I am going to outline how I go about cutting weight and eating and re-hydrating after weigh-ins for contests. I will use as an example my procedure before NASA Northeastern States Championships, held Saturday, June 7, 2008 at Washington High School in Washington, PA.

Weigh-ins were the evening before, at 6:00 pm at the high school. Of course, the following procedure will need to be modified if weigh-ins are at another time, either earlier in the day on Friday or not until the morning of the contest.

For this contest, I competed in the 114 pound weight class, masters (over 40 years old), pure (lifetime drug free) and open pure divisions. On Saturday May 31, one week before the contest, I weighed 121.0 first thing in the morning. The actual weight class limit is 114.5 pounds (52 kilograms), so that meant I needed to cut 6-1/2 pounds in 6-1/2 days.

Let me interject here that it is vital to have a very accurate digital scale. I use a Tanita Body Fat Scale that has proved very accurate every time I have checked it against a contest scale. This is vital as without it, you will not know exactly how much weight you need to lose and how you are progressing through the week. I know of lifters who have starved themselves to make weight, only to find out they were five pounds under when they weighed in.

The Cut Weight Procedure

My final workout plans for this contest got messed up due to a finger becoming infected two weeks before the contest, as discussed in Chapter 15. I originally planned on putting in my last heavy bench workout in on Wednesday (5/28, 10 days out) and deadlift workout in on Thursday (5/29, 9 days out). Then I was going to do a light squat workout on Sunday (6/1) and a light bench workout Monday (6/2).

In that case, I would have started my full cut weight procedure on Saturday morning. That would give my body time to recover from the heavy workouts before restricting food intake. But as it was, I was unable to put in those two heavy workouts, so I did both light squats and light deadlifts on Sunday, working up to my openers.

275

I then put in a light bench workout on Monday, again working up to my opener. I still began cutting weight Saturday morning, but I ate a little more than I would have Sunday afternoon before my workout to give fuel for that workout.

My cut weight procedure is very simple; it is centered on low-fat animal protein and low calorie vegetables.

By low fat animal protein I mean: skinless chicken and turkey breast, tuna fish packed in water, low fat fresh fish like cod and haddock, egg whites, low-fat cottage cheese, and protein powders. A list of low calories vegetables appears in Chapter 19 of this book.

I normally eat six times a day (breakfast, mid-morning snack, lunch, afternoon snack or pre-workout drink, dinner, bedtime snack). I continue this same pattern of eating while cutting. But I am especially careful to always consume one serving of a protein food and one or two servings of veggies with each meal.

Depending on how much weight I have to lose and how my weight loss is going, I might add a few additional foods, mainly sources of healthy carbs and fats. For the carbs, I might eat a serving or two of fruit instead of a serving of veggies. However, this time, I ate half a sprouted grain English muffin for Sunday lunch to give fuel for the light squat/ deadlift workout and used a tablespoon of brown rice syrup in my pre-workout drink. But I ate no grains or other carb sources otherwise.

For healthy fats, if weight allows, the most important thing to eat is fatty fish like salmon or sardines. Next would be nuts and seeds, then olive or other healthy oils. But again, the fruit and these fat sources are only consumed if my weight allows it and usually only early in the week. As weigh-ins draw near, then it is strictly the low fat protein and low calorie vegetables.

I generally use 3-4 grams of creatine in my pre-workout drink, which I drink about 45 minutes before my workouts. Normally, I would stop taking it after my last heavy workout. But with the problems this time, I used a dose before my last two light workouts. But I didn't use it at all during the week after that. But it might have been better to have stopped it earlier, about two weeks pre-weigh-in.

Come Wednesday evening (or 48 hours pre-weigh-in), I'll make one change to my eating plan. I only consume low-salt protein foods from then on. That eliminates all but the turkey and chicken breast. But I continue with most vegetables for the next 24 hours. However, even some veggies are high in sodium (like spinach and celery), so they need to be avoided as well. A software program like *DietPower* (see Appendix #1) or a book like Jean A.T. Pennington's *Food Values of Portions Commonly Used* will provide such information.

Day of Weigh-ins

What is done the day of weigh-ins depends on two things: when I am weighing in and what my weight is first thing that morning.

For this contest and my previous one, I weighed in at 6:00 pm the evening before the contest. For the previous contest, I was still 3.3 pounds over the morning of weigh-ins. To make weight, I had to use some "drastic" measures.

The first was to not eat or drink anything all day long. The second was to take two very hot and long baths. That left me completely dehydrated, and even at that, I still just barely made weight.

I ate and drank as much as I could that night, but I only weighed 117.0 the morning of the contest. In retrospect, I felt like I hadn't started getting "serious" in my restrictions soon enough. One more day, and my weight would have dropped significantly, and thus the drastic measures would not have been needed.

As it was, I never fully re-hydrated. The day of the contest, it ended up being in the mid-80s with wall to wall sunshine, and there was no A/C at the contest site. As a result, I basically "died" by deadlifts, missing my final attempt that I am sure I would have gotten if I had not still been dehydrated.

At that time, I vowed never to cut to 114s again if weigh-ins were not until the evening before, as opposed to 24 hours before. Obviously, if you have all day to eat and re-hydrate, it makes things much easier. But it turned out that the only contest with the gear rules I wanted at the time of the year I wanted once again had a 6:00 pm weigh-in.

But this time, I was determined not to be in the position of having to dehydrate myself the day of weigh-ins, especially since this time it was to be in the 90s with high humidity on contest day. So I started getting stricter on Tuesday. By Thursday, my weight was the same as it had been Friday the previous time, 117.8. I knew then I'd be okay.

Friday morning, my weight was 116.8. I then ate a very small breakfast, consisting of just an ounce or so of turkey breast, and that was it, no veggies this time. I also drank a small amount of water.

I then very fortunately was able to "move my bowels." And believe it or not, I lost a full pound.

I was still at 115.8 at noon, but I still ate a very small lunch, again, consisting of just a small amount of turkey breast. But that was it as far as food intake went for the rest of the day. I also drank a small amount of water. For the rest of the day, at most I would take very small sips of water or suck on ice cubes.

I then drove to my hotel room, taking my scale with me. After I got situated, it was 2:30 pm, and my weight was down to 115.0. By 4:00, I was at 114.8. It was then that I debated on taking a hot bath. But instead, I just began spitting. It would have helped if I had remembered to take some gum with me, but I still managed to get down to 114.2 by 5:30 pm.

I then left for weigh-ins. The meet director was late getting to the contest site for weigh-ins, so I spent that time doing some more spitting. Then right before actually weighing in, I tried to urinate one last time. But by that point, there was nothing left in me to come out.

I didn't actually weigh in until about 6:30 pm. My official weigh-in weight was 114.0, so I made it with half a pound to spare.

The Post-Weigh-In Procedure

To weigh-ins, I took a half gallon jug of water and two bottles with the ingredients for two of my normal pre-workout drinks. As mentioned in the previous chapter, this consists of a scoop of Ultimate' Nutrition's *Pure Muscle* Carbs, a scoop of protein powder, and a teaspoon of olive or MCT oil, along with five grams of creatine (in just one of the bottles). I also added a few dashes of Morton's *Lite Salt*. Immediately after weighing in, I mixed up the drinks and guzzled them down, along with some additional water.

Prior to the contest, I checked Subway's Web site to see if there was a Subway nearby, which there was, right across the street from the high school in fact. After weigh-ins, I ran across the street and picked up a 12" roast beef sub on wheat bread. But if there wasn't a Subway nearby, I probably would have ordered out for a pizza from my hotel.

After getting back to my hotel room, I ate the sub while drinking a glass of *Organic Very Veggie* juice (R.W. Knudsen brand). I also took *Ezekiel Sprouted Grain Bread* and chip steak with me in a cooler to eat latter, along with a bottle of salsa to use on the sandwiches.

I took another serving of creatine with the food, and I drank as much water as possible throughout the evening.

Note that I put two plastic ice packs in the cooler before leaving home. Then at the hotel, I kept putting ice in the cooler to keep everything in it cool. Of course, if there is a fridge in the hotel, that will make things a lot easier. If you go home between weigh-ins and the contest, even better.

For breakfast, I usually eat oatmeal or a multi-grain hot cereal. But unless there is a microwave at the hotel, that is out, so cold cereal will have to do. This time, I took a box of Cascadian Farm's *Oats & Honey*

Granola. I ate quite a bit of it for breakfast, with some almonds on it. I took some protein powder and a shaker cup to mix it up in and used that rather than milk on the cereal.

For the contest, I prepared three bottles with the dry ingredients for my normal pre-workout drink. But only one contained creatine. I took a small bottle of olive oil with me rather than adding it beforehand as I was afraid it would leak. All three drinks also contained two teaspoons of iced tea, and I also added some salt to each. I mixed up and drink the one with creatine after I arrived at the contest site, before warming up for squats, the second immediately after squats, and the third immediately after benches. I also took some Parrillo *Energy Bars* with me in case I was still hungry (see next chapter), along with a bottle of organic orange-carrot juice (Lakewood brand).

I also took in a half gallon water jug and had another gallon of water in my car, just in case I ran out.

The Reasoning Behind the Cut Weight Procedure

This procedure has been arrived at through trial and error from cutting weight for various contests. But there is also sound reasoning behind it. To fully understand this reasoning, it would be helpful to read my *God-given Foods Eating Plan* book as my cut weight procedure is a variant of that eating plan.

It should also be remembered that I suffer from a condition known as reactive hypoglycemia (low blood sugar). I normally eat six times a day, with each meal containing some high quality protein. Eating in this way keeps the blood sugar from fluctuating too much. It also keeps the metabolism elevated as protein has a greater thermogenic effect than fat or carbohydrates, and meat of any sort has a greater thermogenic effect than other protein source. In addition, eating protein this often ensures there is also a supply of amino acids for muscle recovery from hard workouts.

With that background, the rationale behind my cut weight procedure is as follows. I normally wait 36 hours after my last heavy workout to begin to cut weight. The reason here is simple—lifting heavy without eating adequately afterwards can lead to a breakdown of muscle, the last thing you want the week before a contest.

By continuing to eat six times a day with some protein at each meal, the metabolism is kept from dropping, as often happens when going on a "crash diet." Just as importantly, following a high protein diet prevents muscle loss while dieting, as detailed in my *Eating Plan* book. So I basically continue to consume almost as much protein when cutting weight as on my normal diet, with "normal" being about 1.5 grams per pound of bodyweight.

But the focus is on low-fat protein sources as fat contains over twice as many calories per gram as protein. As such, fat needs to be kept to a minimum to keep calories to a minimum while still allowing for sufficient protein intake.

However, if weight allows, the fatty fish, nuts, and seeds will provide essential fatty acids and monounsaturated fats. Both of these are very important for various reasons, as detailed in my other book, but here, the most important point is both help to elevate testosterone levels, which tends to drop when losing weight. The olive oil provides additional monounsaturated fats.

Meanwhile, carbs need to be eliminated in order to deplete glycogen stores. Glycogen is stored carbohydrate in the body. It holds four times its weight in water. As a result, eliminating the stores of glycogen will cause a rapid loss of bodyweight. But if weight allows, a serving or two of fruit will delay this depletion until later in the week. Thus energy levels will not be as low for as long.

Some will run or engage in other cardio during the week to further cut weight. But I warn against that since, as stated, hard exercise without food intake will break down muscle tissue. And besides, rest is vital the week before a contest.

The veggies serve two purposes. First, low-calorie veggies are the most nutrient dense food there is. This means they provide a large amount of nutrients at a very low caloric cost. So eating copious amounts of veggies will ensure adequate nutrition despite the low caloric intake.

Second, veggies are a great source of fiber. That fiber will help prevent constipation, a common problem when dieting and an especially big problem when trying to make weight. The last thing you want is fecal matter clogged up in your intestines when stepping on the weigh-in scale.

Fruit will also aid in this regard. But if you eat fruit, I would suggest sticking with what are called "the best fruits" in Chapter 19.

Some will use laxatives to be sure all fecal matter is eliminated. But I don't recommend that. It can be hard to "time" the effects. If the laxatives kick in too late or continue to have an affect the day of the contest, you might have problems. But I did use Twinlab's *FiberSol* for extra fiber, and that helped. So I would recommend *FiberSol* if you are getting constipated. I have also found a probiotic supplement helps in this regard. I prefer Nature's Way *Primadophilus Bifidus*.

I eliminate all high sodium foods 48 hours pre-weigh-in as sodium holds water; in this way body fluids can be easily lost. The hot baths the day of weigh-ins will eliminate any remaining water. But they are very draining, so try to avoid having to do so if at all possible.

Veggie consumption is stopped about 24 hours pre-weigh-in. Or an even better to look at it, at least 12 hours before your most likely last bowel movement before weigh-ins. Veggies are low in calories, but they do contain bulk. As already stated, this will help to prevent constipation. But you want to be sure your last serving of veggies will have time to pass through your system before weigh-ins. Otherwise, their bulk will still be in your intestines, adding bodyweight.

I have found that creatine causes water retention, so that is why it is eliminated at least a week before weigh-ins.

One question I am sure many are wondering about is if I feel hungry with this cut weight procedure. The answer is, not really. It might bother me on occasion, but with eating some protein and bulky carbs six times a day, I don't feel that hungry. Only the day of weigh-ins if I have to stop eating altogether does hunger become much of a problem.

The Reasoning Behind the Post-Weigh-In Procedure

After weighing in, it is vital to replenish lost liquids, electrolytes, glycogen, and creatine. Another point many do not think of is that cutting weight lowers testosterone and growth hormone levels, but these hormones are vital to have elevated for a contest as they heighten aggression, which is needed to attack the weights.

The post-weigh-in drink provides carbs via the *Pure Muscle Carbs*, to replenish glycogen, protein powder to elevate growth hormone, olive oil or MCT oil for the monounsaturated or saturated fats, which elevate testosterone levels, along with creatine. The water obviously is for re-hydration.

In my *Eating Plan* book I explain the relationship between growth hormone and protein and between fat and testosterone. Also, this mixture of protein, carbs, and fat gives the drink only a moderate glycemic response to keep blood sugar from spiking then crashing.

Morton's *Lite Salt* is a mixture of sodium chloride and potassium chloride. So adding it to the post-workout drinks will begin the process of restoring these electrolytes. But don't use too much, as more sodium and potassium is forthcoming.

The bun for the Subway sandwich obviously provides more carbs for glycogen replenishment. But with the sub, I'll get wheat rather than a white bun as it has a somewhat lower glycemic response. In fact, I tested the sub plus veggie juice meal with my glucose monitor prior to this time, and it produced a low glycemic response. But pizza, even with white crust, has a low glycemic response.

The reason for getting roast beef is red meat is the best food there is for elevating testosterone levels. A Subway sub is also high in sodium (1,800 mg/ 12" sub). Pizza would also be high in sodium. Normally, this is not a good thing, but now, it is vital to replenish sodium.

The chip steak I took with would also provide testosterone elevating red meat, and the bread would further help to replenish glycogen.

The *Very Veggie* juice is extremely high in potassium (740 mg/ cup). It is also high in other nutrients. I usually get the low sodium version as I figure there is more than enough sodium in the sub. But a high sodium version is also available (630 mg/ cup), which I would use if I was only eating my own chip steak sandwiches.

The salsa adds more sodium (140 mg/ tablespoon). I use it rather than ketchup or BBQ sauce as those both contain sugar, which is not good for glycogen replenishment. Ketchup and BBQ sauce also have higher glycemic responses than salsa.

I used to eat cold cereal for breakfast on a normal basis and the morning before a contest. But most cold cereals are high glycemic. That is why I now usually eat oatmeal or a multi-grain hot cereal, as they produce a low glycemic response. But unless there is a microwave at the hotel, that is not an option, so cold cereal will have to do.

Granola is lower glycemic than most cold cereals. Also, it is more caloric dense, with a half a cup providing more calories than found in a full cup of other cereals. Normally, this would not be good and could easily lead to over-eating. But now, the more calories that can be packed in without feeling sick, the better. But be sure the granola is not high in oil or other fats. I used Cascadian Farm's brand as it low-fat. Barbara's Bakery natural cereals are also lower glycemic than most cold cereals and low-fat, so those would also be good options.

Note that I was basically creatine loading from immediately after weigh-ins to before the contest. This of course replenishes creatine levels for the contest. It also causes water retention to help elevate the body weight. But I only used creatine with my first drink during the contest as I am concerned that too much could lead to cramping.

During the contest, I knew it would be important to keep my blood sugar on as an even keel as possible. In fact, another reason deadlifts did not go well at the prior contest is probably because what I was eating caused too much blood sugar fluctuation throughout the day.

282

I also wanted to keep things as normal as possible. Since I am used to my pre-workout drink, I drank one before each lift. It is moderate glycemic and easy to digest. I sometimes eat a Parrillo *Energy Bar* before a workout, as they are also moderate glycemic and easy to digest. These bars would also be good immediately post-weigh-in.

The orange-carrot juice is the only juice I found that is moderate glycemic. All others are very high glycemic. The orange-carrot juice is also high in potassium (365 mg/ cup), to keep that electrolyte from dropping during a contest. It also provides lots of the antioxidants vitamin A (beta carotene actually, 225% of the DV) and vitamin C (75% DV), along with lesser amounts of many other nutrients. The nutrients and especially antioxidants help prevent muscle damage that can occur during a grueling powerlifting contest.

For this contest I also added a few sprinkles of regular salt to the drinks, the reason being the heat. But I used regular salt rather than the *Lite Salt* since the orange-carrot juice would provide the potassium.

Of course, it is important to have plenty of water on hand. That is why I took in a half gallon water jug and had the foresight to have another gallon of water in my car. That way, I was sure not to run out.

One final point worth noting, I did not feel hungry at all during the contest, until I was warming up for deadlifts. As I tried to figure out why, it hit me—I had forgotten to add the oil to the pre-deadlifts drink. That shows why it is important to use some kind of oil in a pre-workout and contest drink. Fortunately, the hunger did not affect my performance, but it very well could have.

Changes for other Weigh-in Times

When I powerlifted in college, weigh-ins were always only the morning of the contest. Since I started competing again, I have avoided any such contests as I knew from back then how difficult that made things.

Obviously, you will not have much time to eat and re-hydrate with a morning of the contest weigh-in. That means you will have to be more realistic about how much weight you can cut for the contest. It will also mean that you need to make every minute and intake count after weigh-ins.

If I would enter such a contest, I would probably follow the same basic plan as above. But the meat would be out as it takes too long to digest. But bread is still good, with maybe a little peanut butter. I would recommend putting brown rice syrup on it rather than jelly, as unlike jelly, all of the carbs in brown rice syrup are good for glycogen replenishment.

Of course, you'd need to take everything with you. Drink the two drinks first, and then eat as much as you can without stuffing yourself. Drink some water otherwise. Then using liquid food during the contest will be even more important as you will still be re-hydrating.

My favorite weigh-in time is a full 24 hours before a contest. With that much time, you can get in several distinct meals through the day. I would recommend spacing out each meal 2-4 hours apart, as should be done for a normal eating plan. Only now, you would eat more than usual and focus on good for replenishing glycogen carbs, like grains. But there is no need to stuff yourself at any one sitting.

Weight Progression

Below is a summary of my weight progression for this contest. Unless otherwise indicated, these are taken first thing in the morning.

Date	Weight
5/31	121.0 (began cutting weight)
6/1	120.0
6/2	118.6
6/3	118.6
6/4	118.2
6/5	117.8
6/6	116.8
	115.6 (9:30 am)
	115.6 (11:30 am)
	115.8 (noon, after lunch)
	115.0 (2:30 pm, at hotel)
	114.8 (4:00 pm)
	114.2 (5:30 pm, after spitting)
	114.0 (official weigh-in)
6/7	118.0 (morning of contest)
6/13	118.8 (first workout post-contest)

The Results

The result of this procedure for this contest was perfection! I went 9/9 and broke eight NASA records. Most importantly, for all three of my final attempts I was able to stick with my original plans. My attempted weights were about the same as I had lifted for my last heavy workouts before the contest except to be rounded down due to the use of kilos at the contest. All three were full max lifts, but I got them.

What this means is, I was able to lose a total of seven pounds in six and a half days with virtually no loss of strength.

My Cutting Weight Eating Plan

Following are two days of my cutting weight eating plan. The first is from Monday, when I was still being a little "free" in my eating, consuming some carbs, fats, and salty foods, and when I put in my last (light) workout. The second is from Thursday, when I got more restrictive in my diet and was my rest day before the contest.

It would be most instructive to compare this eating plan to my normal plan. It is detailed in the final chapter of my *Eating Plan* book. But I will say here, my normal diet at that time averaged:

Calories – 2551
Carbs – 219g (32% of calories)
Protein – 190g (30%)
Fat – 110g (39%)
Sodium – 1170 mg
Potassium – 4810 mg

For other nutrients, my intake ranged from 130% of the RDA for thiamin to 617% for vitamin B_{12}. The emphasis on fat is because fat elevates testosterone levels, as discussed previously. But most of the fat is in the form of healthy monounsaturated fats.

Monday:
Breakfast:
Protein powder – 1 scoop
Almonds – 2 tablespoons
Minola (orange/ tangerine hybrid) – 1 medium

Mid-morning snack:
Cottage cheese – ½ cup
Peach – 1 medium

Lunch:
Stir fry:
Turkey breast – 3 ½ ounces
Green cabbage – ¾ cup chopped

Red cabbage – ¾ cup chopped
Carrots – 1 medium, diced
Onion and garlic – 1 tablespoon chopped
High oleic sunflower oil – 1 teaspoon

Pre-workout drink/ afternoon snack:
Protein powder – 1 scoop
Olive oil – 1 teaspoon
Brown rice syrup – 1 tablespoon

Dinner:
Chicken breast – 4 ounces
Broccoli – 1 cup
Salad (greens, various veggies) – 1 cup
Olive oil – 1 tsp.

Bedtime Snack:
Spinach Omelet:
1 whole egg, 2 egg whites
Spinach – ½ cup
High oleic sunflower oil – 1 teaspoon

Analysis:
Calories – 1341
Carbs – 79g (21%)
Protein – 160g (48%)
Fat – 46g (31%)
Sodium – 1030 mg
Potassium – 2830 mg

Thursday:
Breakfast:
Turkey breast – 3 ounces
Broccoli – 1 cup, raw

Mid-morning snack:
Salmon – 1/3 of 7.5 ounce can
Broccoli – 1 cup, raw

Lunch:
Turkey breast – 3 ounces
Steamed veggies:
Green cabbage – ¾ cup chopped

Red cabbage – ¾ cup chopped
Onion and garlic – 1 tablespoon chopped

Afternoon snack:
Turkey breast – 2 ounces
Broccoli – 1 cup, raw

Dinner:
Chicken breast – 3 ounces
Green beans – ½ cup
Salad (greens, various veggies) – 1 cup
Olive oil – 1 tsp.

Bedtime Snack:
Chicken breast – 2 ounces

Analysis:
Calories – 709
Carbs – 15g (9%)
Protein – 114g (64%)
Fat – 21g (27%)
Sodium – 350 mg
Potassium – 1980 mg

It can been seen that on both days, I kept my protein intake rather high, close to my normal level, but the calories are considerably less by cutting back on carbs and fat. The sodium is also very low on the last day, but the potassium is still reasonably high.

For other nutrients, on Monday I took in from a low of 45% for iron (due mainly to no red meat) up to 277% for vitamin C (thanks to the minola). On Thursday, things were lower, just 27% for vitamin E (due to no nuts and little oil), but still a whopping 1340% of vitamin B_{12} (from all the poultry). So I was able to retain a reasonable degree of nutrients despite the drastic drop in calories.

A Big Mistake

To emphasize some points in this chapter, it would be good to re-late a big mistake I once made after weigh-ins.

For background, there is a restaurant in Pittsburgh that is famous for its sandwiches. What makes the sandwiches unique is they put the French fries and coleslaw right on the sandwich. As I was working on this chapter, they just happened to be discussing this restaurant on a local radio talk show. The host said the idea of putting the fries and slaw on the sandwich originated due to truckers. They needed a meal they could put on their laps and eat with one hand while driving.

In any case, I have eaten at this restaurant twice. The first was when I went to eat at it with a group of guys as a teenager. One of the guys thought the idea of the fries and slaw being on the sandwich was just so neat. I thought it was kind of stupid. It just seemed like a way to pack in as many calories into your mouth as quickly as possible. Personally, I like to enjoy each food I eat; not shove them all at once into my mouth.

I don't remember much from that first visit, but my second visit was much more memorable. It was on September 1, 2006. I know the date because I competed at APF Pennsylvania States the next day, held on the south side of Pittsburgh.

For that contest, weigh-ins started at 9:00 am the day before. To make weight, I lost 9.3 pounds in seven days. I lost that weight mainly by cutting out carbs, thus depleting glycogen stores. Once I weighed in, needless to say, it was time to eat.

I had initially planned on stopping at a Subway on my way home. But then I passed by this particular sandwich shop. I remembered how it seemed like a great way to pack in as many calories into your mouth as quickly as possible, which is what I needed, so I stopped there instead. Big mistake.

Yes, those sandwiches are packed with calories. But it is not due to being high in carbs. The bread that is used is just two slices of normal-sized Italian bread. Where all of the calories come from is the sandwich being stacked high with a large serving of fatty meat, fatty cheese, the fatty French fries, and the fatty coleslaw. In other words, it is a load of fat.

On the aforementioned talk show, the host mentioned that after eating at this restaurant you feel like you have a bowling ball in your stomach. Or better, the host said, think of a Python who has just swallowed a raccoon. The snake will have a big bulge in the middle of its body and won't be hungry again for a month. That is how I felt.

I was left so bloated I wasn't able to eat near as much as I had hoped the rest of that day to get my weight back up for the contest the next day. During that contest, I felt terrible and dragged through it. Part of the reason for that was I never fully replenished my glycogen stores due to the stupidity of eating at that sandwich shop.

For my next contest, I ate at Subway after weighing in. That weigh-in was not until 6:00 pm the evening before the contest. But even with much less time to eat I felt much better for that contest.

Choosing an Appropriate Weight Class

This chapter concerns cutting several pounds very quickly to make weight for a contest, but it assumes that weight will be quickly re-gained after weigh-ins. My *Eating Plan* book addresses losing weight and keeping it off. So there is a difference between "cutting" weight and "losing" weight. The former is short term; the latter is long-term.

But how do you decide if you should reduce your weight to move down a weight class, and when should you move up a weight class?

For your first contest, it would probably be best to just compete at whatever weight you happen to weigh. You might be satisfied at that weight class and want to stick with it. But some might want to lose weight while others might want to gain weight.

Some people get into lifting weights as part of a weight loss pro-gram. Lifting weights is definitely a benefit in that regard, and if you are still carrying extra body fat, then continuing to lose weight and thus dropping a weight class or two could be a very good thing.

On the other hand, very thin people generally do not make good powerlifters. If that is you, then it would probably be beneficial to pack on a few pounds. My *Eating Plan* book discusses ways to do so.

The most important point in either direction is how much fat you are carrying on your body. If you are carrying "extra" body fat, losing weight would be beneficial both health-wise and powerlifting-wise. However, if you have a very low fat percentage, it would not be wise to reduce your bodyweight. Instead, you might want to gain weight.

Chapter 19 discussed the importance of measuring not just your bodyweight but also your fat percentage. It also discussed different methods for doing so and presented charts detailing what are over-weight, average, and athletic fat percentages.

But most people "just know" if they are carrying extra body fat. If you are, then you are in the category of lifters who might benefit from losing weight in general and cutting weight for a contest.

However, if you are so ripped that people tell you that you have nothing to lose, then you probably don't. As such, it would be best not to try to lose or cut weight and maybe even to gain weight.

In addition, most powerlifters over time will gradually gain mus-cular bodyweight due to the hard training. This eventually forces them to move up a weight class.

For instance, back in college, the first contests I entered were at 123s. But I was carrying more body fat than is ideal, so eventually I moved down to 114s. But then later, I was forced to move back up to 123s due to increased muscular bodyweight. If I had continued to lift through my 20s and 30s, I probably would have eventually moved up to at least 132s.

Moreover, this chapter detailed how I lost seven pounds in 6-1/2 days. My starting weight was 121 pounds, so that seven pounds represented a loss of 5.8% of my bodyweight. But at a previous contest I started cutting weight at 123.8 and weighed-in at 114.5 a week later. I thus lost 9.3 pounds, or 7.5%. I wouldn't want to try to cut more than that, so I would say that is about the greatest percentage of bodyweight that can be lost in a week without a loss of strength.

If you need to lose much more than that, then it probably is not wise to try to cut to a lower weight class. With each contest I have entered, it has gotten more difficult to make weight for 114s. It is for this reason that I have been struggling about when it will be time for me to once again move up to 123s.

This issue becomes more exaggerated for those who are still teenagers. Even without lifting weights, most teenagers will gain weight throughout their teen years. Add lifting to that, and a teenager could easily add quite a bit of weight in just a few years. Most importantly, to fight against this natural weight gain through restricted eating would be foolhardy. The teenager could very well end up ruining his health.

I can understand the allure of trying to stay at a lighter weight class. Your competition is not lifting as much in a given weight class as they will be at the next higher weight class. There might also be less competition at the lighter weight class. If I had cut to 114s the second year I entered National Collegiates, I probably would have won again rather than just taking second at 123s.

However, by gaining weight in a smart manner, then moving up a weight class could very well prove to be beneficial performance-wise. In college, pound for pound, my lifts at 123s were far better than my lifts at 114s.

By gaining muscle but little fat, your lifts will improve at a greater percentage than your bodyweight. Adding fat will increase your lifts some, but not near as much as adding muscle. Conversely, losing fat might cause your lifts to drop some, but they will still be better pound for pound. A below average but not extremely low fat percentage is probably ideal for most powerlifters. Only super-heavyweights can afford to carry a lot of extra body fat.

My point is, think carefully before utilizing the cut weight method described in this chapter and about what weight class to enter. And be prepared to change weight classes as your changing body dictates.

Chapter Twenty-two
Supplements for Powerlifters

When I powerlifted in college, I used no supplements whatsoever. No protein powders, no multi-vitamin, no creatine, nothing. And I believe I did very well. This just goes to show that supplements are not necessary for successful powerlifting.

However, back then, I was young and healthy. But over the past decade or so I have wasted a lot of money experimenting with different supplements, first to try to help with my various health problems, and then to aid with my powerlifting.

And "wasted" is the correct term here. Most of what I have tried has proved to be absolutely worthless, or worse. In many cases, I have experienced negative side effects from the supplements I have tried.

On my Fitness Web site are detailed reviews of many of the supplements I have tried over the years and what I am currently using. It is not possible to repeat all of that information here. Instead, I will discuss the types of supplements most commonly used by powerlifters.

The supplements mentioned in this chapter can be purchased from the stores listed in Appendix #1.

Multi-Vitamin/ Mineral Supplement

In my book *God-given Foods Eating Plan*, I write, " God did not intend for us to get our nourishment from pills. He put all that we need in the foods He provided for us. But we need to eat a variety of these God-given foods." Moreover, "In no way can supplements make up for an unhealthy diet" (p15).

These points are important. Before wasting money on supplements, concentrate on improving your eating plan. Eating healthy foods while avoiding unhealthy ones will make a much greater difference in your powerlifting progress than any pill or powder.

However, I also wrote in that book, "This is not to say there is not a place for supplements. But they are just that, a way to supplement or to add a little 'extra' to a healthy diet" (p. 15).

Probably the most important "little extra" would be a basic multi-vitamin and mineral supplement with a wide variety of nutrients in order to ensure you are not deficient in any particular nutrient. But all that is needed in this regard is a supplement containing 100% of the Daily Value (DV) for most essential nutrients.

Where controversy comes in is with mega-dose supplements. By this is meant supplements that contain many times the DV for one or more nutrients. There are many who believe that athletes like powerlifters need far more than the DVs due to the way in which they push their bodies. However, there is little evidence supporting this idea.

Moreover, in most cases, the levels of nutrients that are recommend are far beyond what could be attained from any kind of diet. Given this, mega-dose supplements make little sense. God would not have designed our bodies (or our bodies would not have evolved) to need levels of nutrients that could not be attained from the foods available for human beings to consume. The DVs, and more especially the Recommended Dietary Allowances (RDAs), are set at levels that cover the needs of almost all people and are levels that can be attained from a reasonable dietary plan.

Moreover, there is strong evidence that potential problems can occur with mega-dose supplements. Recent studies for instance have shown that mega-doses of vitamin E *increases* the risk of heart disease, not *decreases* it as is often claimed.

In addition, there is a world of difference between the nutrients found in food and those found in most supplements. Nutrients in food are natural and are generally bound together in "complexes" with other nutrients and helper elements, but supplements generally use synthetic, isolated nutrients. For instance, vitamin E in foods is in the form of d alpha tocopherol, and it is bound together with seven other related compounds. But many supplements only use the isolated and synthetic dl alpha tocopherol form.

Plus, food contains not just vitamins and minerals but also various other antioxidants and photochemicals. All of these nutrients are also found in the appropriate proportions. But when you supplement, you can upset this balance. Mega-doses of zinc for instance can lead to a deficiency of copper.

All that said, going back to the common recommendation for a basic 100% DV type of multi-vitamin/ mineral, many such products are available. But in most the nutrients are synthetic. Much better is a product like Twinlab's *Food Based Ultra Daily* (a.k.a. *Ultra Harvest Premium Multi-Vitamin*). As the first name indicates, this product derives its nutrients from food rather than utilizing synthetic nutrients. The vitamin E for instance comes from vegetable oil.

For this product, three tablets are taken a day. Spreading the intake out over three different meals improves absorption. I have used this product for some time and feel it has bene-fited both my health problems and my power training.

The downside to this product is it is rather pricey as compared to other 100% DV type of products. If finances are tight, then any of a number of commercial available basic multiples will have to do.

However, most multiples contain little calcium and magnesium, so a separate product is needed for these two minerals. One such supplement I used for many years was Twinlab's *Calcium Citrate Caps,* which also contains magnesium. I know it is effective as it helped to keep a neurological condition I have under control.

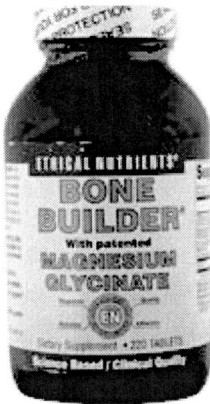

But more recently I began using Ethical Nutrients *Bone Builder with Magnesium Glycinate.* It contains calcium in the form of MCHC, a natural and highly absorbable form of calcium. The magnesium is bound with glycinate, which makes it also very absorbable. It's a little more expensive than the Twinlab product, but I've found it to be even more effective for controlling my condition.

Essential Fatty Acids

In my *Eating Plan* book I discuss the many benefits of eating fish. This is in part due to the Omega 3 fatty acid content of fish. But one benefit I do not mention that is important to powerlifters is Omega 3s can help to prevent and even ease existing joint problems.

However, many people do not like the taste of fish, so they turn to fish oil capsules to attain these healthy omega 3s. This is an alternative, but it is not the same as eating fish. Along with omega 3s, fish also contains many nutrients, as discussed in my *Eating Plan* book. These include protein, niacin, vitamin B_6, vitamin B_{12}, and selenium. In addition, and what I do not mention in that book, fish is the best natural source of vitamin D and iodine.

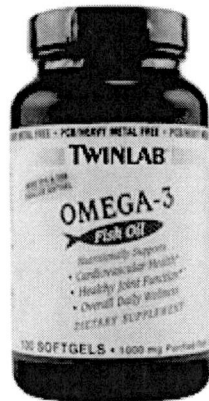

But still, if you are adamant about not liking fish, then capsules will have to do. But you really need to be careful about quality. Be sure the bottle says the fish oil is free of heavy metal contamination. Also, some fish oil supplements still have a fish aftertaste. But I have found Twinlab's *Omega-3 Fish Oil* capsules to be of high quality with little fish aftertaste.

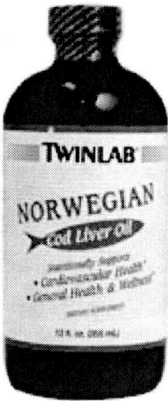

However, a problem with many fish oil capsules is they are rather pricey. A much less expensive alternative is cod liver oil. This was a very popular supplement during the first half of the twentieth century. But by the second half of the twentieth century, cold liver oil fall out of disfavor. This most likely was because of the taste. However, with today's processing methods, cod liver oil does not taste near as bad as it used to. Twinlab's *Cod Liver Oil*, for instance, has little fish taste, even in the unflavored version. It is also available with mint or lemon flavoring, which would further mask the taste.

What separates cod liver oil from other fish oil supplements is that along with being an excellent source of Omega 3s, it is also an incredible source for vitamins A and D. But it this is a double-edged sword as it is possible to attain too much of these nutrients. They are both fat-soluble and thus are stored in the body.

In regards to vitamin D, the RDA is currently 400 IUs while the Upper Limit (the amount above which problems can occur) is 2,000 IUs. But many authorities now believe these numbers are too low and should be raised to 1,000 IUs and 10,000 IUs, respectively. Given this, even if you are already getting 400 IUs from a multi, an additional 400 IUs from a teaspoon of cod liver oil would not be problematic.

But what could be problematic is the vitamin A content of cod liver oil. The DV for vitamin A is 5,000 IUs, which is about what a teaspoon of cod liver oil contains. If you are already getting 5,000 IUs of vitamin A from a multi and add in another 5,000 IUs from cod liver oil, that could be problematic.

However, some supplements use beta carotene (which the body converts to vitamin A). Beta carotene is not problematic even in high doses, so check your multi. The Twinlab *Food Based Ultra Daily* mentioned previously only contains 500 IUs of beta carotene, or just 10% of the DV, so combining it with cod liver oil would work well.

Another source for Omega 3s is flax seeds and flax seed oil. However, the Omega 3s in flax seed is actually in the form of alpha linoleic acid (ALA), while fish contains eicosapentaenoic acid (EPA) and docosahexaenoic acid (DHA). ALA is converted into EPA and DHA in the body, but it is not a very efficient conversion, so fish is a better option.

However, flax seeds are also high in other essen-

tials fatty acids, namely Omega 6s and 9s. The seeds are high in beneficial fiber and protein, so their consumption can be beneficial.

But it should also be noted that flax seed oil is very unstable and should not be heated, so do not use it for sautéing or other cooking purposes. The best way to use it is as a dressing on salad or sprinkled on vegetables.

As with fish oil supplements, a downside to flax seed oil is it is rather pricey. A much cheaper alternative is to use the flax seeds themselves. But it should be noted that it is hard for the body to digest whole flax seeds. They are so small and hard, they tend to pass through the system undigested.

The way around this is to grind the flax seeds. This can easily be done at home with a coffee bean grinder, blender, or *Vitamix*. You can also purchase flax seeds pre-ground, known as flax seed meal.

Flax seed meal can be mixed into hot cereals like oatmeal, sprinkled on cold cereals, or baked into breads and muffins. I personally use it by mixing it into cottage cheese or yogurt for a healthy snack.

All of these products would best be described as "supplemental foods." By this is meant, they are real, natural foods not synthetic products like most supplements, but they are processed in some way to make them easier to take on a regular basis.

I consume at least a couple of servings of fish a week. But during the winter months, on days I don't eat fish, I'll take a teaspoon of Twinlab's *Cod Liver Oil*. During the summer months when I get vitamin D from sunshine, I take Twinlab's *Omega-3 Fish Oil*. I also use a teaspoon of Spectrum Essential's *Flax Seed Oil* on my dinner salad and/ or a teaspoon of flax seed meal at another time during the day.

Have I noticed any benefit of all of this Omega 3s consumption? All I can say is, after six years of powerlifting, I have only had minor joint problems.

Protein Powders

Protein powders were mentioned in Chapter 19 as they are more food than supplements or better "supplemental foods." Protein powders make it easy for powerlifters to attain the extra protein they need. And yes, in this case, I do believe there is strong evidence that powerlifters need more protein than the average person, but at levels that can be attained from diet.

The RDA for protein is only 0.36 grams per pound of bodyweight. But most authorities recommend that powerlifters and other strength athletes attain at least 1.0 grams per pound. I have found my training goes best when I am consuming about 1.5 grams/ pound. Again, that amount could be attained by eating whole foods, but protein powders just make it much easier to do so.

However, there are differences in the rate of absorption of different protein powders. Following is a list of different proteins in the order of fastest to slowest absorption.

Whey protein hydrolysate
Whey protein isolate
Whey protein concentrate
Egg white protein
Casein protein

There are many who recommend consuming a mixture of the three kinds of whey immediately post-workout so that amino acids are available quickly to aid recovery. However, some recent studies show that a blended protein with all of these types is actually more beneficial. In this way, the body receives a steady supply of amino acids from within a few minutes of ingestion to several hours later.

Many brands of blended proteins are available. But I prefer to customize my own at Protein Factory. Below is the "formula" I use.

Membrane Micellar Casein – 35%
Egg White Protein – 15%
Whey Protein Concentrate – 15%
Iso-Chill Whey Isolate – 15%
Hydrolyzed Whey 1400 – 20%

I get it sweetened with stevia and unflavored. I then mix in my own organic cocoa powder or natural vanilla flavoring.

One final point worth mentioning is to be cautious with soy protein powders. As mentioned in chapter 19, soy is a much lower quality protein than the above proteins, and there is evidence that soy can lower testosterone levels.

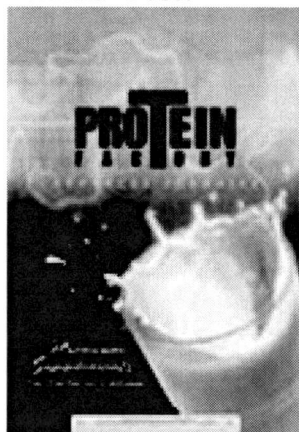

Protein and Energy Bars

This is another type of product that would fall into the supplemental foods category. But in reality, most protein and energy bars are nothing but candy bars, with some added protein powder and vitamins and minerals. But the main protein is often soy and the nutrients are always synthetic, so what you end up with is a poor tasting bar that is not much more nutritious than a candy bar.

In addition, the carb source in most energy bars is some type of sugar. It has already been mentioned that sugar is ineffective for replenishing glycogen and is likely to be stored as body fat. Even when it is a beneficial type of carb source, like oats or brown rice syrup, often the amount of carbs in relationship to protein is too high. There can sometimes be over four times as many grams of carbs as protein. This makes the bars too high glycemic for those like me with blood sugar problems and too low in protein for powerlifters.

The main ingredient in most low-carb/ hi-protein bars is glycerine. Glycerine is a by-product of soap production with no nutritional content other than calories, and it can cause gastrointestinal problems in some people. Sometimes it is a sugar alcohol like maltitol or sorbitol, which again, can cause GI problems if consumed in large amounts.

Plus, some protein and energy bars are high in saturated fat, which is also very likely to be stored as body fat, along with being unhealthy. In addition, many bars use artificial flavorings, artificial colorings, and other unnatural ingredients.

Given all of these points, I have not been able to find a bar I am completely satisfied with. But if you don't mind synthetic vitamins and minerals and soy protein, then the two best commercially available bars I have found are Power Bar's *Protein Plus* and Clif's *Builder's* bars. Both use all natural ingredients other than the nutrients.

The main carb source in the *Protein Plus* bar used to be brown rice syrup, but it now uses glucose syrup. I was initially concerned with this change given the problems I experienced with dextrose described in Chapter 20. But the bar is only moderate glycemic, so it would not have the same problems as high-glycemic dextrose powder.

The *Protein Plus* bar uses a blended protein of soy, whey, and casein. The main fat source is palm kernel oil. The possible benefits of the MCTs in tropical oils were mentioned in Chapter 19. But here, the important point is this bar contains 300 calories and a carb to protein to fat ratio of 3:2:1, the same as for my pre-workout drink. When consumed about 45 minutes pre-workout, it digests just fine. And not surprisingly, I feel energized throughout my workout. There is some glycerine and maltitol, but the amounts are minimal.

The *Builder's* bar uses chicory syrup (from the root of an herb) and brown rice syrup for its carb sources, soy for the protein, and again, palm kernel oil for the fat. It has a 3:2:2 ratio of carbs to protein to fat.

But I do not feel as energized during my workouts when consuming it pre-workout. This could be because it is too low glycemic due to the chicory syrup, which is very low glycemic, and due to the higher fat content. But this makes it ideal for a snack apart from a workout, especially since it is the best tasting bar I have tried. But some find chicory syrup can cause GI problems if consumed in large amounts.

A better option to commercially available bars would be *Parrillo Bars*. They have five different types of bars. All use a use a blended protein consisting of various milk or egg proteins (but no soy) and MCT oil for the fat source. Four of them (pictured) use brown rice syrup for the main carb source.

They are pictured top to bottom in the order of highest carbs/ lowest protein (3:1 ratio) to lowest carbs/ highest protein (1:1 ratio) and thus highest to lowest glycemic. The first two are moderate glycemic and thus are best pre- and post-workout, post-weigh-in, and during a contest. The second two are low glycemic and thus are best for snacks.

Parrillo also has a "High Protein" (low carb) bar. To keep the "net carbs" low, it uses Erythritol rather than brown rice syrup. Erythritol is a natural sugar alcohol that is unlikely to cause gastric side effects.

One downside to Parrillo bars is they all contain artificial flavorings, and some also contain artificial colorings.

Another downside to Parrillo bars is they are all rather pricey. But available on Parrillo's Web site is a sampler bar pack. It can only be ordered once to introduce you to their bars, but it contains all 32 kinds and flavors of their bars for a reasonable price. The bars can be frozen, so the 32 bars should last you quite a while.

Creatine

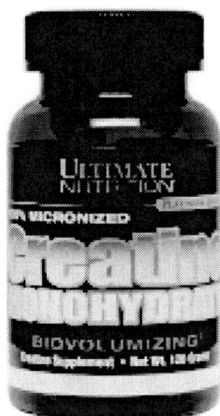

Creatine is one of the most researched sports supplements there is. Most of the research shows it is a safe and effective supplement for those engaging in sports requiring short bursts of high intensity muscle contractions, like powerlifting.

During intensive exercise, the body first uses its muscular stores of ATP (andesine triphosphate). The ATP is converted into ADP (andesine di-phosphate). Once the stored ATP is depleted, the body utilizes stored creatine phosphate (CP) to reconvert the ADP into ATP. Once both ATP and CP are depleted, the exercise must stop long enough to allow the body to restore the ATP levels. But creatine supplementation increases the stores of creatine phosphate (CP).

What this means is, an exercise can be continued for a longer period (i.e., more reps can be done in a given set) and shorter rest times are required between sets as the APT is replenished quicker. I have especially found the latter to be true. With creatine, I can rest a little less time between sets, and I feel stronger on second and subsequent sets of a given exercise.

However, meat, especially red meat, contains ample amounts of creatine, so if you eat a lot of meat, then the effect of creatine would not be as noticeable as for someone who eats little or no meat.

Carbs aid the absorption of creatine, so the best way to use it is to mix it in with your pre- or post-workout drink. But do not mix the creatine in until you are ready to drink it as creatine degrades if left in water for an extended period of time.

I use 3-4 grams in my pre-workout drink. Those larger than me might want to use five grams. But it should be mentioned that some report getting bloated from creatine. I generally gain a few pounds when I use creatine, but it is not excessive. But I only take creatine before or after a workout. If I take it at other times I get excessively bloated. I can only assume the creatine is used up when I take it before a workout or it is used to replenish muscle creatine if I take it afterwards. But if taken apart from a workout, there's no use for the creatine, so for some reason that causes the excessive bloating.

Along these lines, many recommend a "loading" phase, taking five grams of creatine five times a day for the first five days. That is a com-

complete waste of money and the reason many experience bloating from creatine use. The only reason that was ever done was in an initial research study the researchers wanted to get the participants' creatine levels up as quickly as possible to shorten the length and thus cost of the study. But by taking just five grams a day, you will ultimately end up with the same creatine levels; it will just take a couple of weeks. But you'll save yourself the negative side effects and using up half the container of creatine the first week.

Quality is also very important when it comes to creatine. Those who report negative side effects from it are more likely reacting to impurities in the powder they are using, not the actual creatine. For this reason, the brands that I generally use are Jarrow Formula's *CreaPure* or Ultimate Nutrition's *100% Micronized Creatine Monohydrate*.

Glutamine

Glutamine is the most abundant amino acid in muscle cells. It is considered a semi-essential amino acid. What this means is, the human body can manufacture glutamine from other amino acids. However, during times of intense physical stress, like during periods of heavy training or due to various medical conditions or surgery, the body cannot keep up with sufficient production, so an outside source is needed.

Many powerlifters, bodybuilders, and other athletes have found benefit from supplementing with glutamine. Some of the reported benefits include improved recovery, a reduction of post-workout soreness, an increase of human growth hormone (HGH) levels, a decrease in cortisol levels, and a decrease in exercise-induced colds and flu.

But it must be said that glutamine is abundant in any high protein food. It is especially prevalent in whey protein powders. As such, some debate that there is any benefit to supplementing with glutamine above what can be attained from food.

However, I have found glutamine helps with recovery when taken post-workout. Moreover, by comparing my workout logs with my supplement logs, it is apparent I make better progress in my powerlifting training when I am using glutamine.

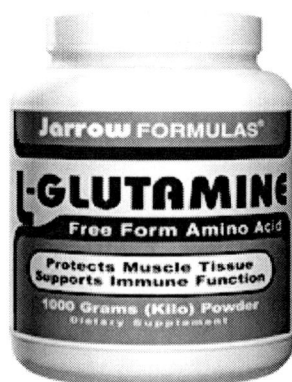

It is best to take glutamine on an empty stomach. This generally means taking it at least two hours after and half an hour before a meal. My practice is to take 3-4 grams immediately post-workout mixed in a large glass of water. I then shower, which gives time for the glutamine to digest. I then eat my dinner immediately thereafter. Those larger than me might want to use 5-10 grams. My favorite brands of glutamine are Jarrow Formula's *L-Glutamine* and Ultimate Nutrition's *Glutapure*. Both brands are 100% pure forms of glutamine.

Desiccated Liver

In the 1960s to 80s, desiccated liver was a very popular bodybuilding supplement. Many old-time bodybuilders swore by it. Desiccated liver is liver that has been made into a dry powder and sold in pill or powder form. It would thus be another supplemental food product.

With desiccated liver you get all of the high quality protein, iron, B vitamins, and other nutrients naturally found in liver but without the less than desirable taste of liver. Desiccated liver is usually defatted, so you also avoid the saturated fat and cholesterol of liver.

However, desiccated liver fell out of favor by the end of the 1980s due to the glut of other products that began arriving on the scene. Now, it can even hard to find it. But companies that still make desiccated liver products are Beverly International, Healthy 'n Fit, NOW, Parrillo, and Universal. It would be best to be sure the liver is derived from hormone-free cattle.

Hormone Enhancing Products

There are many products on the market that are purported to elevate testosterone or human growth hormone (HGH), such as Tribulus, Avena Sativa, Eurycoma, and various homeopathic formulas.

When I was diagnosed with clinically low testosterone levels, I experimented with many of these and found them to have minor effects at best. But I attained much better results by altering my diet in accordance with the hormone optimizing principles laid out in my *Eating Plan* book. By doing so, I tripled my testosterone levels, from being clinically low to being in the middle of the normal range.

Given this experience, I would say, don't waste your money on any of these products. Instead, alter you diet to naturally elevate your hormone levels, as discussed in my *Eating* Plan book.

One such product that deserves special mention is ZMA. The acronym stands for Zinc-Magnesium Aspartate. The potential problem with this supplement is the recommended dose provides 30 mg of zinc, which is almost triple the RDA for men of 11 mg. Moreover, ZMA does not contain copper. As previously stated, taking mega-doses of zinc without being balanced by copper can lead to a copper deficiency.

Arginine/ NOS Products

Like glutamine, arginine is considered to be a semi-essential amino acid. But since arginine is found in almost any high protein food, then a diet adequate in protein should provide sufficient arginine.

However, supplemental arginine is generally taken for two reasons. The first is its role in producing nitric oxide (NO). NO is a vasodilator. This means it leads to an increase in the internal diameter of blood vessels. As a result, blood flow is increased throughout the body. The purported benefits of this are an increased flow of nutrients to the muscles. This then is said to improve recovery rates from intense workouts. Moreover, NO is said to increase the duration of a weightlifting induced muscle "pump."

In addition to increasing blood flow to the muscles, blood flow is also purported to be increased to the penis. It is for this reason that arginine is often included in "sexual enhancement" products.

Along with arginine itself, there are various NOS (Nitric Oxide Stimulator) products on the market. NOS products are actually composed of various derivatives of arginine, e.g. L-Arginine-Alpha-Ketoglutarate (A-AKG), Arginine-Ketoisocaproate (A-KIC), and/ or Arginine Pyroglutamate (APG).

The second reason given for supplementing with arginine is its purported ability to increase HGH levels, so it is often included in HGH enhancement products, along with glutamine and other nutrients.

I tried supplemented with arginine, but I did not notice any vasodilatation or hormone enhancing effects from it. Moreover, arginine is rather expensive. If your diet is sufficient in protein it should thus be sufficient in arginine. As such, I would say it best to spend your money on high protein foods, like meat, rather than on an arginine or NOS supplements. Nuts are also a good source of arginine.

Herbal Supplements

The Tribulus, Avena Sativa, and Eurycoma mentioned previously would be classified as herbal supplements. There are many other herbal supplements available that are purported to help with a wide variety of health conditions.

One of particular interest to some powerlifters is Milk Thistle (Silymarin). The primary use for Milk Thistle is to protect the liver from toxins. One form of liver-damaging toxins would be performance enhancing drugs. If you use such drugs, then taking Milk Thistle would be prudent.

But even for those who do not use such drugs, Milk Thistle might be helpful. A while back, blood tests showed I had elevated liver enzymes. I never did figure out the cause of it. But taking Milk Thistle for several months lowered the liver enzymes back to normal. Specifically, I took Jarrow Formulas *Silymarin 80% Standardized Milk Thistle.*

Specialty Muscle Building Supplements

Pick up any issue of any "muscle mag" and you'll see full page glossy ads for the latest and greatest muscle building supplement. The ad will tout the almost miraculous benefits you'll attain from using the supplement. "Increase your bench press by 38% in two months!" – "Gain ten pounds of muscle in two weeks!"

But try this; pick up a back issue of any of these magazines from a few years ago. You'll see the same companies advertising the then latest and greatest supplements, but they will be different from their currently promoted ones. Then check their Web sites; you'll find that most of those older "great" supplements are no longer even being sold.

The reason they are not is that lifters tried them and found them to be useless. But no matter to the companies, they already made their money. So they've moved on to their latest supplement and a new generation of suckers to buy them.

My point is, don't waste your money on the newest supplement to hit the market. Let someone else waste their money. Stick to supplements that have withstood the test of time.

Conclusion to Supplements

As stated at the beginning of this chapter, food is the best way to attain nutrients. But basic nutrient supplements can add a little extra to a healthy diet. The most natural and best way to attain these extra nutrients is through food-based supplements or supplemental foods. Some other basic supplements might also aid a powerlifter's performance. But most "muscle-building" supplements are simply a waste of money. Be especially wary of the many fly-by-night rip-offs being sold. Stick with tried and true supplements.

Performance Enhancing Drugs

Entire books have been written on the subject of steroids and other performance enhancing drugs, so I will not be able to do justice to the topic here. And I am in no way an expert on this subject given that I have never use any such drugs.

I never have used them as I have always found the idea rather stupid. Working out is supposed to enhance your health, not destroy it. But that is very well what these drugs can do, destroy your health. And for what, a trophy?

It at least makes some sense for a professional football or baseball player to use such drugs given the incredible financial rewards that success on those playing fields can bring. But powerlifting? At best, you might get a $1,000 award. But most powerlifters will never even get that.

However, I can understand the allure. I remember a lifter I trained with back in college, who was also around 20 years old at the time. He had an incredible deadlift, pulling over 500 pounds at 123s. But despite his already great success, he felt the need to use drugs. Within a few months, he had bulked up to 132s and was pulling over 600. But then, he blew out his hip joint and never powerlifted again.

His injury made sense. Steroids will greatly increase the strength and size of your muscles, but they do little for the strength of tendons and ligaments, so his muscular strength outstripped his joint strength. His very early retirement is common among drug users. Natural powerlifters tend to have much longer careers.

But if you want to be a "flash in the pan" and destroy your health for a trophy, go ahead. It's your body; do to it as you want. But at least be honest about it and only compete in federations that allow drug use. Trying to "beat the test" in drug-tested federations is not only dishonest but also unfair to those who compete drug free.

Section Seven

Personal Problems in Powerlifting

Chapter Twenty-three
Gear Problems

As mentioned previously in this book, I began powerlifting again in April 2003. As I write this, it is now spring 2009, so I have been powerlifting for six years. During these years of competition, I have run into many problems.

I love the sport, but these many problems have hindered my progress and have taken much of the "fun" out of it. In this final section of this book, I will detail the many mistakes I have made and the problems I have encountered and give suggestions on how to avoid them.

The purpose of this section is not to denigrate any particular powerlifting federation, gear company, or individual. I understand how very difficult it can be to run a contest, federation, or gear company, and I am thankful for those who do so.

Moreover, the problems I have encountered could easily be encountered in any federation or when dealing with any company or individual. As such, I will not use specific names. But it is my hope this section will enable the reader to avoid the same problems so you can make good progress and truly enjoy the world's strongest sport.

This will be a four-part section. As I said, I've made many mistakes and have encountered many problems, and it will take that amount of space to describe all of them. But I truly hope this section will be an aid to others. This first part will focus on problems related to powerlifting gear.

The Mess that Is Powerlifting

As previously discussed, when I powerlifted in college, there was one federation, the USPF, so everyone competed in that federation and followed its rules. Gear companies were also limited, with little differences between what was sold. As such, everyone wore basically the same supportive gear. But today, there are over 20 different powerlifting federations, each having its one set of rules. Plus, there are many different gear companies, with widely different types of gear available.

This mess has already been discussed, so that is not the focus of this chapter. However, what is important here is that these differing rules and available gear can lead to problems for the lifter.

Initial Gear Problems

As previously mentioned, when I powerlifted in college back around 1980, the basic gear available was a Super Suit and Super Wraps. The Super Suit was single-ply polyester, while the Super Wraps were 2.0 meters long and only somewhat stronger than Ace bandages. Bench shirts were not invented yet. Most importantly, the gear really did not do much. I probably got about 10-15 pounds out of my Super Suit and another 10-15 pounds out of the Super Wraps.

I first thought about powerlifting again in February of 2003. I still had some of my gear from college, but after all of those years, I didn't think it would be safe to use. And besides, I knew the gear had to have improved over all those years. So when I decided on a contest to enter, I knew I needed to get some gear.

However, the contest was in early April, and I didn't order the gear until March. The only thing I was familiar with was single-ply poly gear, so I ordered a single-ply poly squat suit, bench shirt (closed back), and deadlift suit. But when the gear arrived, the company had failed to include the deadlift suit. I called them, and they had to rush ship it to get it to me in time.

When I tried the suits on, the straps were too loose. I used them that way for one workout and then took them to a local seamstress to be altered. But they were not done until the day before I was to leave for the contest, so I never even had a chance to try them on let alone use them for a workout before the contest.

This is a recurring theme in my gear problems, waiting until the last minute to get gear. In this case, it ended up not being a problem. I went 9/9 at that contest. However, that was not the case later that year.

For my second contest I used the same gear as for my first. But I wasn't completely satisfied with it. It was better than what I used in college, but not by that much. I estimate I was getting about 20-25 pounds out of the suit and the same out of the wraps.

Meanwhile, since I hadn't used a bench shirt before, the company had sent me a shirt that was probably a couple of sizes too large. I was only getting a few pounds out of it at best. This was a far cry from the numbers I heard other lifters saying they were getting out of their gear.

The federation I was competing in allowed double-ply gear, so I decided to get a double-ply poly squat suit and bench shirt. I also ordered a pair of 2.5 meter wraps, since the longer length was also allowed. I thought I ordered it in plenty of time, but the company delayed in getting it to me. This meant once again, I was only able to get in one workout for each lift before the contest.

At the contest, on squats, I got two white lights and one red light on my first attempt. But on my second attempt, I got two red lights. The strange thing was I felt like I was squatting more than deep enough. After that attempt, I asked a side judge how high I was, and he said I was on only about an inch high.

On my third attempt, I really felt I had adjusted and sunk that extra depth, but once again, two red lights. That meant I came one red light from bombing out! The best I could figure was the double-ply suit and extra half meter of wraps threw off my sense of depth. As a result, inexperience in the new gear almost caused me to bomb out.

On benches, the new shirt was also closed back, but three sizes smaller than my first shirt. It was so tight I could barely breathe. I had a hard time getting psyched up and putting full effort into the lift. I got my first attempt, but missed my second and third attempts.

I ended up going 1/3 on both squats and benches. However, on deadlifts, I used the same suit I had worn for my previous two contests, and I went 3/3. So it was clearly the new gear and not just me having a bad day that caused my problems. In retrospect, I should have either used my single-ply gear for that contest or just skipped the contest. Either way, I would have given myself more time to get used to the new gear before competing in it.

After that contest, I had the shirt altered so that it was open back, since such was allowed in the federation I was competing in. That solved the problem of it being too hard to breathe in. It also made it much easier to get into and out of. I knew then I would only enter federations that allowed open back shirts.

More Gear Problems

I still was not that satisfied with my double-ply poly gear. I was only getting about 50 pounds out of the suit and another 30 or so out of the shirt. Again, this was a far cry from what others report getting, especially out of double-ply gear.

As such, I decided to try a double-denim shirt. The shirt seemed to fit okay when I got it. But when I tried it for a workout, I could barely bend my arms with 30 pounds over my 1RM, so I sent the shirt back to be altered. This time, I could touch with my then current 1RM, but it took that much to touch, and I wasn't able to bench any more than that. This meant it was not any better than the shirt I had been using.

I sent it back once again to be altered. I also ordered a double-denim suit at that time. But when the gear was sent to me, the post office lost the package! The company offered to redo the gear and send it to me again, but I was so frustrated at that point that I decided to go unequipped for my next contest and canceled the order. Fortunately, the package was lost on its way from the company to me, so the company nicely refunded my money. But another time, the post office lost a package containing gear when I was sending it back to the company. That time, I was out the money.

Two points to note here. First off, my problem with using denim was probably because I simply do not bench enough weight to make a denim shirt work for me. If it fits tight enough to actually do something, I cannot handle enough weight to get the bar to touch. But if it fits loose enough to touch with a reasonable weight, it doesn't do much. Given this, I would say, double denim shirts are best left of those with hefty benches. For those of us with more average benches, a material with some stretch to it like poly will have to do.

Second, on the lost packages, after those experiences, if I send something through the post office, I will always get delivery confirmation. If it is something expensive like powerlifting gear, I will get insurance as well. But I think it is even better to use UPS or Fed Ex where you can track the packages online.

After the experience with denim gear, I competed unequipped at my next contest. But due to some minor injuries, I decided to try using gear again. I ordered some new double-ply poly gear from a different company. The gear fit okay the first try, but it didn't help even as much as my previous gear. But since the squat suit was not real tight, I decided to try wearing briefs under the suit, since briefs were allowed in the federation I was entering.

However, I tried three different briefs from three different companies. But none of them really fit right or did much. Then I came up with a "bright" idea. I had the straps removed from my initial single-ply poly suit and would use that as a pair of briefs.

But once again, I didn't get this done until right before a contest. I stupidly tried wearing the newly made briefs at the contest for the first time. In the warm-up room, I put on the briefs for one set, and that went okay. But then, when I put the suit on over it, the gear was digging into my testicles! The pain was unbearable. There was not way I could squat that way, so I had to take off the suit and briefs.

Fortunately, I had the foresight to bring my old squat suit with me, so I changed into that. But all the putting on and taking off of gear really tired me out, so I was fighting exhaustion the rest of the day.

The suggestion here should be obvious—never use gear at a contest that you have not tried out in training.

More New Gear

I was not satisfied with my newest gear, so after that contest, I decided to try gear another company had just come out with that used the new "super-poly" fabric. This fabric was purported to be much better than the older poly. I ordered a double-ply squat suit and bench shirt.

I ordered the gear in mid-November. My plan was to enter a contest in March; I figured that would be plenty of time. However, ordering in mid-November was a big mistake. I should have known that with the holidays coming, it would delay the gear. And it did. I didn't get the gear until the end of the year. But when I got it, both the suit and shirt were too large, so I had to send them back to exchange for a smaller size. That is when the real nightmare began.

Over the next three months, I called and emailed the company repeatedly. But every time I was told "We're working on it." At one point, I was told in an email that "We'll get you out something early next week." When the next week came and went, and nothing arrived, I called again. The person I talked to was who had sent me the email, but he denied ever writing that. It was at that point that I canceled the order. But it was another month fight to get them to refund my money.

In the last email I received from the company, a different person admitted to me that they had just come out with the gear in single-ply and were not really prepared yet to be selling double-ply gear, and that was the reason for the delays. But with all of the delays, I ended up having to cancel my plans to enter the March contest.

My suggestion here is when a company first comes out with new gear, resist the temptation to go for the "newest and best" as there is sure to be problems with it. It would be best to let someone else work out the problems. Instead, stick with gear a company has been producing for an extended time and has worked out all the production bugs.

In any case, six months after I first ordered the new gear, all I had gotten was a lot of hassles, but no new gear. Given these latest problems, I once again decided to go raw. But I ended up injured, so I once again, decided to go back to using gear.

I ordered a new double-ply poly shirt from yet another company. They said it would take two weeks to be delivered. But three weeks later, I hadn't received it, so I called them. I was told it had just been sent out that morning. I waited a few days and still didn't receive it. I called again. Now I was told it hadn't even been shipped yet! But they said it would be sent out the next day.

A few days later it still had not arrived, so I called again. I was told it still had not yet been sent. But they finally sent it the next day, and they even sent it overnight delivery at their expense to make up for the delays. But I tried it for a workout and did not like it. It was no better than the old shirt I already had, so after all of that, I ended up returning it.

Next I decided to try a canvas suit. The suit came in a reasonable amount of time, but it didn't fit right. I sent it back to be altered. But again, that only took a short while, so I had it in plenty of time for my next contest.

However, I still had not found a pair of briefs I really liked. I ended up using a pair I had gotten some time before. But at the contest, I once again had depth problems, getting two red lights on my third attempt. The frustrating thing was, several other lifters told me they thought the lift was good. Even the president of the federation told me it was "close."

After that contest, I got a new pair of briefs from the same company I got the canvas suit from. This time, I had to send them back twice to get them to fit right. Between the suit and briefs, I had to send gear back three times to this company. They eventually got it all right, but all that postage added to the total cost of the gear.

But the main problem was that between the briefs and the suit, I was having a hard time hitting depth in training. And the combination still was not much better than my initial double-poly gear. I estimate I was getting about 50 pounds out of the combination.

Summary on Gear Problems

Some of my problems with gear had to do with waiting until too close to a contest to get new gear. That is mistake that is easily corrected; don't wait until close to a contest to get new gear! And even if you get new gear just in time for a contest, don't use it! As my experiences show, unexpected problems can too easily occur.

Another set of problems I have had is in getting gear to fit me properly. There is not much you can do about this as it is doubtful that gear "off the rack" will fit exactly right. But you should always figure that you will need to get gear altered at least once, so plan on that when ordering gear. Allot time not just for the gear to come the first time, but enough time to send it back to the company to alter it and for them to get it back to you, and for you to use it for at least several workouts before planning on using it in a contest.

But most of all, I've wasted a lot of time, energy and money trying to get just the right gear that would work well for me. All I got for all of that trying different gear is a lot of hassles and a lot of wasted money. In retrospect, I would have been better off if I had just stuck with the single-ply poly gear I started with, at least for a year or two.

That leads to my next suggestion. Start with some basic gear and stick with it for quite some time before trying something else. Yes, there is probably something better out there, but it simply is not worth it to keep trying out new gear. I probably would have learned to get more out of my gear if I had just stuck with one kind of gear rather than constantly trying new stuff. Do some investigation before first ordering the gear, but then stick with it!

Thinking over all of my experiences, I would have been plenty happy if things hadn't changed; if all powerlifters just wore the old Super Suits and no bench shirts. That way, things would be much simpler and everyone would be using the same gear, so there would be an even playing field. But as it is, the gear situation is truly difficult and confusing.

Moreover, for me, there is an added problem that most do not have to deal with, my health situation. Specifically, I have fibromyalgia. If you don't know what that is, it is basically chronic pain with chronic fatigue. The fatigue is an ever present problem. And I have found that using gear is very exhausting.

I only have limited energy to devout to a workout before getting exhausted. This means part of my frustration with gear is that I needed to find something that was not too difficult to get on and off but still was worthwhile. But that I was never able to do. That is why I have gone back and forth between using gear and lifting raw. That struggle will be addressed in the next chapter. But first, it will be good to provide a few tips on getting gear on and off.

Tips on Getting Gear On and Off

The way to put on a squat suit is pretty obvious; you put your legs inside of the suit then into the leg holes. But the difficulty is, once you get to your knees, it will get very difficult to pull it up any further as the hole will seem too small for your legs, at least if it is a poly suit and fitting the way it should, which is to say, very tight.

To make it easier to pull the legs up further some gear companies offer what are called Power Slickers, Suit Slippers, or the like. These are basically very slick stockings. You pull them all the way up your legs first, and this then makes it much easier to slide the suit up over them. You then pull the slickers out from under the suit and off.

But the real difficulty is getting the suit over your buttocks and hips. This is where you need two helpers, one standing on either side.

The helpers need to grasp the suit by the sides and pull up. But for someone my size, what would usually happen is they would pick me up into the air and then have to "shake" me into the suit. The helpers are then needed to pull the suit straps up onto your shoulders.

If you wear a jock strap, it will help in getting the suit over your butt and hips if you put baby powder on them. But even better is to wear a tight-fitting pair of underwear made with a silk-like material. Neither option sounds very manly, but getting a suit over a sweaty, bare bottom is not easy. Note also, in most federations that allow supportive briefs, you are allowed to wear a jock strap or underwear in addition to the briefs.

If you're alone, you might be able to get the suit over your hips yourself by hooking one suit strap at a time over the end of a bar placed in a power rack or on squat racks, just be sure there are sufficient weights on the other side so the bar doesn't flip. Alternatively, place one of the safety bars high up in a power rack and use it. With the strap over the bar, you then sit down into the suit.

But be forewarned, this approach could stretch out the straps, especially if it is a single-ply poly suit. But with a double-ply poly or canvas suit, it probably will not be a problem.

This approach is easier if you have Velcro on the straps. That way, you can stand in the middle of a bar placed on squat racks, open the straps and connect them over the bar, and sit into the suit. The Velcro will also make it easier for you to get the straps over your shoulders yourself. However, Velcro on straps is not allowed in all federations, so be sure to check before getting Velcro on your suit straps.

To get the suit off, you do the reverse. Have the two helpers stand on either side and pull down. Or place the safety bars low in a power rack, squat down, and loop the straps over the bar, then stand up.

To get a closed back shirt on, you again need two helpers. You first put your arms inside the shirt and into the arms. The helpers then help to pull the sleeves up as far up as possible. Then one helper stands in front and grasps the material in the back of shirt, bunching it up to the back of the neck. He then pulls the neck opening over your head. The other helper stands behind and grabs the material and pulls down. The helpers then move around your body and pull down the shirt, smoothing out any bunching. Reverse the process to get the shirt off.

With an open back shirt things are much easier. When alone, I will first hold the shirt with the back in front and draped down just to connect the Velcro at the bottom. I will then spin the shirt around and slip my arms into the sleeves and work them up.

If you have a helper, then put the arms on first and use help to get the sleeves up, and then have the helper tighten the Velcro in the back.

314

Chapter Twenty-four
Raw Problems

The first chapter in this section looked at problems I have had with powerlifting gear. This second chapter of this section will look at problems I've encountered trying to lift raw or unequipped.

Raw Background

As mentioned at the end of the previous chapter, I have fibromyalgia. The fibromyalgia fatigue makes using gear very difficult. A lot of energy can be expended getting into and out of gear. That expenditure of energy leaves me with little energy for the actual workout. Moreover, I have found I need to keep my workouts to less than an hour and a half. Any longer, and I simply get too fatigued.

However, it is virtually impossible to get in a full gear squat workout within that timeframe. In fact, most of my equipped squat workouts would take about two hours. It simply takes time to get into briefs and a suit, to wrap knees, put up suit straps, and to tighten a belt, then to undo all of that afterwards.

But even without my health situation, there are still many reasons to lift without gear. The first is simply that it is a pain to use the gear. I can even remember back in college, my roommate would always complain about the Super Suits. "Belts and wraps are fine, but the suits are stupid and a pain."

I never complained about the suits back then. I just figured that I had no choice but to wear them since my competitors did. However, when I decided to powerlift again, another lifter at my gym was very much into "raw" powerlifting and was trying to get me to compete in the same raw federation that he was.

However, that federation allowed only a belt, but no wraps. I was very leery about doing max squats without knee wraps. When I powerlifted in college, I often had people tell me I would hurt my knees by doing squats. But I rarely had problems with my knees back then. But I always wore knee wraps when doing heavy squats and knee sleeves when pulling heavy deadlifts.

After I stopped powerlifting, I hurt my right knee in a bicycle accident and then my left knee in a different accident. My knees bothered me from then on. It was actually kind of ironic—little knee pain while I was powerlifting, but chronic knee pain after I stopped.

In any case, with the pre-existing knee pain, it seemed too dangerous to do heavy squats and deadlifts without knee wraps. And time has proved me right in this regard. After I started powerlifting again, my knee pain disappeared and has only rarely been a problem. But I have usually used knee wraps or knee sleeves when doing heavy squats and knee sleeves when pulling heavy deadlifts. The only times my knees have bothered me is when I have lifted heavy without knee support.

In addition to knee wraps in college, I also always wore wrist wraps on all three lifts. I did so as my wrists would bother me if I did heavy lifting without them. So that was another reason I didn't want to enter the federation that didn't allow any wraps. In fact, I considered it kind of silly not to allow them. Under no stretch of the imagination can wrist wraps add to what can be lifted. They are purely protective.

First Two Attempts at Going Raw

However, after all of the problems I had with the suits and shirts, in the winter of 2006 I decided to attempt to compete raw. The federation I was competing in at that time had a raw division that allowed a belt and wrist wraps, but no knee wraps, so I figured I'd give that a try.

But a couple of weeks in, I tried a 1RM squat and hurt my groin. That could have been due to being used to wearing a suit. It had been protecting my groin area when doing heavy squats, so possibly the area was not as strong as my legs. But it is also possible it was due to no knee wraps. I know that sounds strange, but hear me out.

I felt the pain was when I was at the bottom of the lift, and I could tell I was really struggling to get out of the hole. I simply wasn't used to handling a heavy weight at that point without some "lift" from gear. A suit will provide such lift, but so do knee wraps. As such, I figured that if I just wore knee wraps that might suffice.

I then looked around and found a federation that allowed knee wraps in its raw (or better, unequipped) division. I found one and began to train for it. However, I also hurt my left pec and right hip in training for it. These would again be body parts that are supported by gear. As a result, after that contest, I went back to using gear.

However, my gear problems continued, so a year later, I again decided to attempt to go raw. I figured the main problem with my first attempt was that I tried going heavy too quickly, and that was definitely a factor. Trying a 1RM squat without any gear after a couple of years of using gear was just plain stupid.

Moreover, it was when I was doing wide grip benches that I hurt my pec, not when I was using my regular grip. I figured that wide grip benches would help the drive off of the chest that is needed when benching raw. But I now knew they were too dangerous for me to do.

The hip was hurt about a month before the contest when trying and missing a 1RM deadlift. After that missed attempt, I backed off some the last couple of week before the contest, and then ironically, I got that same lift at the contest without any problems. I figured the problem initially was again, trying it too soon, along with being a little overtrained.

With this second attempt at raw lifting I figured I'd follow a basic cycle of staring with higher reps and less weight and then gradually dropping the reps and increasing the weight until the contest. Most importantly, I would not do a 1RM until the contest. However, when I dropped down to just four reps, I hurt my knee while deadlifting.

The next week when I tried pulling again, the knee still bothered me. I then put on a pair of knee sleeves, and just that amount of support sufficed, and I was able to put in a workout. But that told me I needed to wear the knees sleeves for deadlifts. And that much more, I would need to wear knee support for squats. This meant lifting raw without knee support was out for me, so I went back to using gear for my next couple of contests.

But by the winter of 2008, I was again fed up with the gear problems. I knew I couldn't lift raw without wraps, but by that time, I found another federation with an unequipped division that allowed knee wraps that was holding a contest in my area in the summer of that year. That would give me plenty of time to get used to lifting unequipped to do it safely.

However, by this time just wrapping my knees was too exhausting due to my fibromyalgia, so I only wore knee sleeves for squats.

With that limited support, the contest went great. I went 9/9, with all three of my final attempts being full max lifts. But most important for this chapter, I did not get injured while training for the contest or at the contest itself. But it should be noted that I used a 20 week cycle to prepare for that contest. That gave me plenty of time to get used to lifting unequipped.

Third Attempt and Current Plans

After the very successful unequipped contest, my plans were to stick to lifting unequipped. I began training for a contest that federation was holding in November of that year. But then I the suffered the hamstring injury that was mentioned previously in this book along with other health setbacks and had to cancel those plans.

Meanwhile, my health situation was such now that it would be very difficult for me to travel very far to contests, so if I were to continue to compete, I would need to stick to contests within a couple of hours of my home. But as mentioned in Chapter Four, the options in the Pittsburgh area where I live are not that great. However, after some investigation, I found that I would many more contest options if I could just compete raw, without wraps, than if I continued to compete unequipped with wraps or even with gear.

As such, after my break over Christmas 2008, I began training in January 2009 for a possible raw contest in the late spring or early summer of that year. That gave me several months to prepare. However, my knees once again began bothering me when I dropped down to 3-4 reps on squats and deadlifts. This can be seen in my workout logs from this time period included in Chapter Fifteen.

It was then that I discovered a new federation that allows knee sleeves in its "raw" division, so at this writing, I am training for a contest with that federation.

Going Back and Forth

It should be obvious by now, I have gone back a forth a lot when it comes to gear. I started out with single-ply poly gear, switched to double-ply poly, tried double-ply denim, different polys, and lastly canvas. In the middle of this ever changing gear, I tried going both raw and unequipped.

Needless to say, all of this going back and forth has really hurt my progress. It simply is not possible to make any steady progress if you are constantly changing things. Given this fact, my main advice on gear would be to make a decision and stick with it.

If you decide you want to compete with gear, fine. Do so. But decide what kind of gear you will use, get the best you can find, and then work with it to learn how to get the most out of it.

If you decide no gear is the way to go, then decide if you will go raw without knee support or unequipped with knee support. Either way, stick with your decision.

But if you ignore this advice and go from one type of lifting to the other, at least be sure to give yourself plenty of time to prepare. It takes time to get used to lifting raw if you have been lifting with gear. The reverse is also true. If you have been lifting raw, it will take time to get used to using gear.

Chapter Twenty-five
Gym Problems

This third part to this final section of this book will address gym problems I have encountered since I started powerlifting again.

Gym Problems Background

When I powerlifted in college, I was a member of the Penn State Barbell Club. It wasn't that often when the whole club would be working out at the same time. But when it did, it produced without a doubt the best workouts I've ever engaged in. We'd be screaming and yelling for each other, psyching each other up. You just couldn't help but train harder than ever. We'd make a great ruckus, but no one in the packed weight room at "Rec Hall" ever complained.

But even without the whole team there, some yelling was always a part of the workouts of all of us, so I just naturally did the same when I was training alone. Again, never once was an eyebrow raised or did anyone complain. It was just common for serious lifters to make a ruckus while they were lifting. Those who were not serious lifters seemed to just accept it as part of the weight room atmosphere.

The same goes for the use of chalk. We'd always use chalk in our workouts, and chalk would be all over the floor when we were done. Yet not a word was raised about it. I always used chalk when lifting alone, and I never once thought of it being some kind of problem if I got any on the floor.

We also always piled our gym bags up against a wall in the gym, and there was a bench right behind the deadlift platform and squat racks for us to sit on when we wrapped our knees or simply to rest between heavy sets. And yes, every gym I trained at had a deadlift platform and at least one set of squats racks and/ or power racks.

It was also standard at any gym for hard rock and heavy metal music to be blaring. We all just knew then that such music was ideal for getting psyched up for heavy lifting. And again, no one complained about the music.

However, after not using free weights for over 20 years, how things had changed when I started back. It seems that yelling is no longer acceptable in most gyms. Gym owners don't like it, and people will actually complain about it.

Gym owners also can get very nasty about lifters getting even a speck of chalk on the floor. I can understand them wanting you to clean it up if you spill a whole container of chalk. But what does a little chalk dust hurt? It is a gym after all, not a CSI lab.

Gym owners can also get nasty if you bring a gym bag into the gym. You would think the two go together.

And just try to find someplace to sit down to wrap your knees or rest between heavy sets. Most gyms don't seem to think about this. That's probably because most gyms do not have deadlift platforms, while squat racks and power racks are rare.

Meanwhile, the music at gyms can be anything but the hard driving music that is needed for heavy workouts.

It's no wonder the average person doesn't make much progress at most gyms these days.

From Gym to Gym

With that background, when I first decided to try using free weights again, there was a gym within walking distance of my home. The owner was someone I knew from high school, a former bodybuilder who had trained at the same gym I did when I wasn't away at college, so I just naturally went there. But the problem was, he was moving to Ohio, so the gym was closing a month later. I worked out there for that month, mostly in the afternoons by myself. But it gave me a chance to get used to lifting again.

The next closest gym was about 20 minutes away. At that gym there were several powerlifters. It felt really good to be working out with other powerlifters again. I also already knew this owner as he was also a former bodybuilder. There was a deadlift platform, two power racks, three benches, and plenty of free weights. I figured I had found a great gym. But that was not to be the case.

It seems that despite his background, the owner really did not want the hardcore lifters there. He started complaining about us making too much noise and about chalk on the floor. He'd even complain if we turned the music up too loud.

He then started talking about building us a separate "powerlifting room." That would have been just fine by me, until he showed me the "rules" he had for it. They included no yelling, no chalk on the floor, and worst of all, no music allowed!

It was then that I saw the writing on the wall and left for another gym. As it turned out, he moved the gym shortly thereafter. For the new location, he got rid of the deadlift platform, one of the power racks, one of the benches, and most of the free weights. In their place was a walking track taking up half of the floor space of his new gym.

The reason for this change was he had advance notice of the new gym cash cow, the "Silver Sneakers" program. Medicare was now going to be paying for the gym memberships of senior citizens. This was great news for seniors, but terrible news for powerlifters. This program has done more to ruin gyms for powerlifters than anything else. It is the seniors that will complain about powerlifting practices, as I would soon find out.

The next gym I tried was also about 20 minutes away. Before I joined it, I specifically asked the person signing me up about yelling, chalk, and the like. He said it wouldn't be a problem—he lied. It was. It was mainly the old ladies on the treadmills that would complain. But the problem really was that I was the only powerlifter in the gym.

I even got into trouble for bringing in a folding chair to sit on while wrapping my knees. I was given permission by one employee, but another not only complained about it, but he began screaming and swearing at me over it. You would think an employee screaming and swearing at a customer would be cause for the employee's dismissal. But he just happened to be the owner's brother-in-law, so I was the one who was asked to leave!

I then joined a YMCA not too far from my home. I was once again the only powerlifter there. They only had one power rack. Initially that wasn't a problem as it seemed that no one else in the gym ever did squats. There was the occasionally squint who would tie it up doing curls. But beyond that, for a few months I had little problems using it for as long as I needed for my workouts.

There was no deadlift platform, but I would put some mats down to deadlift on. But the problem was, the floor wasn't level, so the bar would keep rolling away from me!

The seniors mainly stayed in the Nautilus room, so I had no complaints from them. However, the music for the weight room was also pumped into the Nautilus room. For that reason, I wasn't allowed to turn it up very loud or to put on really good music. But I solved that by wearing a MP3 player. There were even wooden boxes in the gym that I could use for sitting on. Overall, it was not a bad place to train.

However, the biggest problem with the Y was it was closed on Sundays and holidays, and that messed up my training schedule. There also began to be someone coming in the same time as me that needed the power rack. Since he was much taller than me, there was no way we could work out together, so it became a "fight" as to who got to use the power rack.

I could have solved that problem by changing my workout days. But I had previously heard of a "key entry" gym. That meant the doors stayed locked, but each member was given a key and could work out anytime, 24/7/365. That sounded great.

The gym also had two power racks, so I wouldn't have a problem in that respect. And it had plenty of free weights and seemed like more of a hardcore gym than any I'd been at before.

However, it was about 30 minutes away. With my worsening fibromyalgia that distance proved to be rather difficult to travel back and forth for a workout. And again, I was the only powerlifter there. In fact, given the sparse membership, I was often the only person in the gym for most of my workout. That made it hard to get psyched up for a workout. But at least I could crank the music up as loud as I wanted.

MCS and Home Gym Problems

I stayed at the key-entry gym about a year. But then Hurricane Katrina hit and gas prices skyrocketed. As a result, that drive was getting to be not only tiring but also rather expensive. In addition, by this time the serious problem I had with allergies had worsened to the point that would be best described as "multiple chemical sensitivity" (MCS).

To describe MCS would require a whole chapter in itself. But basically, I am terrible allergic to any kind of chemicals, including any kind of cosmetic products. It is to the point that I have a hard time being around people as people have chemicals on their bodies and clothing (perfume, cologne, make-up, hair spray, cigarette smoke, remnants of soap and detergent, etc.).

As mentioned, I was alone most of the time at the key-entry gym, but if people came in before I was finished, that could cause me problems. As a result, I had no choice but to set up a home gym. I figured the gym would pay for itself through savings in gas and gym memberships within a year or so.

However, I had many problems in setting up my home gym. I won't detail those here as I do so in the section "Setting Up a Home Gym" on the Powerlifting section of my fitness Web site.

I will simply say here, that yes it is convenient to have a home gym, but it is also difficult to train by yourself. As I said, it can be hard to get psyched up for a workout when lifting alone. But again, I always really crank up the music.

A way to rectify this would be to get a workout partner or two. I would strongly encourage that if you have a home gym. But for me, due to my MCS, that is not really an option. I rarely have visitors to my home as I cannot risk them bringing in smells and contaminating my home. That can cause me problems even after they leave, so there is no way I can have a workout partner coming several times a week.

Incidentally, I have never really had a problem with my MCS during a contest. But then I usually have a flare-up afterwards. At one contest, I had no problems the whole day I competed, even though I arrived at the contest site at 8:00 a.m. and was not out of there until 7:30 p.m. But the next day, I went into the very same hotel ballroom to watch the heavyweights compete, and it bothered me so much being there that I had to leave before squats were even finished. The best I can figure is the adrenaline suppresses the allergic response while I'm competing. But of course, there is no way to keep that up long term.

The Ideal Gym

In college, I majored in nutrition science. My plans were that I would make a name for myself with my lifting, and then between my lifting experience and my degree, I would open a gym and be able to counsel people in both exercise and diet. Basically, I had planned on starting a personal trainer service long before "personal trainer" even became a term, let alone a profession.

For the gym, I had planned on following the pattern seen in a gym I trained at when I was home from college. The ground floor was the main gym, with some free weights but mostly weight machines, along with treadmills and other cardio equipment. But then in the basement were a power rack, a bench, a deadlift platform, a couple of bars, and lots of weights. The basement also had a sound system separate from the main gym. Very often, I was the only person down in that musty old basement. But I put in some of my best workouts ever down there.

That basic design of one floor for the hardcore powerlifters and bodybuilders and another for the "fluff" trainees seemed like a great way to design a gym. But due to my health problems, I never pursued my plans.

When I started powerlifting again and was looking around for a gym to train at, I found one with just this very design. The top floor had all the machines and stuff for the fluff trainees, but the bottom floor was a fully equipped powerlifter's gym: power racks, benches, deadlift platforms, even a monolift, along chains, bands, and boards.

Unfortunately, that gym was 45 minutes from my home. Driving an hour and a half on top of a workout would be too much for me. But for the average person, if would be no big deal. In fact, I would say if you are at all serious about making progress in powerlifting, then if there is such a gym anywhere near you, then it would be worth the drive if it is at all feasible, at least for an occasional workout.

As indicated at the beginning of this chapter, my best workouts without a doubt occurred when we had the whole Penn State Barbell Club working out together. Training with a bunch of other powerlifters in a fully equipped power gym is the best situation possible.

Second to this would to set up a home gym with at least the basics of a power rack, a bench, a deadlift platform, a power bar, and plenty of weights, and then to get a good workout partner or two.

The worst situation is to be stuck working out at a fluff gym where there are no other powerlifters. That atmosphere can seriously hinder your progress.

In Defense of Screaming

Before closing this chapter, I want to address the issue that got me into trouble, yelling before and during a heavy lift. Does this actually help?

This question was addressed in an episode of the TV show *Sports Science* seen on FSN. The show first showed clips of different athletes screaming before and/ or during their respective events. One such athlete was a black belt karate expert, who was brought into their lab.

They set up a two stacks of five concrete slabs. For the first stack, the karate expert screamed while hitting the stack. He promptly broke through all five slabs. But then he did not scream while hitting the second stack, and he only broke four of the five slabs.

They had set a pressure pad on the top of each stack. The readings showed the karate guy exerted 25% greater force when he screamed than without screaming.

The show than detailed how much of a difference that 25% would make in different sports. They mentioned Olympic Weightlifting and said that screaming could mean the difference between a 500 pound clean and jerk versus a 400 pound lift.

I doubt screaming would add that much to a lift, but I do believe it can make a significant difference. That is why I and many other powerlifters scream before and/ or during a lift.

Of course, this can be taken to ridiculous extremes, with lifters making much more ruckus than is necessary, screaming on every rep of every set of every exercise. You really don't need to scream while doing say calves raises. But for gyms to get upset about powerlifters screaming before a heavy deadlift is to ignore this science about how much screaming can help when performing a heavy lift.

324

Chapter Twenty-six
Contest Problems

This final chapter in this final section of this book will address various problems I have encountered at contests and related issues.

Bench Press Handoffs

The Introduction to this book related the very bad experience I had at my first contest, a high school bench press meet. Part of the reason for my bomb out was the problem I had with the handoff.

For background, on benches, many powerlifters in training and at a contest have someone handoff the weight to them. This is allowed by the rules. The handoff person usually stands behind the head of the lifter and lifts the weight up off the racks and over the lifter. This saves the lifter energy in having to lift the weight to that point. In training, the handoff person should then stay behind the lifter and spot him or her as needed. But if it is a contest, the handoff person must get off of the platform, as mentioned in Chapter Nine.

It is best if there are preset signals between the lifter and the handoff person. Usually, a three-count is used for when the handoff person should lift the weight. But I would suggest it is the lifter who does the counting, not the handoff person. Then after the bar is over the lifter, the lifter should nod. It is then that the handoff person should let go.

Now back to that first contest, as mentioned in the Introduction, at that time I was lifting at home alone. That meant I usually had to un-rack the weight myself. However, at times, my brother would handoff for me, if he happened to be around. But I never had two people handing off the weight, one standing at each end of the bar, so I was doing something at the contest that I was not used to.

That was bad enough. But even worse is that it is never a good idea to use two handoff people. There are several problems with that situation. First, the lifter cannot see the handoff people, so he does not know when they actually let go of the bar. Second, they cannot see him for him to nod to them to let go. Third, it is almost impossible for both handoff people to let go at the same time; so inevitably, the weight will immediately be unbalanced. All of these problems led to that weight almost crashing down on me.

But that contest is not the only time I have had problems with the handoff. More recently, when I was working out at public gyms, I would often ask someone in the gym to handoff and spot for me. But I would always be sure to instruct them as to how to proceed. But each time I used a "new" person there was inevitably some problems. It just takes time for a lifter and handoff person to get into synch. And that leads to my first suggestion.

It is best is if you have the same person handoff to you each and every workout. That is the ideal, but not practical for most lifters. But at least try to use as few different people as possible. It would then be best if you are able to take a person you are used to handing off to you to the contest with you.

In college, my brother attended a few of my contests. When he did, I would have him handoff for me. If he wasn't there, I would have one of the other members of the Penn State Barbell Club handoff.

However, since I started competing again in 2003, I have not been able to have someone at contests I knew from training. So at my first couple of contests, I asked one of the spotters to handoff for me from behind. That went okay the first couple of times, but then at one contest, it did not work out so well. The spotter lifted the bar up too much and pulled me up out of my arch.

After that contest, I would then look for someone in the warm-up room who was not competing but who I knew from a previous contest and I was sure knew what he was doing. I would then ask him if he was willing to handoff for me. I would then practice with him in the warm-up room by having him handoff to me for all of my warm-up sets. That way, he would know what I wanted and there would be little chance of problems on the platform.

But since I set up my home gym, I work out alone. That means I am used to un-racking the weight myself. So for my next contest, I figured I would not use a handoff person. But on my first attempt, the spotters took it upon themselves to handoff the weight to me, each lifting the bar from the side. Just like at my first contest that really threw me off. I almost lost control of the bar. But fortunately, this time I was able to control it enough to get the lift, but barely.

For my next atempt, I made sure to tell both spotters that I did not need their help. I would un-rack the bar myself. You would think that would be the "default" position. The spotters should know to not touch the bar unless the lifter (or one of the judges) asks them to. But from now on, I will not assume that is the case. I always make sure to tell the spotters before my first attempt that I will be un-racking the weight myself, so please do not touch the bar.

The main point of this section is it is best to try to keep contest conditions as close to what you are used to doing in the gym. If you are used to a handoff person, then use one at a contest. If it can be the same person you use in training, great. If not, then be sure to practice with the handoff person in the warm-up room. If you are not used to a handoff, then it would be best to not use one at a contest. But be sure to tell the spotters that is what you are doing.

Of course, the first point is good advice in general and has been mentioned previously, but it bears repeating. If at all possible, do not do anything at a contest that you are not used to in training.

Videotaping Workouts and Contests

Back in my college lifting days, video cameras had not been invented yet, or at least, they were still way too expensive for the average person to purchase. But a few years after I had stopped competing, my dad got a video camera. I can remember thinking back then how nice it would have been to have had a video camera when I was powerlifting. I could have videotaped myself working out and been able to review my form, and having videos of competitions would have been really nice.

When I started powerlifting again in 2003, there were now many different recording options around. I looked into buying a camcorder. But it just seemed too expensive, so I didn't bother. Big mistake. It really would have been a worthwhile investment.

In the first chapter of this section, I mentioned about missing my third squat attempt at two different contests due to depth. But on both occasions I really thought I was deep enough. It would have been so nice to have had a video to review just so I knew how deep I had gone. Even more important would be to be able to record squats in training to be sure I was hitting proper depth all the time. That way, it will become second nature, and there'd be no problems come contest time.

For Christmas 2005 I got a digital camera. I had my dad use it to take pictures of me at the two contests I entered in 2006. Some of these pictures are seen in this book. I also took many pictures with the camera of my home gym and the equipment contained therein to post on my Web site. But I never thought to check to see if the camera had a video function.

In May of 2007 I bought a cheap WebCam. I ran cables from my PC in my home office into my home gym area to take videos of me squatting. But that was a real pain to do, and the quality was terrible. But even with the poor quality, I could see I was squatting too high, so I knew I needed a way to be recording my workouts more often.

It was then that I thought of checking my digital camera. And sure enough, it had a video function. The quality was very good, and it was very easy to use. I began taking videos of not just squats but many other lifts. This proved invaluable in reviewing my form. I also began posting these videos on my Web site in order to demonstrate proper form for a wide variety of exercises for visitors to my Web site.

Given the wide variety of recording options available today, there is no excuse for powerlifters to not avail themselves of this technology and record your workouts, at least occasionally. In this way you can review your form and be sure you are hitting proper depth on squats.

Moreover, I do not see why it is not common practice for meet directors to record contests. I would love to have a DVD of the entire contest to review afterwards, and I am sure many other lifters would as well. With today's technology, it would be so easy for the meet director to record the contest and to make copies available afterwards. He could let people know at the contest that meet DVDs would be available for ordering. I am sure many would order copies, and that would thus be another revenue stream for the meet director. But for some reason, this has never been the case for any contest I have entered.

Formula Calculations

At most contests, a "Best Lifter" award is given out. This is for the lifter who totals the most on a pound for pound basis.

At some contests, this is calculated using simple division. Divide the total weight lifted by the lifter's bodyweight. Using myself as an example, at one contest I totaled 1030 at 114.5 pounds bodyweight. That would be 1030 / 114.5 = 8.99, meaning I totaled just shy of nine times bodyweight. If someone else totals 1450 at 165 pounds, that would be 8.78 times bodyweight. I would thus be the better lifter.

However, simple division tends to favor the lighter weight lifters, so very complicated formulas have been invented and are used instead at most contests. There are various formulas used: Schwartz, Wilkes, Glossbrenner, and others. The formulas are based on the all-time world records at the time they were calculated. Each formula gives a "coefficient" for each possible bodyweight. You need to have a chart with all of the coefficients to do the calculations. The charts are available on various federation Web sites.

For instance, at the aforementioned contest I did win Best Lifter, but that contest used the Schwartz formula. My bodyweight would be rounded up to 115 pounds. The coefficient for that weight is 0.9481. You multiply the coefficient by the total, so 1030 x 0.9481 = 976.534. For the person totaling 1450 at 165 pounds bodyweight, their coefficient is 0.6656 and their result would only be 965.120, so I again, I would be the better lifter.

However, getting the same result is not always the case. Different formulas or simple division could produce different results as to who wins Best Lifter. With different federations using different formulas, it can all get very confusing.

Sometimes, such formulas are also used for the regular placing at contests, especially at smaller contests. Rather than there being separate awards for each weight class, all lifters are grouped together, with awards given out based on the formula. That was the situation for the highs school bench press contests mentioned in the Introduction to this book, where the Schwartz formula was used. Sometimes, just the teenage, female, or masters lifters awards are figured out by formula.

With that background, at one contest I entered, given the caliber of lifters at the contest, I thought that I might win Best Lifter. But I didn't get it. It instead went to someone in the 165 pound weight class. I talked to the meet director afterwards, and he said that three of us were "very close."

But a couple of months later, I saw the full meet results for the contest in *Powerlifting USA* magazine. I did some calculations, and it looked like I should have won Best Lifter, and it wasn't even close. I should have won it by a wide margin. But that was calculated using the Schwartz formula and the weight class limit for the person who beat me. But I wasn't sure if that was the formula that was used and what that person actually weighed in at. But in order to have actually beaten me, he would have had to weigh-in at 149 pounds, which is almost at the next lower class. That was possible, but not very likely.

I tried contacting the meet director, but did not get a reply at that time. I also emailed the president of the federation about it. I was told the meet director probably still did not have a record of the weigh-in weights, so there was nothing that could be done about it. I didn't expect that anything could be, but I still would have liked an explanation.

Much later, I finally heard from the meet director. He did still have a record of the weigh-in weights. The person who had beaten me had weighed in at 164 pounds. He also said he used simple division at that contest not a formula for figuring out Best Lifter. But due to my having raised questions about it, he now uses the Schwartz formula.

He tried to explain his calculations, but frankly, I could not figure out how he arrived at his results. When I did the math myself, it still looked like I should have easily won Best Lifter. With weighing in at 164, there was no way it was mathematically possible for the other lifter to have beaten me no matter what calculation method was used. So it was apparent that a mistake had been made.

Not that it mattered at that point, but the whole situation was frustrating. I was less than satisfied with my performance at that contest. If

I had known then I had won Best Lifter that would have "saved the day" so to speak. But at least I was able to work things out enough with the meet director that I might enter another of his contests.

My point is, if you think you have a chance for Best Lifter, or if awards are based on formula, you need to be prepared. Find out beforehand which formula or if simple division is being used. Then take a calculator and (if needed) a copy of the chart with the coefficients for that formula to the contest with you. Before the event is over, request the actual bodyweights for your closest competitors and do the calculations. Don't assume mistakes will not be made. If you have concerns about the results, you need to raise them then; you won't be able to do anything about it later. You may not even be able to find out the needed information afterwards.

It is also important to know the actual weigh-in weights of your competitors for placing within weight classes. It two lifters tie in their totals, the person with the lighter weigh-in weight is declared the winner, so you really need to find out this information during the contest.

If you're a meet director, it would be good to include on the entry form what method will be used to figure out Best Lifter. It would also be good to post at the contest a list of the actual weigh-in weights of all lifters. I would also suggest that after the contest, you keep a record of the full contest results, weigh-in weights included, just in case questions are asked later. If questions are raised, please have the courtesy of responding in a timely manner and providing an explanation.

Contest Announcing and Projections

At powerlifting contests, an announcer will announce the lifters who are: "up," "on deck," and "in the hole." These terms of course come from baseball, where the player who is "up" is in the batter's box, the next one who will bat is "on deck" and the next is "in the hole" meaning still in the dugout. In powerlifting, the meanings are about the same, except the lifter who is "up" should be prepared to step onto the platform, while the "on deck " and "in the hole" lifers will be the next two to lift. Sometimes they might also announce the lifter who is "fourth up."

However, sometimes it can be hard to hear and understand the announcer. Personally, I have always had a hard time understanding people in a crowed room. At one contest in particular, I simply could not understand the announcer at all.

As a result, I kept having to go up to the scorer's table and peer over their shoulders to look at the schedule of lifters. Eventually, the announcer realized I had problems, so starting when I was "fourth up" he would look straight at me and motion that my turn was coming. I really appreciated that he was willing to do that for me. However, the need for it could have easily been avoided with some readily available technology.

At the first contest I entered when I started competing again, rather than doing all of the scoring with paper and pencil, the scorer used a notebook computer with an Excel spreadsheet. The spreadsheet was then projected onto a large screen. On the spreadsheet were all of the lifters' names, their weight classes, their actual weigh-in weights, and then their opening attempts. The names were arranged in the order they would be lifting in the first flight.

When the contest started, the lifter who was up would be highlighted. That way, all one had to do was to look up at the screen, and at a glance, you could see how long it would be until you were up.

As the flight progressed, the attempts would be scratched through if the lifter missed the lift, so you could see clearly how the contest was progressing. Then for the second attempts, the names were rearranged according to the new order of lifters. After benches, the subtotals were indicated. Then at the end of the contest the final results were projected.

The use of such technology has several benefits besides enabling lifters to know when they are up. You could very easily follow the contest, knowing who is in your weight class, who your closest competitors are, and thus figure out how to adjust your lifts for the win.

It also provides benefits for the audience. Let's face it; powerlifting contests can get rather boring to watch. All the audience sees is a series of lifts, with no way of really knowing how the competition is going. But with this technology, the audience can see at a glance how the contest is progressing, who is competing against whom, and where the close races are. As a result, it becomes a true competition.

This is the way it is for any other sport. If you go late to a football game, just by glancing at the scoreboard you can see the score, what quarter it is, how much time is left, what down it is, and how many yards is needed for a first down. You are immediately "caught up" and can begin to enjoy the game. The same goes for baseball, hockey, basketball, and just about any other sport.

After that first contest, I just assumed that such technology would be standard at every contest. But much to my dismay, I have never seen such a "scoreboard" since. Even when I entered that very same contest two years later, the Excel projection was not being used.

In my opinion, it should be commonplace for such technology to be used. If it was, maybe powerlifter would become more of a spectator's sport, and you'd see more people in the audience than just the lifters' family and friends.

The use of such technology would also solve a problem described previously. I could have just glanced at the screen and seen what the weigh-in weight was for the person who won Best Lifter.

Moreover, there are now specialty software programs that have been designed just for powerlifting contests. These programs would be even more beneficial than a basic spreadsheet. They would do the calculations automatically for placing in weight classes and for the Best Lifter award. As such, as long as the information is imputed correctly, mistakes would be eliminated.

In addition, all that would be needed would be for a printer to be brought to the contest, and the full contests results could be printed up and made available to all of the lifters before they even left the contest facility. As it is, most lifters do not even see the full meet results until they are posted on the Internet or even until months later when they appear in *Powerlifting USA*. It was this delay that caused my problems over the Best Lifter award.

And finally, with the meet results on a computer file, it would simple for the meet director to save the full results indefinitely. So just a little technology could make contests more enjoyable for both lifers and audience and eliminate any questions about the results.

Contest Friendliness

At most contests I have been at, the meet officials and other lifters have been very friendly and helpful, but not always. I remember one contest where I needed help getting my squat suit off. I asked everyone in the warm-up room who was not lifting for help, but everyone was "too busy" to be bothered. I then had to start asking people in the audience, and finally, after about 20 minutes, I found a couple of college students who were willing to help.

What was strange, though, was the students who helped me actually recognized me. It seems they went to Kutztown University, which had hosted National Collegiates the year I won. That was way back in 1981, but pictures from that contest were still having on the wall of the university's weight room, including a picture of me. Small world.

In any case, the situation could have been avoided if I had a "helper" to go to the contest with me, but I have never had that luxury. But if at all possible, I would suggest the reader try to take a friend along to help you out at a contest. But for me, after that experience, I figured out how to get my suit on and off myself so I wouldn't run into such problems again. Good thing too, as it was not too long after that when I set up my home gym and now had no choice but to get my gear on and off by myself.

At another contest, I got the impression that most of the lifters and officials had been at contests together before, so I was the "outsider" so to speak, and felt like such. That really lessened my enjoyment of that contest. There's not much you can do about this, except try to be as friendly as you can yourself. And again, it would help if you do not go to a contest alone.

Hotel Problems

The first contest I entered was held in the ballroom of a hotel, so I, like probably most every other competitor, stayed at that hotel. That was incredibly convenient. No worries about traveling to the contest on meet day; just get up and go downstairs. However, the hotel was rather expensive, $89/ night plus tax. I stayed two nights, so just the hotel for that contest cost me almost $200.

The next two contests I entered were held at a convention center. The hotel to stay at was just across the parking lot from the meet site, so again, incredibly convenient, but also incredibly expensive, $119/ night plus tax. For the first contest I stayed two nights, but the second contest I stayed three nights. I did so in order to take full advantage of the "24 hour weigh-in rule" of the federation and thus to weigh-in the morning before the contest. But those five nights in that hotel cost me over $600.

When I was just about ready to leave after the second contest, another lifter mentioned he was staying at a hotel a mile away, and it cost only $69/ night. I was so kicking myself. Sure, having to travel a whole mile would not have been as convenient as walking across the parking lot, but it would have been worth it to save over $250.

After that experience I started doing what I should have done in the first place, checking the Internet for hotels near the contest site. You can almost always find a hotel or motel that is much cheaper than the hotel listed on the contest form. You just might have to drive a little bit further to get to the contest.

Of course, the least expensive option would be to find a contest close enough to your home that it does not require a hotel stay. Also, due to my fibromyalgia, I find driving to be very tiring. From the time I started powerlifting again, I had restricted myself to contests within a four hour drive. But after a while, even that distance was proving to be too much.

As a result, in 2006, I entered two contests within an hour from my home. That did make things much easier and less expensive. But I have to admit, I kind of missed the excuse to stay at a hotel. It is simply nice to get away, if even only for a couple of days.

In 2007 I entered one contest. For it I stayed at a very cheap motel I found on the Internet. It only cost $90 for both nights, including tax. That was half of what the hotel listed on the entry form would have cost, and it was only a half a mile farther away from the contest site.

However, this time, I had a serious problem due to my multiple chemical sensitivity. As soon as I walked into the motel room, I could tell it was going to be a problem. I barely slept both nights I stayed there. When I got home, I had to wash everything I took with me into the motel room, if I wore it or not.

The last time I stayed at a hotel was a year and a half before this, but that was at a much nicer hotel. So I wasn't sure if the problem was due to it being a cheap motel or I had gotten worse in those 1½ years.

But a year later, I stayed at another inexpensive hotel for a contest. This time, despite being rather inexpensive, it was actually a very nice room, and I didn't have any problems this time. So I can only guess the quality of the hotel can make a big difference, which is not necessarily related to price.

T-Shirt Problems

It was mentioned a couple of times in this book that some federations do not allow a pocket on your T-shirt. The reason this is an issue for me is I wear a mouthpiece when lifting. It is similar to the type of mouth guard football players and boxers wear.

The reason I wear it is I suffer from TMJ, which is a jaw joint problem. Grinding my teeth aggravates the condition. A dentist recommended I wear such a guard at night and when working out since I tend to grind my teeth at both times. But wearing it makes it difficult to talk, so I take it out when doing so. A pocket makes for a convenient place to put it so I don't have to stand there holding the salvia-dripping mouthpiece and so that I don't lose it.

In addition, all of the colored T-shirts I own have pockets on them, by design. I just find it very convenient to have a shirt pocket for putting miscellaneous stuff into as needed.

Also, during warmer weather, I usually wear a sleeveless T-shirt around my home and when working out. It is simply cooler than a short-sleeved shirt.

The first several contests I entered allowed a pocket and sleeveless T-shirt. But the first time I entered a contest that did not allow either, I couldn't find a colored T-shirt to wear, so I ended up wearing a plain white T-shirt. Not very nice looking, but it's all I could find.

I find the no pocket and must have sleeves rules to be rather silly. Really, what possible difference can it make? But be that as it may, for the most recent Christmas, I got two plain red T-shirts, without pockets but with sleeves just to use for contests. Red will look nice under the new black singlet I recently got, so I am ready for the next time I enter a contest with such T-shirt rules.

Cash Awards

A few contests I have entered, there have been cash awards of around $1,000. That is a good step in powerlifting. But I find it disturbing when the awards go to the lifter with the *biggest* squat, bench, and deadlift. Why should only the heavier-weight lifters have a shot at the cash awards? The prizes should be given to the lifter with the *best* lifts on a pound for pound basis. Give everyone a chance at the cash.

Not Entering Planned Contests

I've already mentioned in this book about the time I had to cancel my plans to enter a contest due to sustaining a hamstring injury and another time due to not receiving ordered gear. But those are not the only times I've had to cancel contest plans. There have actually been many such occasions.

When I set up my home gym, I had previously planned on entering a contest a couple of months later. But due to the many problems I encountered, I ended up having to take over a week off of lifting, and that ended those plans.

Most of the time, however, I've had to cancel contest plans due setbacks health-wise causing me to miss training time. Even the contest in 2008 that I did enter and went 9/9 at, I almost didn't enter due to contracting an infected finger two weeks before the contest.

When such things occur, there really is not much you can do about it. But it is frustrating, especially when you've been preparing weeks or even months for a contest. All you can do is take it in stride, cancel those plans and begin looking for another contest.

Conclusion to Section Seven

Given all of the problems I have had in the six years since I started powerlifting again and given my health problems, I have been struggling with if it is time for me to just give up on powerlifting. But I really enjoy the sport. Moreover, I like to enter a contest or two a year to give me an extra incentive to keep working out, which is important for me to do for my health.

But for those who are reading this who do not have such health problems, I hope this section does not discourage you from powerlifting. It is a great and very satisfying sport. It is my desire that this section and this book in general will enable you to avoid the many problems I have experienced. But I thank the LORD that I have been able to accomplish as much as I have despite all of the problems.

Conclusion to Book

Due to my health situation, I am only able to spend a very limited amount of time writing each day, but I still thought it wouldn't take me very long to write this book. But it ended up taking eight months, about twice as long as I originally thought.

It took me that long as I was continually writing, re-writing, and revising sections. I did so as I was struggling over exactly what to include and how to word various sections.

After I finished the rough draft, when there was a blank space at the end of a chapter I tried to fill it in with a something that was at least somewhat related to the chapter, such as the "Contest Anecdotes" at the end of Chapter 16. When the book was just about finished, I proofread it several times in an effort to eliminate typos.

In addition, this was the first time I used pictures in a book, and it took quite a while to get them formatted and displayed properly.

After all that time spent revising, I finally got this book to where I am fully satisfied with it and was able to include everything I thought would be helpful or interesting to the reader.

As such, I truly believe this book is a "comprehensive guide" to powerlifting. It covers all of the areas that are of importance to the person interested in the great sport of powerlifting. It is my hope and prayer that all of this information will enable the reader to make very good progress in your training and competitions and to truly enjoy the world's strongest sport.

Section Eight

Appendixes

Appendix One
Product Companies

This first appendix lists companies where the products mentioned in this book can be purchased. These are all companies the author has ordered from. They are listed in alphabetical order.

Powerlifting Gear and Weightlifting Equipment Companies

APT Pro Weightlifting Gear – www.prowriststraps.com/store ~ 888-236-1258 ~ APT Inc. Pro Gear, 19 Baron Park Rd, Unit 103, Fredericksburg, VA 22405.

High quality wraps, also bands, chains, and other powerlifting and weightlifting equipment available. Plus, "APT's APEX Powerlifting Shirt for Bench Pressing is THE NEWEST State of the art Bench Press Shirt. Brand New for Jan 2009." Excellent and fast service.

BigFitness – www.bigfitness.com ~ 508-336-3879 ~ 5 Progress Street, Seekonk, MA 02771.

"Exercise Equipment Super Store. For 16 Years we have been offering a great selection of quality Fitness Equipment." Good service. I especially like the "Quicklee collars" available here. They work as advertised: very easy to put on and take off once you get the knack for it, and they hold very well even on deadlifts.

Crain.ws – www.crain.ws ~ 800-272-0051 ~ 405-275-3689 ~ 3803 North Bryan Road, Shawnee, Oklahoma 74804-2314

"We are the manufacturer of the Okie Power Bars, Power Suit, Genesis Power Suit, CX1 & CX2 Squat & Deadlift Suits and Bench Shirts." Crain's CX1 & CX2 gear is top of the line gear that is less expensive than similar gear from other companies. Even less expensive Genesis power gear also available.

Elite Fitness – www.elitefts.com ~ 888-854-8806 ~ 138 Maple Street, London, Ohio 43140.

Metal and other powerlifting gear and weightlifting equipment available, including the Texas Power Bar, which I got from here for my home gym. Also, quality articles on powerlifting, featuring the "Westside" training method. Very good and fast service.

Frantz Power Gear – www.frantzpowergear.com ~ (630) 596-5989 or (630) 892-1491.

Custom-made powerlifting suits, briefs, and shirts. Wraps and other gear also available. The polyester gear is very inexpensive and great for "starter" gear. The denim and canvas gear is more advanced gear. All are of high quality. Excellent and fast service.

Ginny's Power Gear – www.ginnyspowergear.com ~ 506-466-1879 (Canada) ~ ginny@ginnyspowergear.com.

Makes customized double-canvas squat suits and double-denim bench shirts. The optional "front loops" on the straps for the squat suit makes it very easy to adjust the straps by yourself. Excellent service. She'll alter the gear as many times as it takes to get it just right.

Inzer Advance Designs – www.inzernet.com ~ 800-222-6897 ~ PO Box 2981, Longview, TX 75606.

"The most extremely advanced squat and deadlift suits ever made." Also bench shirts, wraps, and other gear. Many powerlifters swear by Inzer gear, but I never had much luck with it.

Karen's Xtreme Powerwear – www.karinsxtremepower.com ~ xtremeshirts@alltel.net ~ 740-366-9513 ~ 244 Sherwood Downs North, Newark, Ohio, 43055.

Karen makes customized double-denim shirts and suits. Excellent service. Will alter the gear as needed.

MonsterMuscle – www.monstermuscle.com ~ 800-319-0711 ~ 208-765-5033 ~ PO BOX 3224, CDA, ID 83816.

"The Powerlifting Superstore." Marketer of Inzer gear. Also, other weightlifting gear. Good service.

New York Barbell – www.newyorkbarbells.com ~ 800-446-1833 ~ 160 Home Street, Elmira, NY 14904.

Has everything needed to set up a home or commercial gym. I purchased much of what I needed for my home gym from NYB. Most of their stuff is high-quality. However, I must warn the reader against getting their "FID Bench." It is much higher and narrower than a standard bench, making it very difficult to use.

Topper Supply Company – www.toppersupply.com ~ 866-424-2467.

Good source for powerlifting chains.

York Barbell – www.yorkbarbell.com ~ store@yorkbarbell.com ~ 800-358-9675 ~ 3300 Board Road, York, PA 17406.

"As the 'Strongest Name in Fitness' we will develop, manufacture and distribute quality strength and fitness products that enhance athletic performance and improve quality of life." Has everything needed to set up a home or commercial gym.

Titan Support Systems – www.titansupport.com ~ 800-627-3145 ~ 1214 Ricky, Corpus Christy, TX 78412.

Many swear by Titan gear. I've only used their briefs and wraps, and those worked well. The problem is their service is very slow. It takes 6-8 weeks to get gear, and the same when getting it altered. For much quicker service, it is better to order from either of the following dealers. Both provide very good and quick service for in-stock items.

LiftingLarge – www.liftinglarge.com ~ 877-266-90-60.

PL Gear Online – www.plgearonline.com ~ priscilla@plgearonline.com ~ 888-495-6045 ~ 509-533-5375.

Supplement Companies

Bodybuilding.com – www.bodybuilding.com ~ 866-236-8969 ~ service@bodybuilding.com ~ 2026 South Silverstone Way, Meridian, ID 83642.

Great prices on a wide variety of supplements and brands. Also available is select weightlifting gear, along with many articles about supplements and training, and a forum, Excellent and fast service.

iHealthTree – www.ihealthtree.com ~ sales@ihealthtree.com ~ 888-225-7778 ~ 803 Sentous Street, City of Industry, CA 91748.

"We carry over 20,000 products including vitamins, herbs, diet pills, low carb foods, beauty and personal care products. We offer professional service and attractive low prices." Good service.

iHerb – www.iherb.com ~ info@iherb.com ~ 866-328-1171 ~ 5012 4th Street, Irwindale, CA 91706.

"A world-class online store, supplying a vast selection of brand name natural products. We believe iHerb offers the best overall value, period." When checking out, use referral code HOP815 to receive $5.00 off your first order. Excellent and fast service.

MuscleSurf – www.musclesurf.com ~ service@musclesurf.com ~ 877-304-8615 ~ 455 Whitney Street, Northborough MA 01532-2503

MuscleSurf offers many nutritional supplements at reduced prices. They have a full line of supplements for powerlifters and other athletes. Good service.

Parrillo Performance – www.parrillo.com ~ 800.344.3404 ~ 6200 Union Centre Boulevard, Fairfield, OH 45014.

As discussed in the text, makers of very worthwhile energy and protein bars. Many other high quality supplements. Excellent and fast service. Their *Parrillo Performance Press* is a very good muscle mag. It is mostly geared towards bodybuilders, but powerlifters will benefit from it as well. Available free online or in hardcopy for a fee.

Protein Factory – www.proteinfactory.com ~ 800-343-1803 ~ info@proteinfactory.com ~ 991 Cedar Bridge Ave, Brick, NJ.

All types of protein powders sold by the pound. You can customize your own blended protein. Also available are various powdered carb and fat sources, along with other supplements. Very good prices and service.

Vitacost – www.vitacost.com ~ customerSupport@vitacost.com ~ 800-381-0759.

Excellent prices and service on a wide variety of supplements.

WebVitamins – www.webvitamins.com ~ 800-919-9122 ~ 920 River Street, Suite E, Windsor, CT 06095.

WebVitamins offers very low prices on vitamins, herbs, health and beauty product, and much more. Good service.

Miscellaneous Companies

DietPower – www.dietpower.com ~ sales@dietpower.com ~ 800-852-8446 ~ Diet Power, Inc., 7 Kilian Drive, Danbury, CT 06811.

DietPower is an excellent software program for keeping track of your eating plan. It evaluates your diet for calories, protein, carbs, fat, and 24 nutrients. It automatically adjusts its caloric recommendations based on your diet history and weight goals. Includes a database of over 21,000 foods, and you can easily add additional foods.

Powerlifting USA – 800-448-7693 ~ Box 467, Camarillo, CA 93011.

The premiere powerlifting magazine. It's "Coming Events," Top 100 and Top 20 charts, meet results, and many high quality articles make it invaluable to the powerlifter.

Tanita – www.tanita.com ~ 847-640-9241 ~ 2625 South Clearbrook Drive, Arlington Heights, Illinois 60005.

As compared to contest weigh-in scales, my Tanita body fat scale has proved to be very accurate. The body fat percentage is not quite as accurate as it can be affected by hydration levels. But I have still found it to provide a rough estimate of the proportions of fat versus muscle I am gaining or losing.

Appendix Two
Additional Books by the Author

The author of this book is also the author of nine additional books and is the translator of a very unique version of the New Testament. All ten of these books are available in Microsoft Reader® eBook format from the "Books and eBooks by the Director" section of the author's Darkness to Light Web site (www.dtl.org/books).

These books are also available in hardcopy and Acrobat Reader® eBook formats from AuthorHouse (www.AuthorHouse.com ~ 1-888-280-7715) or from Lulu Publishing (www.lulu.com). Most are also available from online bookstores like Amazon.com.

God-given Foods Eating Plan
For Lifelong Health, Optimization of Hormones, Improved Athletic Performance
(paperback, hardback, and eBook from Lulu)

This book studies different foods and food groups, with a chapter devoted to each group. Both the Biblical evidence and modern-day scientific research are considered. Foods are classified as "God-given foods" and "non-God-given foods." A healthy eating plan is composed of a variety of God-given foods and avoids non-God-given foods.

Creationist Diet
Nutrition and God-given Foods According to the Bible
(paperback and eBook from AuthorHouse)

This book is superseded by the above book, but it is still available.

Overcoming Back Pain:
A Mind-Body Solution
(paperback and eBook from Lulu)

I was crippled with low back pain for six years. But I was able to completely overcome the back pain, so much so that I was able to not only start powerlifting again but to be very successful at it. This eBook discusses all of the treatments I tried and what finally worked.

Analytical-Literal Translation
(paperback, hardback, eBook from AuthorHouse and Lulu)

The ALT is the only New Testament that is a literal translation of the *Byzantine Majority Greek Text*, brings out nuances of the Greek text, and includes study aids within the text. No other English translation gets as close to the original Greek text as the ALT.

Companion Volume to the ALT
(paperback, hardback, and eBook from Lulu)

This book provides aids in understanding the translations seen in the ALT. It includes a glossary for important words in the ALT, an eight part "Grammatical Renderings" section to explain the unique translations in the ALT, along with much additional information.

Complete Concordance for the ALT
(paperback, hardback, and eBook from Lulu)

This book indexes every occurrence of most words in the ALT. Only minor words are omitted. Sufficient context is provided for the reader to recognize the verse or to get the gist of it. Invaluable for finding verses and for doing word studies and topical studies in the NT.

Scripture Workbook
For Personal and Group Bible Study
and Teaching the Bible:
Second Edition; Volume I
The Essentials of "The Faith"
(paperback, hardback, and eBook from Lulu)

This is the first of what will be two volumes. This first volume covers the essential doctrines of the Christian faith. It is these doctrines that separate the true Christian faith from cultic and other deviations. Included here are studies on such essential doctrines as the authority and reliability of the Scriptures, the attributes of God, the Trinity, and forgiveness and salvation.

Scripture Workbook
For Personal and Group Bible Study
and Teaching the Bible:

This book contains twenty-two individual "Scripture Studies." Each study focuses on one general area of study. These studies enable individuals to do in-depth, topical studies of the Bible. They are also invaluable to the Bible study teacher preparing lessons for Sunday School or a home Bible study.

This book is being superseded by the *Scripture Workbook: Second Edition*. That will be a two volume set, but only the first volume is currently available. So this one volume, first edition is still available.

Differences Between Bible Versions
(paperback and eBook from AuthorHouse)

Why do Bible versions differ? Why does the same verse read differently in different versions? Why do some versions contain words, phrases, and even entire verses that other versions omit? Which Bible versions are the most reliable? In answering these questions, over 30 versions of the Bible are evaluated.

The New World Translation:
A Reliable Bible Version?
(paperback and eBook from Lulu)

The NWT is the Bible of Jehovah's Witnesses. This review evaluates it by looking at passages from Paul's Epistle to the Ephesians.

Appendix Three
Author's Web Sites

This appendix provides details on my three Web sites and related sites.

Zeolla.org
www.Zeolla.org

Zeolla.org is the personal Web site for Gary F. Zeolla, author of Christian and of fitness books, ebooks, Web sites, and newsletters, and a top ranked and multi-record holding powerlifter. This site provides links to all of my writings, along with information about my Christian faith, my powerlifting, and other personal details.

Fitness for One and All
www.FitnessforOneandAll.com

I have a B.S. in Nutrition Science and am a top ranked powerlifter, holding 39 powerlifting records, set in four different powerlifting federations. These records were set after over 20 years of dealing with a variety of serious health problems. But I am dealing with these problems sufficiently to be able to compete successfully in powerlifting.

With all I have been through, dealt with, and accomplished, it is now my passion to help others achieve their health, fitness, and performance goals. To that end, I set up Fitness for One and All Web site.

Currently available on the site are over 400 Web pages, dozens of videos, four books and eBooks, and a free email newsletter.

Subjects covered on the site include general fitness, powerlifting and strength training, nutrition, supplements, and various health difficulties. These materials are directed towards a wide range of people, including beginning fitness enthusiasts, athletes, powerlifters, and those dealing with health problems. The name "Fitness for One and All" reflects this diversity of covered topics.

Darkness to Light
www.DTL.org

Darkness to Light ministry is dedicated to explaining and defending the Christian faith. Currently available on the site are over 900 Web pages, ten books and eBooks, and a free email newsletter.

In these materials, a wide range of topics are covered, including: theology, apologetics (defending the faith), cults, ethics, Bible versions, and much more, so you are sure to find something of interest.

The words "darkness" and "light" have a wide range of meanings when used metaphorically in Scripture, but basically, "darkness" refers to falsehood and unrighteousness while "light" refers to truth and righteousness. People turn from darkness to light when they come to believe the teachings of the Bible and live in accordance with them.

MySpace Page
www.MySpace.com/Gary114

On my MySpace page, there is a short biography, videos from my workouts, weekly workout logs, announcements about my planned upcoming contests, contest reports, and other personal details.

Weight Trainers United
www.weighttrainersunited.com

This is the forum I participate in. Follow the "Message Board" link near the top of the home page. "Weight Trainers United is primarily a Powerlifting forum; however we also welcome the discussion of other facets of the iron game, such as strongman, bodybuilding, or just recreational lifting."

I like WTU as it is a moderated forum, so crass language and bashing of federations and other lifters is not allowed. But what you will get is lots of encouragement for your training.

However, there is a chance by the time this is published the main site will be down. However, the forum can still be accessed by following the "Discussion Boards" link at www.deepsquatter.com

Contacting the Author

The author can be contacted by using the email link on any of his Web sites. Click on the "Contact Information" link near the bottom of any page on any site.

The author can also be sent a message through his MySpace page. Plus, the author can be contact via postal mail at:

Gary F. Zeolla
PO Box 138
Natrona Heights, PA 15065

CPSIA information can be obtained at www.ICGtesting.com
Printed in the USA
BVOW012252191112

305998BV00019B/158/P

9 780578 025162